SECURITY EDUCATION, AWARENESS, AND TRAINING

SECURITY EDUCATION, AWARENESS, AND TRAINING:

From Theory to Practice

By Carl Roper, Joseph Grau, and Lynn Fischer

AMSTERDAM • BOSTON • HEIDELBERG • LONDON
NEW YORK • OXFORD • PARIS • SAN DIEGO
SAN FRANCISCO • SINGAPORE • SYDNEY • TOKYO

Elsevier Butterworth–Heinemann
30 Corporate Drive, Suite 400, Burlington, MA 01803, USA
Linacre House, Jordan Hill, Oxford OX2 8DP, UK

Library of Congress Cataloging-in-Publication Data
Roper, C. A. (Carl A.)
    Security education, awareness, and training : from theory to practice / Carl Roper,
Joseph Grau, Lynn Fischer.
        p. cm.
    ISBN 0-7506-7803-8
    1. Security systems.   2. Private security services.   I. Grau, Joseph J.   II. Fischer, Lynn F.
III. Title.
    HV8290.R656 2005
    363.28—dc22

                                                                    2005009792

British Library Cataloguing-in-Publication Data
A catalogue record for this book is available from the British Library.

ISBN 13:   978-0-7506-7803-2

Transferred to Digital Printing 2009

For information on all Elsevier Butterworth–Heinemann publications
visit our Web site at www.books.elsevier.com

Dedication

To the faculty and staff of the former Department of Defense Security Institute, Richmond, Virginia, for their 25 years of excellence in providing instruction, guidance, mentoring, advice, and assistance to those many dedicated security people who go that extra step to help protect our nation's multivaried assets.

Contents

Contributing Authors

The authors are former employees of the Department of Defense Security Institute, the premier security educational training institute for a quarter century until it closed in the mid-1990s. During their tenure at the DODSI, the authors were instrumental in the development and presentation of the Strategies for Security Education Seminar course, on which this book is based. Their background and experience, prior to and since the course was developed, have all gone into the creation of this book.

DR. LYNN FISCHER
LYNNFSCHR@AOL.COM

Currently on the research staff of the Department of Defense Personnel Security Research Center (PERSEREC) in Monterey, California, since May of 1998 and in recent months Dr. Fischer has headed up a number of research projects on professional development and training for the newly established Joint Security Training Consortium.

Prior to his joining PERSEREC, he was responsible for developing security awareness publications and products at the Department of Defense Security Institute (DoDSI) in Richmond Virginia, where he also edited the *Security Awareness Bulletin* and *Security Awareness News*.

Before entering civilian government service at DoDSI in 1983, Dr. Fischer taught political science in several universities, primarily in West Africa.

He earned his Ph.D. in political science at Northwestern University in 1970. His first experience with government security programs was gained in the

United States Air Force from 1962 to 1966 while serving as an intelligence officer.

Chapters: 8, 9, 15

JOSEPH A. GRAU
GRAU@CHEK.COM

Joe Grau is a graduate of Duquesne University and the U.S. Naval War College (with distinction). A senior instructor and department head at the DoD Security Institute, Mr. Grau specialized in the field of security education and the DoD Information Security Program. He was a member of the Presidential Review Directive 29 Task Force, the National Disclosure Policy Committee, and principal drafter of the DoD Regulation 5200.1-R, Information Security Program (1997 edition). Over the years, he has had numerous articles published.

Chapters: 1, 2, 3, 4, 6, 7, 11, 14, 16

CARL A. ROPER
ROPERC@RCN.COM

Carl Roper holds an MSA in Security Management from Central Michigan University. As a DoD Security Institute lead instructor, he specialized in information security, physical security, risk management, and security education. Currently, he is a security consultant and trainer. He was a member of the U.S. Security Policy Board Risk Management Group Training Team, responsible for developing a national risk management course of instruction. He is also a retired U.S. Army Counterintelligence Special Agent. Mr. Roper is also the author of several other security books.

Chapters: 5, 10, 12, 13

Preface

From past experience, people understand that they don't know everything, and when push comes to shove, they may have a hard time finding what they need to know in order to properly perform their job functions and responsibilities. Security education is one of these areas. Many people assume that if you can stand up and tell a group of people something with a modicum of authority, you know what you're talking about and that it's good. This is far from the truth in the security arena. Security education is a field that requires background, study, and experience in the varied subject areas within the security environment that are only accomplished through learning over time. No one knows everything, but to know where to look for the right answers is truly the beginning of enlightenment. This book, then, is your enlightenment. It is also the first step in learning how to craft a relevant program that will be meaningful to your organizational employees. This is where you start to learn or, if you are already in the field of security education, where you can further expand and improve your abilities and then really motivate people to support the program in a worthwhile manner.

In writing this book, the authors have called on decades of hands-on experience within the government, military, and private sectors in order to provide a critical balance of knowledge, theory, and experience.

Naturally, we could not have done this alone. Over the years, we had coworkers, students, and others who provided us with personal insights and new directions of thought for the advancement of security education practices. We thank those many unsung persons.

We should like to thank the staff of American Society for Industrial Security (ASIS) International, particularly the O. P. Norton Resource Center personnel, for their time, efforts, and assistance in obtaining background materials for this book.

As former instructors in security education, we also rely on the many products from a variety of government and industry organizations. Never one to start over, various items from government sources, where they have definite value to the security educator — all approved for public release — have been included, particularly those items in the appendixes that can be used for organizational or security newsletters, pamphlets, or other handouts.

Lastly, thanks to our families and close friends, for their support and allowing us to take time away from various endeavors so that we had the time and effort to produce this book.

To contact the authors with questions or comments, please write them through this publisher.

1

Security Programs, Security Education, and This Book

WHAT IT'S ALL ABOUT

This book is about making your security program work better. It is as simple as that. If you have a really good program now, we're going to try to help you make it even better — perhaps with a little (or a lot) less cost and effort. If you have a program that needs fixing, we'll give you some ideas on how to do that, minus the wheel spinning we've all seen and probably experienced. What sort of security programs are we talking about? All kinds: air transport security, information systems security, retail security, security in the health care and hospitality industries, security of government classified information, security programs that address the protection of trade secrets and proprietary information, security in industrial environments, and any other kind you can think of.

How can we hope to cover all these widely varied security programs in one slim book? Simply because they all have one critical element in common. Every type of security program you can name is ultimately dependent on people to make it work. And that's what this book is about: people. We're going to be looking at ways to get the active participation of people in and around your organization to make your security program work. And we mean all sorts of people, not just your security staff and security force. They're vitally important to the success of your program, all right. But we need to look beyond them, too, to recruit people throughout the organization as willing and able contributors to effective security.

Air transport security — very much a subject of interest these days — provides us with a perfect example. We have a security staff at the airport that plans and supervises the security program. These are security professionals, of course.

We have other professional security people operating the security checkpoints and patrolling the premises. But these people — competent as they may be — aren't enough. We also count on others who are not "security people" to perform roles in the program. The airline employees staffing the check-in counters are responsible for verifying passenger identities by checking picture IDs. We count on gate personnel and flight crews to observe and report suspicious behavior. We look to all of the airport and airline workers to let us know about situations that might signal a security problem. We even ask the customers — the passengers — to help out by keeping an eye on their luggage and refusing to carry packages on board for others. (You've probably heard those announcements in the airports.)

Years of experience have firmly convinced us that this same sort of thing — the need to get nonsecurity personnel in organizations to participate in making the program work — holds true for every type of security effort we have ever been involved in. There are no exceptions. The level of their participation that you'll need will vary based on the situation and the type of asset you're protecting, but the need will always be there. If my program protects large, bulky items in a static environment (big diesel engines in a rarely accessed, securely constructed storage building, for example), the need for operating employee participation in the program will be relatively low. My security force alone will probably fill most of the bill pretty nicely. On the other extreme, programs that protect information — trade secrets, marketing plans, government-classified information, corporate proprietary data, personal information, and so on — are by their nature heavily dependent on the nonsecurity people who work with the information to protect it. We guarantee you that any information protection program that relies only on the organization's security professionals for its success won't have much.

If we're going to get the effective participation of people within our organizations in our security efforts, we need to make sure that they are able to carry out their roles in the program properly, and then we need to get them to do it. Our efforts to accomplish that goal are what this book is all about. That's what we call security education. Let's try a formal definition:

Security education is *everything* we do to enable people in our organization to carry out their roles in our security program effectively and reliably, plus everything we do to influence them to do just that.

In this book, we'll be looking at security education from a variety of angles, and we're going to be taking a holistic view. Notice we said that security education was *everything* we do to get those goals accomplished. We mean it! Effective security education can't be something that happens only in a training room, or once a year at an annual security briefing, or only when you conduct training for security force members, or only when a new employee comes on board, or only when corporate headquarters lays a requirement on us for changes. Security education should, can, and must be something that happens all the time, in all sorts of settings, and in all sorts of ways. One of our goals in this book is to help you find ways to make that happen.

SOME COMMON PROBLEMS

In our years of practicing the security profession and teaching it to others, we've found several unfortunately common shortcomings in security education efforts in both government and in the private sector. These shortcomings do not occur everywhere, of course. Lots of smart people in the security business have been using common sense and management savvy and have been doing lots of smart things for years to make security education happen. But there are some widespread ailments that we've seen limiting the effectiveness of much good work. At the risk of sounding too negative, let us lay them out for you. If they seem uncomfortably familiar, this book is definitely for you.

1. Security education consists of "briefings," classes, lectures, and that sort of thing, plus maybe a few posters.

2. Security education efforts are fragmented, not coordinated and mutually supporting.

3. Security education is driven more by government regulations or corporate directives than by security program needs.

4. Security educators look only within the security profession for ideas, not outside it.

5. Security education target populations are limited to narrowly defined segments of the workforce, or the program is the same for everyone.

6. Security education consists of telling people what to do and then exhorting them to do it or threatening them if they don't.

7. Security education activities are the same year after year.

Whew! Sounds like everything's a disaster, huh? Keep in mind that there are plenty of people in our business making a lot of fine advances when it comes to security education. We're going to try to help you learn from their successes. We're also going to attack the problems we've just listed. We'll be looking at dozens of means, mechanisms, gimmicks, and activities that can be a part of security education. We'll work on making sure all our security education efforts are coordinated and mutually supporting. We'll look at figuring out what our security program needs and then using security education to supply those needs (while still complying with those pesky regulations and directives). We'll roam around in other professional fields to steal every good idea we can use. We'll make sure we've thought about what contributions everyone in the organization can make to security success and how one can get them to make them. We'll make sure we cover all the bases when it comes to what security education can and should do with people. Finally, we'll try to load you with enough good ideas that nobody will ever accuse your security education program of being "more of the same old thing."

THEORIES

As we go along, we'll introduce you to or remind you of some theories and models that apply to security education. Some people get itchy at this. *Theory* and *theoretical* seem to be almost dirty words to some people. Many people don't want to be bothered with theories; they want something practical. Well, as somebody once said, there's nothing more practical than a good theory. Theories about and models of human behavior are frameworks on which we can hang our real-world observations and practical experiences. They help us see the shapes of things, understand how all the pieces fit together, and consider all the possibilities. That's what we'll be using them for in this book. We'll be presenting you with some theories and models — stolen from psychology, performance technology, educational technology, and marketing — that we and others have found useful in designing and carrying out security education efforts. In most cases, we've whittled them down to the basics and stripped off the gobbledygook to make them understandable and usable by busy people. (This isn't a psychology textbook or performance technology handbook.) Give these theories and models some thought, and you may be surprised at how practical they suddenly seem.

DEFINITIONS

There are a few terms that we'll be using in very specific ways in this book, so we'd better take a quick look at some of them:

- We'll be using the word *program*, as in "security education program," to mean your overall effort, not a specific briefing (or training session) or activity. We'll call those *presentations* or *activities*.

- *Problem*, as we use this term, refers to a situation you need to do something about. It doesn't necessarily mean that something's wrong. Things may be going well, but you recognize a need to boost quality just a bit. Or you may recognize a need to reinforce good performance so it will continue. Think of *problem* more along the lines of an arithmetic problem: something to be solved.

- A *task* is a specific action or small set of actions. Examples include activating the intrusion detection system when closing the store, determining whether a document contains corporate proprietary data, verifying the identity of a visitor, securing a vehicle when parking it in the motor pool, or deciding whether key X should be issued to employee Y. Notice that tasks may be pretty simple (securing the vehicle) or quite complex (deciding about the proprietary data). But they're all specific actions with a specific end result.

- A person's *role* in our security program is the whole set of tasks we expect him or her to perform for the program. Examples of roles that would involve some of these tasks include securing the store at closing time, reviewing documents for proposed public release, acting as a security receptionist, taking required security measures when driving a company vehicle, or operating the facility's key control station. People will often perform multiple roles in the program, and their roles may change with the circumstances. For instance, a member of your security force might, at various times, staff a static observation post, operate the key control station, work as a security receptionist, perform foot patrols, perform vehicle patrols, staff your security control center, serve as an escort for moving cash or sensitive items, and so on. Each of these functions represents a specific role, and each includes a variety of tasks.

Enough introduction. Let's get started!

2

Starting with Some Basics

In this chapter we cover a few issues that have important influences on the other material you'll find in this book. We want to get you thinking about concepts that we believe can have strong, positive effects on the quality of security education but that haven't always been as much a part of your thinking as they should be. We'll be talking in generalities, but we'll offer specific examples of how these concepts have impact. As we move through other chapters, we'll be coming back to these concepts and hitting them again from different angles with more specific examples.

A PERFORMANCE FOCUS

As you move through this book, you'll notice one significant and somewhat unusual characteristic of our approach to security education. Our focus is almost entirely on performance — people *doing* things that either support or hinder your security program. We'll talk about information and knowledge, but only as they are needed for performance. We'll discuss attitudes, but only as they affect performance. We'll examine that favorite security icon, security awareness, but only as a trigger to performance. Although all of those factors are important, our premise is that it's not what people know, or feel, or are aware of that is the final determinant of the quality of security — it's what they *do*. If the purpose of security education is to establish, enhance, and maintain quality security, we should keep our eyes firmly fixed on performance.

There are a couple of reasons for this focus, and both have to do with cost-effectiveness. Unless you start by looking at what people actually do (or should do) in the security program, you can't possibly figure out what information they need to do it. The default is usually to give people too much information. Now that would be fine if you and they had all the time in the world for this stuff, but you know that's not the case. When you load unnecessary information onto your performers, you're wasting their time and yours — time that could be put to better use. So we'll always start out asking what we want people to do (or not to do), then move on to figuring out how to get them to do it (or keep them from doing it).

The second reason has to do with attitudes. People's attitudes toward the organization, its security program, and specific security functions and tasks are often important influences on performance. Many of you have probably run across people who performed their security responsibilities poorly because they were disgruntled or dissatisfied with their situation. We will be alert for attitudes that influence performance, and we may try to do something about them. But the performance technology folks tell us that it's usually a whole lot easier to change performance than to change attitudes. Often there's some other, more cost-effective way to work around the attitude problem. So we'll make sure we keep our focus on performance and see if we can't find one of those ways.

Awareness is important, too, and its something we'll be careful to consider. But I can be as aware as all get-out yet it may still be meaningless when it comes to what I do. Two of the authors are smokers. Both are very much aware that they would be better off if they quit. Their expected life span would increase, they'd probably feel better, they'd save a bundle of money, and they wouldn't have to bother emptying those cruddy ashtrays. One of them was completely aware of all that as he wrote this statement — then he reached for the cigarette pack. Making people aware of the need for security is important, but something more is needed. I can make my store's sales force 100% aware of the threat posed by shoplifters, but unless they know how to counter it and are motivated to do so, being aware won't stop the merchandise from walking out the door.

PERCEPTIONS VERSUS REALITY

A security officer who was having serious problems getting cooperation from the workforce once complained, "I don't know what's wrong with these people. Security's important. But they just don't act like it." We've heard that same complaint, in a variety of words, time after time. What these folks have run afoul of is a basic but often overlooked truth of human psychology: People don't react to reality; they react to their *perceptions* of reality. That's a critical idea to keep in mind as you work on your security education program, particularly when it comes to motivating people.

A favorite story about perception versus reality comes from Fort Sumter at the start of the War between the States. A southern official was at the fort trying to negotiate its surrender. He happened to be sitting in the dispensary and saw a bottle on the table. *Perception:* It's a bottle of medicinal whiskey. (They had a lot of that in dispensaries in those days.) So he snuck a healthy swig. *Reality:* He ended up outside with a doctor pumping the iodine out of his stomach. Like Civil War stories? Here's another one. Major General George B. McClellan was moving his huge Army of the Potomac up the Virginia peninsula to attack Richmond and end the war. He encountered Confederate fortifications at Yorktown. *Perception:* The Federals face fortifications bristling with dozens of heavy artillery pieces. McClellan spent a month moving up a hundred heavy guns to counter the Confederate artillery. *Reality:* When the Confederates suddenly abandon the fortifications and fall back to other positions, the Union troops discover that most of the Rebel artillery consists of "Quaker guns" — trunks of felled trees painted black to look like cannons.

Security is important. But unless the people in your organization understand and believe that security is important, they won't act like it. Perhaps your specific security requirements and procedures have been carefully developed, make good sense, and are necessary, but unless your workforce understands and believes that these procedures are necessary, they won't act like it. There may be a real, credible threat to the assets you're protecting, but unless people understand and believe there is a threat, they won't act like it. And sure, people should understand that security's important. But what people should believe, should understand, or should think doesn't matter one bit when it comes to performance. It's what they do understand, think, and believe that counts. As you work on your security education program, you need to be on the lookout for the possibility of misperceptions that could hurt you.

One newly assigned security officer of a facility decided that a good way to get to know the organization was to just wander around, get to know people, and get to see the operation firsthand. She mentioned her intentions at a staff meeting and said she'd like to hear about problems people might be having so she could see what she could do to help. And she meant it. She believed strongly in developing a good, cooperative working relationship with people in the operating activities. When she began her "management-by-walking-around," she was surprised and puzzled by the reactions she got. "People treated me like I was a rabid dog," she said. The people in the offices and labs watched her like a hawk, answered questions with one-word answers, and seemed to have expressions that were somewhere between wary and terrified. After a couple of weeks of this, she was having lunch in the employee cafeteria with a branch chief she'd gotten to know. He teased her: "Well, where are you going to cause panic today?" When she asked what he meant, he told her, and their subsequent discussion was an eye-opener. It turned out that her predecessor had been an old-school, hard-line security dinosaur who had seen his principal duty as catching people messing up and hanging them. He had even told one colleague: "My job's to get out there and find out what's going on, then kick ____ and take names!" No wonder she was perceived as a threat. The reality that she was there to learn about the organization, meet people, and give them a hand with program problems didn't matter. Their reaction to her was based on their perceptions of her, which were based on their experiences with her predecessor.

PROGRAM DRIVERS

We've found that there are three basic ways that people decide what goes into their security education programs. There are requirements-driven programs, means-driven programs, and needs-driven programs. Most programs are combinations of two or all three of these types, with one or the other predominating. There is nothing wrong with that approach, but you have to be careful.

In a requirements-driven program, the program developer sets his or her sights on fulfilling a set of requirements imposed by an outside authority. If you work in a large corporation, your corporate headquarters may have issued a directive stating mandatory requirements for security education. In government, your higher headquarters has included security education requirements in its security regulations. In industry, you may have to abide by requirements established by law or regulations issued by government agencies covering your type of business. The security education program is developed with a focus on making sure those requirements are met.

A means-driven program is shaped by "stuff" — what sort of materials (or maybe people) are available for use in the program. "Huh? You're kidding, right?" Not at all. We've seen a truly unfortunate number of security education programs that were put together very obviously on the basis of what a hard-pressed security officer could find to use in the program. One of the authors spent some time on a military department staff working with security education. Often, he'd get calls from security staffers at subordinate command levels asking for help with their security education efforts. Quite a few of them would start off like this: "Hi. I'm so-and-so at such-and-such command. I'm putting together our annual security education program, and I was wondering if you knew of a good videotape I could use." When he'd ask what subject matter they wanted the tape to cover, there would sometimes be an uncomfortable silence. (His favorite story was the time he asked a caller, "What do you want the tape to be about?" and got the reply, "Oh, about 15 or 20 minutes.") We've also seen security posters prominently displayed in organizations that had nothing whatever to do with the specific security programs in those organizations (such as posters exhorting folks to protect classified information in organizations where nobody ever had access to any classified information). Why were they there? Because they were really nifty posters with one compelling advantage: they were available. Another case illustrates a program driven by the people available. When looking at the security education program of a particular large organization, we found that it was an active effort. It used a variety of means to reach the people in the organization, and everything was very well done. But then we noticed a problem. The organization had a wide variety of assets to protect and faced some serious threats, but the security education program dealt almost entirely with only one facet of the security program: personnel security and surety. All other aspects of the program were only rarely mentioned, and then only briefly. Why? Well, it was all because of George. George handled personnel security for the organization. George also happened to be an excellent and enthusiastic public speaker and a good writer. So when it came time to put together presentations or written material, the solution was literally "let George do it." You ended up with high-quality stuff that covered only a small segment of the organization's security needs.

Finally, there's the needs-driven program. In this sort of effort, the security staff looks at the security program and figures out just what needs to be done to make the program work. Then they look at the people in the organization to figure out who it is that should be doing those things. Then they decide what needs to be done with those people to make those things happen. That's their basis for deciding how their security education program can make its best contribution to the quality of security in the organization. That's how they go about starting to design their program. Now, if you think that's just common sense and that it's obviously the way things ought to be done, we agree with you 100%. You want to think about requirements and means, of course. Many of us work in organizations where we have to abide by instructions issued from higher echelons of the organizational hierarchy, so we want to make sure we cover those bases. It's just smart management to make sure we take good advantage of special talents we can tap or really good support materials we find. But basing our program fundamentally on the needs we have that it can fulfill is definitely the way to go.

So why isn't this approach followed all the time? Why do we find programs that are primarily requirements driven or means driven? After looking at this problem for many years, we've come to the conclusion that the most common factor is lack of confidence. It's not intelligence or ability. We've seen lots of smart and capable people snared in the requirements/means trap. They were lured and caught because they lacked confidence in themselves when it came to security education. They didn't have confidence in their own ability to put together an effective security education program, so they decided that it was a given that the security staff at their higher headquarters (who were probably a couple notches above them on the pay scale) knew what to do better than they did. They looked to the directives to shape their program. Or they didn't have confidence they could put together a good program so they looked for crutches.

The lack-of-confidence problem is also one reason behind security education programs that stay basically the same from year to year, whether they work or not. If someone doesn't have confidence that they can do something different and better, they tend to do the same thing that was done before, which, if not much of a success, at least hasn't been enough of a disaster to get anyone fired. At one organization, two relatively new security specialists were assigned to develop a security education presentation that was to be used as the activity's annual security education effort. (We'll talk about the fallacy of the annual or any other periodic efforts later.) Being new to security and the organization, they had zero confidence that they could do the job, and they dug out the previous year's program and modeled their work after it. They weren't satisfied with the result. They had some ideas that they thought would be improvements, but they didn't quite have the confidence to give them a try. So the organization's population was treated to pretty much the same program they had the year before, which was basically the same program used the year before that, and so on. That went on until one of the organization's top managers sat through one of the presentations and made a phone call to the chief of security, which included the question: "How many times do you people intend to make me sit through the same, tired old thing?"

EFFECTS PERSPECTIVE VERSUS CONTENT PERSPECTIVE

Throughout this book, we encourage you to adopt a particular perspective as you develop your security education program: an effects perspective. When you adopt an effects perspective, you constantly ask yourself, what effects do I need to have on my target audience and its security performance, and what effects might what I'm doing have? Notice the two-part question. You figure out what effects on performance you need to have, but you're also alert to other effects your activities might have — including unintended, perhaps harmful ones.

The alternative is to take a content perspective. With this perspective, you focus on subject matter or topics to cover. This is not a bad strategy by any means. It's useful in some ways, but not as effective as the effects perspective. (No pun intended.) You can tell when people have adopted a content perspective by listening to the way they talk about the effort. They discuss what they need to cover. They use the word *about* a lot: "We need to include something about . . ." or "make sure we talk about . . ." or "tell them about. . . ." The focus here is not on performance. Just what is it we're going to include about such-and-such? A content perspective is fine for a first, broad-brush whack at planning a program or activity, but unless you do some whittling down, you'll probably end up including a lot of useless or only marginally useful content. When you whittle it down properly, however, you'll end up taking an effects perspective almost automatically. So why not start off that way in the first place and save yourself some effort?

One of the authors was once discussing a security education project with his supervisor. The supervisor was taking a content perspective. At one point, the supervisor commented, "We better make sure we tell them about such-and-such." The response was, "Okay. Good. What about such-and-such?" The supervisor then explained, "Well, when we've done inspections, we've been finding that people don't know how to do so-and-so." (So-and-so was one step in the such-and-such process.) The response was, "Okay. Great. I'll put a section in explaining how to do so-and-so." *Content perspective*: Tell them about such-and-such. *Effects perspective*: Teach them how to do so-and-so. The difference was that the subject of such-and-such took up three whole pages in the organization's security directive. Doing so-and-so was covered in one small paragraph. "Telling them about such-and-such" would have eaten up most of the time available for the presentation. "Explaining how to do so-and-so" took a few minutes.

The other side of the effects perspective coin is that it can help you avoid unintended, counterproductive effects. For an example, we'll use one of our least favorite security education techniques. You may have run across it in security and in other fields. It's the common practice of periodically circulating reading materials — often copies of directives — and having people "read and initial" them. Let's look at the intended effects. People will learn or have their memories refreshed about the material covered in the reading matter. If you believe this will happen, we have a nice bridge in Brooklyn we'd be happy to sell you. If you've been around longer than yesterday, you know darn well that hardly anybody ever reads that stuff. The trick is to see how fast you can scribble your initials on the routing sheet and pass the bundle along to the next victim. "Well, yeah," you say, "but at least it puts the people on notice that there are requirements." Okay, we'll give it that much. "And the initials give you some documentation that the employee has been put on notice." All right. We'll grant that, too. That doesn't do anything much for your security program, but it might make your legal department happy. But now let's look at a probable, unintended, and very damaging effect.

When one particular company put in the new promotion system, the vice president for employee relations has an all-hands meeting in the company auditorium to explain it. The meeting is important. The branch chief spends most of the last branch meeting talking about the inventory control system and how important it is that everyone use it properly. It is important. There's an annual, three-hour class on equal employment opportunity. It's important. The company fire department holds monthly fire drills. They're important. Security passes around a bundle of directives, which nobody reads anyway. How important will people think security is? Is this directives circulation business promoting the dangerous misperception that security is a relatively unimportant, purely administrative nuisance? You tell us.

TAILORING

Taking an effects perspective leads us to another important, sometimes overlooked aspect of good security education: tailoring. By tailoring we mean working to ensure that specific people are provided with the specific security education they need to perform their specific roles in the program in ways that are most effective for them. We want to tailor our efforts as much as we possibly can to the specific needs, interests, and abilities of the people we're trying to reach.

People's security education needs depend in large part on the roles they're expected to play in the program. Your senior executives have very different roles to play in the program than workers on your production line. The members of your security force have different roles than sales personnel. Information systems technicians have different roles than public affairs specialists. So it's simply common sense that different employees need to be provided with different information, perhaps need to be made aware of different threats, need to have different aspects of the program explained to them, and perhaps need to be motivated in different ways. There will almost certainly be some parts of the security education program that will apply to all of the employees, or at least most of them. But there will also be many aspects that are necessary and applicable to only a small segment of the population. As much as we possibly can, we should make sure we provide people with what is necessary for them to fulfill their roles and avoid cluttering their lives with concerns that don't apply to them.

So much for needs. How about interests? It's sad but true that you're probably going to be dealing with a lot of folks in your organization who just aren't interested in your security program — at least, not until you *get* them interested. But maybe you can find a subject that you know will interest certain segments of your population and that you can use to grab their attention and get your security message across. For example, if you're dealing with your information systems specialists, they're probably interested in the world of computers. So using a few examples from that arena might be worth trying. With marketing people, examples of leaks of marketing data and the damage caused might pique their interest. This strategy not only gets people's attention, it also sends a subtle signal that you're talking to this specific person, not somebody else. These are the ones whose roles in your security program are important.

Tailoring your efforts to the abilities of people you're trying to reach is such a common-sense idea that we shouldn't even have to mention it. Unfortunately, we do, because it's all too often been neglected. Here's a horrible example. At one military installation some years back, security education for new employees with security clearances consisted of handing them a copy of the military department's information security regulation and a form, with instructions to read the regulation and initial a block on the form, which indicated they had "read and understood" the regulation. Unfortunately, many of these employees were industrial workers and didn't have the reading skills or vocabulary to make sense of the bureaucratic gobbledygook with which the regulation of that day was loaded.

When making presentations, we need to make sure that the words we're using are understandable to our audience. This is especially true when we find ourselves using the jargon of the security business. There's nothing wrong with jargon as long as the folks on both sides of the communication attempt to understand it. If you're not sure that others understand your language, make sure. Written material poses another problem. It's estimated that around 90 million American adults have limited literacy skills. Some of those people are in your organization. We're not suggesting that you "dumb down" everything you write; plenty of good tools are available to help you make sure your written material is understandable to the people you're trying to reach. If your message isn't comprehensible, it's a waste of your time and theirs.

Unfortunately, tailoring is something we've often found lacking in security education programs. There's an unfortunate tendency to treat everyone the same in security education. When we've presented the idea of tailoring to security educators, the reaction has often been that it's a nice idea but impractical in the real world. We disagree. We recognize that you're not going to be able to tailor your programs 100% to individual needs, but we can do a whole lot more to focus a program than has been traditionally done. We're going to be providing you with ideas for tailoring as we move through the following chapters, but let us give you a couple of quick examples now, just to get you thinking that it may be a realistic possibility for you.

Suppose that you have an opportunity to conduct some security education presentations for one of your operating elements. The organization includes managers, the administrative support team, engineers, information-processing specialists, and clerks/typists. It's a large organization, but the conference room is rather small. You're going to have to do five presentations in order to include everyone. You take a nontailored approach and put together a good presentation that includes a lot of important material. Then you fill up that conference room five times and present the same presentation to everyone. Some of the material is applicable to the engineers but not the clerks and typists. Some is extremely important for the managers but has nothing to do with the information systems folks, and so on.

Now take a tailored approach. Instead of filling up the room five times with mixed audiences, you divide the staff up according to the roles they play in the security program and schedule five sessions with specific groups. At each session, you present the material that's appropriate to everyone and the other material that's appropriate only for that specific group. You're able to spend more time covering the material that is relevant to the specific audience.

Consider this second example. You get creative and use different means of reaching different groups. For material that's appropriate to all, you may present to a large group. For aspects of the plan that are management specific, you may get some time on the agenda of the department staff meeting. For items that apply only to the information systems staff, you may use e-mail or a Web site to communicate your message. For the clerks and typists, you may wangle some time in a training course they all attend. For workers with limited reading ability, you may concentrate on oral rather than written material. Again, you're taking a tailored, focused approach, which will probably be much more efficient and effective and will avoid wasting time and effort.

You can probably see that tailoring your efforts to specific roles people play will help you avoid wasting their time and yours. But it will also help you avoid something else. Remember the effects perspective? What unintended, negative effect might the old, mass coverage approach have? Actually, there are a couple.

The first negative effect flows from the fact that busy people hate to have people waste their time. Oh, we all waste time now and then, but people resent it when others do it to them. (How many times have we heard people grumble about something being a "waste of time"?) When people waste our time, we take it as a lack of respect. Could the people subjected to the mass approach to security education see it as a lack of respect for their roles in security?

The second possible negative effect is promoting the perception that security is for someone else to worry about. A security specialist happened to be standing outside the door of an auditorium where a coworker was making a presentation to a large group of employees. Suddenly the door opened and one of the employees walked out. He was a warehouseman in the organization's central supply facility. The security specialist knew him. He said hello, followed by "Have to leave, huh?" The warehouseman's response was, "Hey, I'm sorry, but that guy ain't talking to me. I don't have anything to do with that classified stuff." The first part of the program covered issues related to the security of classified information, and the warehouseman was right — none of that applied to him. But later in the program, items would be discussed that *did* apply to him: pilferage control, some physical security subjects, and so on. He left, but his coworkers stayed. They were reading material unrelated to the meeting, chatting quietly with each other, and a couple people were having nice naps. Being told about things that were obviously not applicable to their work had signaled them that the whole program was meant for someone else, not them. And there was the real possibility that this would carry over to their attitudes toward the security program in general.

Tailoring our security education efforts as much as we can to specific segments of our organization's population helps us do the job more cost-effectively and promotes the attitude that security is a specific, important element of everyone's job.

SOUND GOOD SO FAR?

We hope that what you've read in this chapter sounds like common sense to you. Throughout the rest of this book, we'll give you the weapons and ammunition you need to make these basic principles a reality in your security education program.

3

Goals, Objectives, and a Model

We want to use security education as a means of improving the quality of our security program. That's our basic goal. Now let's look at some specific objectives. We'll break them up into three handy categories or phases: *installation, maintenance,* and *enhancement.* It's useful to think about these categories because you may want to use different tactics, depending on which type you're doing. They are also a good way to start thinking about when security education can and should be having a positive impact on your program.

INSTALLATION SECURITY EDUCATION

In the installation category of security education, you're dealing with something new. It might be a new task to be performed. It might be a new person in the organization. It might be a person who's been around a while, but now has to perform a task that he or she hasn't done before. It might be a new method of performing a task — either a change you've made or one that's been imposed by higher-ups in your agency or corporate management structure. So far, things are obvious. When we get new people in our organizations, we give them a good grounding in security rules. If people change jobs, we make sure they know what their responsibilities are in their new positions. If there's a new security requirement, we make sure people know about it. When we change a procedure, common sense leads us to get the word out.

The one area that falls under the installation category but that is sometimes overlooked is what happens when the environment changes. For example, your corporate headquarters moves from its comfortable but slightly shabby old facility, buried in the middle of your manufacturing compound, to a fine new building in an office park. The assets to be protected — trade secrets, proprietary information, marketing data, and, of course, all that high-tech and high-dollar office equipment — are the same. The rules people have to go by to protect those assets are the same. The tasks they have to accomplish to implement the rules are basically the same. But those tasks need to be performed in a totally new environment. To make sure that this is done effectively, the staff will need some security education. Installation security education is what we do to enable people to do things that are new for them — or to do things in a new way — and to motivate them to start doing what's needed.

MAINTENANCE SECURITY EDUCATION

Security programs are like cars. They need maintenance. Security education must be a central part of that maintenance. We'll talk later about something called the *forgetting curve* — which simply means that if people don't do something for a while, they forget how. (Can anybody tell me how to find the square root of a number? I knew how when I took high school algebra.) Awareness of threats and the need for security tend to fade into the backgrounds of busy people's lives unless they're reminded of them. People need to be reminded that security is an important part of their jobs, and that management also believes security is important. So we do maintenance security education — not to teach people new things or correct problems in the program; instead we just keep the program running at an optimum level. There's a tendency to take corrective action when things go wrong, but to keep hands off when things are going right. It's probably a natural consequence of following the good old adage, "If it ain't broke, don't fix it." If we followed that idea with our cars, never giving them periodic preventive maintenance, we'd soon be walking. If we do it with our security programs, we'll see them sitting on the side of the road with their hoods up, too.

ENHANCEMENT SECURITY EDUCATION

Enhancement security education is what we do when we need to improve the performance of tasks in our security program. Notice that we *didn't* say it's what we do when things go wrong. Things may be going well, but we see that there still could be some improvement. We do enhancement security education whenever we want to raise the level of performance from unacceptable to acceptable and when we want to boost it from acceptable to even better. We use it when we want people to stop doing things they shouldn't be doing, like propping the door of the secure area open so they won't have to key in their access codes as they go in and out. We use it when we want to help people sharpen their skills or gain more information, like how to more effectively use security classification guides or how to find guides that would be useful. And we use it when we want people to pay more attention to security tasks and put more effort into them, like being more alert for suspicious loiterers in the hospital parking lot.

One thing to remember when doing enhancement security education: If the purpose is to raise acceptable performance to an even higher level, make sure the people you're dealing with know and understand that. If not, you could run across a problem. One of the authors once had some ideas for improving the effectiveness of his security police's motorized patrols. The security force was already doing a good job in that area, but he wanted to pass along some hints and tips he'd learned. He told his training officer he wanted to devote part of a training session to the subject. He started out reviewing some of the basics, which wasn't a bad idea. It doesn't hurt to remind people of the basics once in a while. But as he went along, he noticed that his audience wasn't exactly enthusiastic. Their body language and facial expressions sent clear signals that they weren't at all happy with what they were being told. When he finished the presentation (which didn't take as long as he'd planned because there were no questions from the group), he knew something had gone wrong but couldn't figure out what. One of his police sergeants clued him in. He hadn't made clear what he was doing. By failing to do that and starting out with a review of basic patrol techniques, he'd sent the signal to the audience that he didn't think they were doing the job right. That wasn't the case, of course, but remember that people react to their perceptions, not reality, and the police officers had resented what they perceived as an unfair implication of incompetence. If you're working with people who are already doing a good job but you want to help them do it even better, make sure they understand and believe that right from the start.

A MODEL FOR SECURITY EDUCATION PROGRAMS

No matter what kind of security education you're doing — installation, maintenance, or enhancement — you'll want to make sure you've covered all the necessary bases. To help you make sure your security education program has all the necessary effects on your organization's population and that you get the maximum payoff for your time and resources, we suggest you use a model for your program that we call the TEAM model.

TEAM is an acronym for training, education, awareness, and motivation. (We love acronyms. They're great ways to remember things. More about them later.) First, let's look quickly at what each of the elements of the model is all about, then we'll talk about using it to help shape your program. We'll cover each element in detail in other chapters.

ELEMENTS OF THE TEAM MODEL

Each of the four elements of the TEAM model is aimed at producing a specific type of effect on your organization's population. Each type of effect is an essential aspect of good security performance.

- *Training.* Training enables people to perform their roles in the program with the needed quality by helping them gain needed skills and knowledge or have ready access to needed information. Training is what we do to make sure people have the skills, knowledge, and information they need to perform their roles in the security program. Traditionally, training has been thought of as helping people stuff information into their heads for later use. We use the term in a broader sense, because we're also going to try to find situations where we can use other, more cost-effective alternatives to that approach. However we do it, training produces skills, knowledge, and information needed for job performance.

- *Education.* Education helps people gain an understanding of security program principles, policies, purposes, and rationales so they can and will make intelligent contributions to program quality. The education component of the TEAM model goes one step beyond training to produce an understanding of the reasons behind our security requirements. If you think of training as helping people know the who, what, when, and where of security tasks, education can be seen as getting them to understand why. This is perhaps the most neglected aspect of security education. That's a shame, because it can have positive effects on your security program.

- *Awareness.* Increasing awareness involves promoting the probability that people will consider security as they go about their work and personal lives by building a recognition of the reality and presence of the threat so countermeasures are recognized as necessary. When security educators use this term, they often mean awareness of a threat. Threat awareness is important, but you'll see that we use the term in a different way. In the TEAM model, we use *awareness* to mean getting people to think about security and specific security requirements when it makes a difference in what they do. Threat awareness is one way to help make that happen, but there are other ways, too, and we want to take advantage of them.

- *Motivation.* Motivation involves working to raise the probability that people will make choices that are positive in terms of our security program and to increase the amount of effort they devote to security performance. At this point, we have people who are able to do their job for security (training), understand what they're doing (education), and think about doing it when it counts (awareness). Now we have to get them to *do* it. That's what the motivation component of the TEAM model is all about. Your population can know everything there is to know about security, understand the program perfectly, think about it all the time, and still not perform the way we need them to. We need to motivate them to give security requirements the time, effort, and attention they deserve.

Let's look at it another way:

People will not do . . .	So we do . . .
What they don't know they should do or don't know how to do	Training
What they don't think makes sense	Education
What they never think of doing	Awareness
What they have no reason to do	Motivation

Notice that our TEAM model practices what we preached in the previous chapter. Everything is laid out in terms of the effects we want to have on our population: make them more skilled, knowledgeable, or informed; heighten their understanding; make them more aware; and so on. This concentration on effects makes this approach different from the more traditional content-based or subject-matter-based approaches to security education. We believe it's a much more powerful way to attack the subject.

USING THE MODEL

So now we have a nice model with a nifty acronym and four elements that seem to make sense. But just how do we go about using the thing? The answer is really amazingly simple: Think about it when you're planning your program and specific presentations and activities. Now we know you're probably thinking that it couldn't possibly be that simple, but it really is. You see, the purpose of the model is to help you make sure you've covered all the bases and taken advantage of all the possibilities, so just thinking about the four elements will remind you to do that.

Do you have to include all four elements in everything you do in your security education program? Of course not. Sometimes, you'll be doing just one thing or the other. You may produce or obtain a good poster that you distribute purely to create some awareness. Or you may conduct a class for your guard force that's specifically intended to train them on using some new piece of equipment. You may say a few words at a staff meeting just to educate managers about the reasons behind a new security requirement. Or you may take a minute to thank an employee for contributing to the security program, in hopes of motivating him or her to keep up the good work.

Although individual presentations and activities in your security education program may just address one element of the TEAM model, and there's nothing at all wrong with that, your program as a whole *must* include all four elements if it's to have the maximum payoff for quality security. Look back at the chart. Wipe out any one of the elements in the left-hand column, and you're left with an employee who's not doing the job. Leave any of the elements out of your security education program, and you're going to have poor or nonexistent performance somewhere in the security program.

And something else — one of the real advantages of using a model like this is that you're going to find it hard to do just one of these things at a time. That means you get more payoff with very little added effort. Say you start out intending only to do some training on a new security procedure. But you think about TEAM and you toss in a few words explaining the reason for the change, then you remember to close with a quick pitch on the importance of making the new requirement work. One of your staff members is sketching out a new poster you're going to have printed. Its purpose is to keep people aware of the need to watch out for virus infections on their computers. But, thinking of TEAM, you suggest he plop a couple of quick dos and don'ts at the bottom. You're providing information, and that's part of what we call training. In both cases you've spent very little extra effort but increased the potential payoff.

Using the TEAM model helps you make sure your program is doing all it can to promote quality security in your organization. It also helps you make sure you don't miss any worthwhile opportunities.

4

Performance Problem Solving:
Figuring Out What's Going On

WHAT'S REALLY THE PROBLEM?

Time and money are always scarce in a security operation. The last thing we want to do is waste them. When it comes to security education, however, we sometimes have done just that. Like managers in all fields, we tend to want to *do* something about a problem, and do it now. We're wary of studying the problem to death. But sometimes that leads us to take action without impact — solve the wrong problem — and waste our time and our organization's resources while we're doing it. Performance problem solving (PPS) is all about making sure we understand the problem before we attack it. Actually, it's just common sense. It's doing what we would probably do anyway. The key is that PPS gives us a method of systematically applying that common sense, of making sure we've looked at all the angles, and of helping us consider all the possibilities.

PPS is based on the simple idea that all sorts of factors influence employee performance — of security functions as well as all their other job responsibilities. There are factors that promote good performance and factors that get in its way. To improve performance, you want to accentuate the positive and eliminate the negative. (Hmm, that would make a good song lyric.) But to influence these factors properly, you have to know what they are and how they're operating first. Now, that's not exactly rocket science. We all knew that already. The problem is that even though we know it, we don't always act like it. There's a tendency to look for *the* cause of a performance problem and solve it. But there may be just one factor involved, and perhaps not the most important one. Or we apply a standard, stock solution, which can be worse than useless. Let us give you an example.

A few years ago, one of the authors was working at the headquarters of one of the military departments. He was reviewing reports of security violations: instances where classified information had been put at risk because proper security procedures were not followed. He focused on the part of the reports where the responsible officials described what corrective actions they'd taken to keep that sort of thing from happening again. Sometimes they took disciplinary action against the people involved. In almost every case, they reported that remedial training had been given to the person involved, or even to everyone in their part of the organization. This response appeared in the reports so often that it was obviously the standard solution: if somebody screws up, give the person remedial training.

The problem with this was that, quite often, it was just as obvious to somebody who was attuned to a PPS approach that training was a completely meaningless response to the real cause of the problem. Recall that training helps a performer know the who, what, when, where, and how of a task. But in so many of these cases, the people already knew all that. There was some *other* reason for the poor performance, and training just wasn't the answer. And what about giving the training to everybody in the organization? Talk about wasting time and effort! What sort of attitude toward security would you imagine those people had, after their time was wasted by this training just because somebody else messed up? You can just hear the grumbling: "Why do I have to sit through this when it was George who fouled up? What makes these people think I'm not doing my job right? I've got better things to do than sit here while they tell me a bunch of stuff I already know! Why are they wasting my time like this?"

PPS AND THE FRONT-END ANALYSIS

PPS is a method of taking a systematic approach to analyzing a performance situation, whether it's poor performance you need to correct or good performance you want to improve. It's a systematic application of common sense that helps you avoid missing possibilities. The tool it uses to do this is called a front-end analysis, or FEA.

At this point, I can imagine you might be thinking that this all sounds nice and might be just wonderful for people who have time to do all this analysis stuff, but not for busy people like you. Fair enough. FEAs of complex performance situations can take weeks of work by skilled performance technologists observing and studying work processes. But a useful, worthwhile FEA can also be done by you in a couple of minutes while you're walking down the hall to that next meeting. We're going to ask you to remember three sets of letters — nine little letters — and think about them when you're figuring out what to do about a performance problem. If you do that, you'll automatically end up with a quick-and-dirty FEA.

INFLUENCES ON PERFORMANCE

Performance technologists have found that there are three basic types of influences on employee performance. Hundreds of different influences are involved, but they all clump together nicely into these three categories. What makes this grouping important is that a different type of intervention is appropriate for each of the three types, so figuring out which category is involved gives us a head start in finding a solution. The three categories also give us a nice mnemonic to help us make sure we haven't overlooked something. Here they are:

- Environmental (ENV)

- Skills, knowledge, and information (SKI)

- Motivation, attitudes, and incentives (MIA)

You usually see these categories listed in a different order, but we've rearranged them to fit the particular situation of the security world. Now let's dig in and see how you use this stuff.

THE QUICK-AND-DIRTY FEA

You identify a performance problem. Some security function isn't being performed well enough or is being done fairly well but you want to improve it. The very first thing you do is make sure you're clear in your mind as to exactly what the problem is. A good way to do that is to think about the problem and work it around until you can state it in one sentence:

- "Store employees are not changing the tapes in the surveillance cameras every eight hours."

- "Security guards are not spot-checking enough doors (50%) on the office floors."

- "Employees are discussing sensitive company information in the local restaurants."

- "Security badges are not being worn by all employees while in the restricted areas."

- "Clothing department salespeople are not reporting suspicious activities by customers to the security staff."

Notice two things about these sentences. First, they state exactly who is involved: all employees, security guards, clothing department salespeople, and so on. Second, they state exactly what you want them to do (change tapes every eight hours, wear badges in the restricted areas) or not to do (discuss sensitive information in the restaurant). The more specific you can be in describing the problem, the more cost-effective you'll be in solving it.

Now you move on to using your ENV-SKI-MIA model to figure out what's causing the problem. If you're lucky, you'll be able to discover a single cause and work on it. Be prepared, though, to find that several — maybe quite a few — influences may be involved. This is often the case.

ENV FACTORS

First, consider environmental (ENV) factors. We suggest doing this first, because in security programs they are probably the least likely to be important and also the easiest to fix. Get them out of the way. In the ENV category, you want to consider the task itself, the work situation, and the tools available. Consider the following examples:

- Store employees are not changing the tapes in the surveillance cameras every eight hours. When you look at the task itself and the situation, you see that the tape deck is mounted on a shelf beside the surveillance camera. To change the tape, the employee has to get a ladder from the stockroom, take it out to the camera mount, climb up, change the tape, and return the ladder. The employees are letting it go because it takes a good bit of time and they don't like having to climb up the somewhat shaky ladder. That's a function of the task and the situation: an ENV factor. You find a quick solution: Lower the shelf with the tape deck to eye level.

- One of your security specialists is making too many errors when reviewing documents to sanitize them of sensitive proprietary data. Looking at her work environment, you realize that her desk is right on the main aisle through your office. People are constantly interrupting her work by stopping to ask questions or just say hello. That makes careful reading of the documents much harder — nearly impossible. You move her desk to the back of the office where she won't be constantly distracted.

- Engineers are not using security classification guides to determine the classification of information they're working with. Considering the ENV category in your FEA, you realize that the guides are all carefully maintained in a neat library in the security office down the hall from the engineering offices. Every time an engineer wants to use one, he or she has to walk down and get it. The tools needed aren't readily available — ENV again. Your solution is to make copies of the specific guides the engineers use so they can keep them right at their desks.

When you're looking at the ENV side of things, don't forget time. Time is an important factor in everyone's work environment. We get tired of hearing people say they "don't have time" for their security responsibilities, but don't let that blind you to the fact that time just may be an important issue. One of the authors worked part-time for a security guard service company while in college. One assignment was night duty on a local junior college campus. The major requirement was to make guard rounds of the campus buildings using one of those old, round watchmen's clocks, recording the times with keys mounted at various points. A complete round had to be made every two hours. Now, making a round at a reasonable pace — one that would let you observe the surroundings and note anything out of order — took one hour and 55 minutes, give or take a couple. You could then sit down at the guard station for a grand total of three or four minutes before starting the trudging and stair-climbing all over again. So what happened? By the second or third round of the night, the guards walked faster (trotted, actually) so they'd get the round done in time for a reasonable 10 minutes or so off their feet. Observe the surroundings? Not hardly. There simply wasn't enough time allowed for them to do the job the way it should have been done. Make sure this isn't happening in your performance situation.

Please notice something at this point. In three of the cases we've looked at, the ENV factor you identified wasn't the only factor that had a bearing on the problem. If the store employees, the engineers, and the security guards had been motivated enough to do the job right, they would have overcome the environmental obstacles. But moving the shelf and copying the guides was a whole heck of a lot easier and more cost-effective than doing a lot of motivating. And allowing two and a half hours for the rounds produced more effective patrolling. Often, solving ENV problems can let you avoid tackling tougher ones. As you do your FEA, be aware that there may be (and probably are) multiple influences at work and that taking care of one of them may make the others disappear. Notice also that nobody needed any training. Their environment was the main factor involved.

When we look at ENV factors, we are trying to figure out if there are things in the environment that are making the task impossible or difficult. If so, we change things if we can. This doesn't sit well with some people in security management and supervisory positions. One of the authors once suggested a change to a procedure that would make a security task simpler for the people in the organization. The security director's response was that he wasn't there to make life easy for people; his job was to make sure the facility was secure. Not very smart. If we can make a task easier to do, we reduce the probability of error. And when we look at motivation, we'll see that it's easier to motivate people to do easy things than it is to get them to do hard things. Sometimes a change in the task itself (called work simplification by the management engineering folks), the work environment, or the availability of needed tools will move us a long way in the right direction.

SKI FACTORS

Now that we've looked for ENV factors, we move on to skills, knowledge, and information (SKI). Does the performer know what is supposed to be done, who is supposed to do it, when (or under what circumstances) it's supposed to be done, where to do it (if that's a factor), and how it's to be done properly? And how do we *know* he or she knows? There are three basic ways of finding out. The first is to examine the product of the task, whatever that is. Maybe that will tip you off that there's an SKI problem here. Many security people in government and industry deal with classified government information. There are specific and rather complicated rules on how documents containing that information have to be marked. Often, just by looking at a document, you can tell that the person who marked it just doesn't know the rules or how to apply them to that specific document. You've found an SKI problem.

The second way is to observe the person performing the task. Is he doing it properly? Is she putting forth enough effort, but just doing the wrong tasks? Has your experience shown you that there are common errors that people make when doing the task, and this person is making them? You may well run into a problem here. If you have problem performers who just aren't putting out enough effort to do the job right, and they know you're watching them work, they're probably going to mend their ways — at least while you're watching. You won't be getting a true picture of how they're doing the task when they're not being watched. That's not all bad, though. You've ruled out an SKI deficiency! If they know how to do the task while they're being watched, they know how to do it at other times, too. They're performing poorly for some other reason.

The third way to find SKI deficiencies is to talk to the people involved about the task and how they do it. Please don't make it an inquisition. Some seemingly casual conversation can often produce just as good a result without creating an adversarial atmosphere. One good technique is to ask the person if he or she has run into any problems in doing the task. When one of us asked a technical specialist if he'd run into any problems using the organization's classification guide, he replied, "What's a classification guide?" Another time a question about checking property passes in a sensitive items warehouse brought the response that "somebody else takes care of that." (That response was from one of the people who was supposed to be doing it.) A question about possible problems in applying corporate information disclosure policy brought the response, "You know, I hate to admit it, but I'm not sure I really know what I'm doing with that." Another subtle, nonthreatening way of discovering SKI problems is to ask the people doing the task if they have any suggestions for improving it. The added benefit of this technique is that you might actually get a good suggestion or two!

Keep in mind as you're doing this that there are five elements in the SKI category. The people who are supposed to be doing the task must know (1) that the task needs to be done, (2) that they are supposed to be doing it, (3) when or under what circumstances it must be done, (4) where to do it (if that's a factor), and (5) how to do the task properly. Those involved must know what, who, when, where, and how.

As you look at the SKI part of the FEA, there's something else to consider. There are three terms in the category: skills, knowledge, and information. They have specific and very different meanings. A *skill* is an ability, usually developed through practice. It's more than something you know; it's something you can do. I could read a dozen books on how to play the piano and memorize all their contents, but I still wouldn't want to have to listen to me try to play. *Information* is just that — something that can be known: facts, steps in a procedure, conditions that signal the need for something to be done, and so on. *Information* is data, no matter where it happens to be. Knowledge is information too, but it's information that is stored in a performer's brain so he or she can take it out and use it when needed.

In considering SKI issues, it's extremely important to get straight which is which and which is *really* what's needed. We often assume people have the basic skills needed to do their jobs, and their security responsibilities are part of their job. That's a dangerous assumption. Sometimes, problems with what we consider basic skills can get in the way of performing security tasks. Let us give you an example from our classroom experience to illustrate how the same thing could happen in your workplace. We had a student in one of our classes whom we all considered one of the good ones. He was obviously intelligent, asked good questions in class, volunteered worthwhile answers to the instructors' questions occasionally, and was alert and interested in the subject matter. Then came the first exam; it was a disaster. He failed it miserably. We were all astounded when we saw his score. So one of us tried a little quick-and-dirty FEA. There was nothing unusual about the test-taking setting, and he hadn't seemed to be suffering from a terminal hangover or the flu. No motivation issue seemed at work, because he had been putting forth effort in the classroom and failing the course would have serious consequences for him back on the job. SKI didn't seem to be at fault, because we were sure from his performance in the classroom that he was able to handle the lesson material. Then we took a closer look at the *S* in SKI, and we noticed something odd. He answered almost every question in the first two-thirds of the exam correctly, but he answered almost none correctly in the final third. From the right-wrong pattern of his answers and having eliminated every other possibility we could think of, we figured we were looking at a skill problem. A talk with the student confirmed it. He was dyslexic. Reading (including our questions and answers) took him much longer than it would take most people. He ran out of time two-thirds of the way through the test. We were easily able to accommodate his disability, and his score on the final exam was 96%. Dyslexia aside, today's problems with low literacy levels in adults and other educational issues make watching out for a lack of basic skills a must in an FEA.

Determining whether it's information or knowledge that's needed can have a major impact on how you approach solving an SKI problem. This is going to become crystal clear in a later chapter, but for now, let's just leave it this way: Never try to stuff information in people's heads if there's a better place to put it.

MIA FACTORS

We've looked at how ENV and SKI factors may affect performance. Now we move on to motivation, attitudes, and incentives (MIA). Are people failing to do the task because they aren't motivated enough to do it? Is there some sort of attitude problem that's keeping the task from being done? What are the incentives for people to do the task right? We're going to be spending a lot of time looking at motivation in security programs, because that's always been a tough issue for people to deal with. For right now, we'll keep it short and simple. What factors can we find that will influence people to do the task and make sure they do it well? On the down side, what factors might keep them from doing the task or putting in enough effort to do it right? The influences that promote good performance, we'll call *incentives*; the ones that get in the way, we'll call *disincentives*.

Every time we decide whether or not to do something or how much effort to put into it, there are plusses and minuses: incentives and disincentives. Sometimes, the solution to an MIA problem will be to increase the incentives for proper performance. Other times, we'll work on removing or lessening disincentives. As you do your FEA, you want to be alert for both.

And now you're done with your FEA. As you can see from the examples, it may only have taken you a couple of minutes. You've taken a good, systematic approach to applying your common sense to the problem. You've made sure you've thought of all the possibilities. You've discovered what real issues are involved. You may, with luck, have already found an easy solution. And you've gone a long way toward figuring out how to solve your performance problem.

SOLUTION GUIDELINES

You've taken a major step toward a solution to your problem because you're not going to waste time tilting at windmills, doing things that aren't really going to make a difference. Just plopping the relevant factors into the ENV-SKI-MIA categories lets you apply some proven guidelines for action. Now we'll look at these quick-and-dirty guidelines for handling the issues you've identified in your quick-and-dirty FEA.

1. If you're dealing with an ENV factor, you have to either change the environment, increase the performer's motivation, or both. You might try to simplify the task, change it in other ways so it's easier to perform, make tools more available or provide better tools, or change the work environment so it's easier on the employee. If you can't do enough to take care of the problem, you then consider boosting the person's incentives to do the job right, even though it's hard.

2. The traditional approach to handling an SKI problem is training, which many times is the best solution. But many other times, there are far less expensive alternatives (in both time and money) that are often more effective in the long run. We'll be looking hard at one of these alternatives, called "job aiding," but for now we'll just say that training or an alternative is the solution of choice for most SKI problems where a knowledge or information deficiency is involved. When the lack of a skill is at fault, you may be able to help the employee to develop the needed skill. Some on-the-job training or a formal training course may be the answer. Or, if worse comes to worst, it may turn out that the person lacks some basic ability. That's when you and the person's chain of supervision may have some tough decisions to make about whether that person should be doing the task. Don't overlook the possibility that shifting duties around may leave you with better qualified people doing particular functions.

3. MIA problems require specific efforts to increase incentives, reduce disincentives, or both. One caution: Don't fall into the common trap of trying to use training to solve an MIA problem. It doesn't work. Period. There are a couple of cases where training activities can have a place in working with motivational issues, but training someone in hopes they'll magically get motivated is misguided, to put it nicely. Remember that training is only an appropriate solution if you have certain types of SKI problems.

Now we're going to look at possibilities for attacking some of these problems we've uncovered. When we discuss training, we'll be carrying part of our FEA a bit further. Before we leave FEAs, though, let us offer one piece of advice: *Do them!* Do a full-blown, detailed FEA if you have a serious, complex performance problem and enough time. Otherwise, do a quick-and-dirty FEA while you wait for the office coffee to perk. But do one. A little time spent thinking about ENV-SKI-MIA as you consider the problem can pay off big time down the road. We guarantee it.

5

Security Education and the Employment Life Cycle

No matter what your official job title or position is labeled, the key word will always be *security*. Security education, as such, is implicit in your day-to-day activities and interaction with organizational personnel. It must be a continuing influence during the employment life cycle of each and every individual. It is not only the responsibility of security people, but that of all people.

MEETING PROGRAM NEEDS

To ensure the continuing influence of security education for all employees of an organization, you — the security educator and trainer — must, to the extent possible, tailor the employees' educational needs to meet the specific requirements of your overall program. You must determine the means and methods of providing education and training, to include standard briefings, videos, the dissemination of desktop instructional materials, formal training in specific security subject areas, posters, flyers, the use of daily or weekly bulletins, and any other possible ideas that will assist in instilling a positive view and support of your fellow employees for the overall security program.

Frequency of Training

The frequency of the security education and training cycle must not be haphazard either. The frequency must be ongoing and continuous, while varying in specific topic content, in accordance to your organization's security program. The frequency of various topics and their content can be developed and organized based on overall program subject requirements, subject areas and concerns within the organization, and areas prone to potential threats and vulnerabilities, using as background continual local, regional, and worldwide news items that may have a direct or indirect bearing and impact on the organization's mission and your understanding of employee personnel duties and responsibilities wherein such duties and responsibilities have a potential impact from a security viewpoint.

Security Standards

Typically, every security manager and program has evolved a set of standards — even informal and unwritten ones — to which the security department would like all employees to attain. Such standards are, at times, hard to delineate, but would be recognized as reasonable standards that should be sustained and nurtured by all in order to protect those physical, electronic, personal, and intellectual assets of the organization.

Determined standards are not intended to be all inclusive, but the individual(s) responsible for the security education and training program must in some fashion delineate a minimum and then continue to expand or modify such subject matter coverage according to the needs of the organization's overall security program, coupled with the goals and objectives of the organization.

Training as a Continual Process

The education and training of employees is continual throughout the life of the organization and throughout the life of an employee as a worker within the organization. Education and training elements include the initial coverage of minimal education and training for everyone in terms of basic security policies, principles, and practices, and they are typically provided in conjunction with the granting of access to certain documents or work areas or controls within the organization. This is the initial briefing and is an introduction to security for the individual. Beyond this come the refresher, travel security, and termination security training. Other areas of education and training can include conferences and meetings, protection of documents in the office, transportation of documents, control of documents, protection of classified/intellectual/sensitive information, computer security controls and procedures, proper destruction of sensitive data, security and government-classified information, financial and budgeting security, contracts security, personnel documents and privacy security concerns, identification and access control to sensitive or controlled areas of the organization, and so on.

As you can surmise, security is just not a few items or areas, but from it two things can be determined: security is an integral part of the organization's lifeblood, and security education and training are a critical part of each and every employee's employment life cycle within the organization.

As you move through this chapter, discussion will touch on some security concepts and concerns, a bit of theory, and reasoning for the employee's life cycle security involvement. Some examples are drawn from the author's personal experience. A practical exercise at this chapter's end has been included to further involve you in brainstorming potential security education solutions.

Because this book must address both government and private-sector security concerns, several pages are devoted specifically to the identification of concerns wherein government sensitive or classified information is important to employees. As such, a delineation of government security standards and responsibilities are highlighted. For the private sector, wherein government-classified concerns are not part of daily work life, the classification level may be changed by inserting words like *company confidential, company sensitive,* or just *sensitive* so the full effect of these pages can also be used for the benefit of all.

Training as Part of Employee Responsibilities

Each security education and training individual must take the minimum training requirements that are delineated in your security program, so add to them, and tie them to the overall security program goals to ensure a viable program. As you will to come to understand from various examples in this chapter, all types of people throughout the organization need to understand that security is part of their job responsibilities, not just something that arises once a year or when a problem arises.

Each and every security education program should do the following:

- Advise

- Indoctrinate

- Familiarize

- Inform

- Instruct

Thus, the varied training, that is minimally required, will include a variety of formal briefings, hands-on projects, examples, readings, security posters, and discussions. The areas involved in initial briefings will be the initial and refresher; foreign travel; meetings, conferences, and symposia; threat; protection of intellectual property; personnel and financial data; termination; and other specialized subject areas, each of which will also be necessary to the organization.

SECURITY EDUCATION AS A JOB RESPONSIBILITY

You don't see motivation listed as part of any formal security education program. You have the training and awareness, but motivation is an implied part of the process; it is important to the program's success. If individuals who attend training and education are not motivated for the better, then the program becomes useless — to you and to them.

Now comes the big question: *Is it a briefing or a learning experience?* We tend to put all the presentations given into the "briefing" category. A briefing, at its baseline, usually infers a form of lecture, usually without any questions asked during the presentation, although perhaps some questions are allowed at the end, and we have the assumption that all participants will learn from it everything that you wanted them to learn. Regretfully, this is not the case.

A technical presentation for scientists and engineers, all of whom are closely tied to the subject matter, will certainly entail numerous questions, visuals, handouts, and other technical data. This is because the participants have come for a specific reason. Security presentations are different.

In many cases, those attending the presentation have come because of a requirement. As such, it interrupts their daily work flow, breaks the chain of thought on a project, takes them away from something they deem much more important than another briefing; therefore they do not have the motivation to support the program and the goals via a new presentation.

For this reason you must tailor the presentation (never a briefing) to them so all participants will take away at least one important concept and then use the concept and its value in their daily activities. It may seem hard to visualize this, but that is the bottom line — and it works.

Because the training, education, awareness, and motivation (TEAM) process must be a *continuing influence* during the employment life cycle of each individual within the organization, you must take the basic security education requirements and expand on them, tying them to the TEAM goals of your organization. As security educators, we cannot afford to fall into the "fallacy of the assumption of knowledge" by our fellow employees.

Remember the five program points listed previously? Let's take a closer look at them, recalling what the security education program is used for:

- *Advise.* To advise personnel of the adverse effects to the organization and its security that can result from the unauthorized disclosure of either classified, corporate sensitive, personnel, privacy, or financial data.

- *Indoctrinate.* To indoctrinate personnel in the principles, criteria, and procedures for the protection of various forms of information from its birth to death.

- *Familiarize.* To familiarize personnel with the procedures necessary to ensure that proper decisions that have security implications are carefully thought out before action is taken.

- *Inform.* To inform personnel of the techniques employed by foreign intelligence, foreign and domestic industrial spies, and others attempting to gain access to sensitive organizational information and then to emphasize the responsibility to report all such attempts. Also, to inform personnel of any penalties that can arise for the violation or willful disobedience of various protective safeguards and policies of the security program.

- *Instruct.* To instruct personnel that individuals having knowledge, possession, or control of information in their possession must determine *before* any dissemination of such information that the recipient is authorized to receive such information in the performance of his or her duties. And if such information is passed to the employee, the recipient is in a position to properly safeguard it from falling into unauthorized hands.

In terms of the employment life cycle of each employee, these five points must be used. As such, the TEAM process has to become a continuing influence. These minimal tenets for security education training essentially become the starting point for all security education; but we cannot view these as our only responsibility much less allow them to stand alone when educating our employees. We must take these requirements — and more — and tie them to the TEAM concept goals in ensuring a viable program.

Continuing further, the promotion of understanding of *security as a job responsibility* must also be understood by everyone within the organization. Lastly, we must ensure that as security educators we do not fall into the fallacy of the assumption of knowledge.

As we establish the security program to advise, indoctrinate, familiarize, inform, and instruct personnel, we carefully consider how it will be performed within the initial security presentations that should be tailored to each employee segment. These will be a minimum of four basic level presentations within the employee life cycle: initial ("welcome aboard the company"), refresher (annual update and reminders), travel (inside or outside the country), and termination (discharge, retirement, transfer, etc.). Optional training and education, depending on the circumstances, cover most of the other types of presentations that are given to employees.

At the outset, though, regarding these presentations, the security education program must continue to be positive in all aspects. This means that we emphasize the balance between the need to release a maximum amount of information to employees but, at the same time, we consider the long-term interests of the organization (or government under the Freedom of Information Act (FOIA) and privacy acts) to protect in terms of overall security.

So a presentation (briefing) must be made to new employees, a refresher to multiyear employees, and so on, and you must now consider exactly who will be receiving each presentation. Everyone? A selected few? Scientists, engineers, technical personnel? Administrative staffers? Security force guards? The in-house janitorial staff? Actually, all of these should receive presentations in some form on a continuing basis.

At a minimum, personnel who are authorized or expected to be authorized access to sensitive company information (technical data, concepts, design, financial, personnel and other privacy data, customer listings, sales records, administrative controls, security plans, and operational procedures) or government-classified or unclassified sensitive data must be included.

The security force, for example, has the potential to obtain information in the normal course of its duties. Throughout the day, security personnel interact with employees, may have reason to look at documents in briefcases entering or leaving the facility to ascertain the legality for them to be removed or entered, have access to employee personal and privacy data through the access control accounts on the computer, and overhear discussions from which they can accumulate a variety of sensitive data. During off-hour periods, they make the rounds of offices, inspect security containers, check desks and waste baskets for sensitive or classified information that should have been locked up (e.g., they have the opportunity to read such information), and check sensitive or controlled areas to ensure materials therein are properly secured. In any of these situations, the possibility exists that they will be in a position to find information that should have been secured. What do they do? Without the proper knowledge of specifically what is to be protected and secured, they may well overlook sensitive information, leave it lying around, or see it in the trash and let it go to the dumpster — where, down the road, someone outside the organization can obtain the information and can use it for unauthorized purposes.

CUSTOMIZING THE PROGRAM TO EMPLOYEE GROUPS

The need arises, then, to design the program to fit the requirements for different groups of people. Here, the security guards are specifically recognized as an important cog to the program's success. Likewise, just about everyone in the organization can use this type of information and learn what the proper actions are to be taken when the need arises. Each group of employees has differing specific needs according to their job functions, but from a security view, they all need certain basic levels of security training and education. Then they are all on the same wavelength when you talk about a specific security-related issue. They can visualize the situation in their mind and see the positive benefits accruing when they handle the situation appropriately. Everyone comes out ahead, because everyone is motivated to support the program in a positive manner.

Continuing in this vein with a given program item, we also must ensure that the program does not evolve into a perfunctory compliance to a formal requirement *without achieving* the real goals of the program. Here we speak of the more broad formal requirements of the program. The program states there will be an incoming briefing, a refresher, and so on. The refresher can be standardized or even tailored to the differing groups of employees, but what many trainers do is forget that without educational specifics and ensuring that some motivating factors are included, the process becomes perfunctory and just a time filler to meet the stated requirement.

The refresher briefing at one organization I worked with was very perfunctory — 30 to 45 minutes and then a question-and-answer period. It became a standard practice to ensure that everyone signed a log indicating they had attended the presentation. Whether they learned from it is unknown, but the requirement was met because the trainer (briefer) had a log sheet showing that the training goal had been met. It must have gone well because he said "there were never any questions" and people rushed out to get back to their offices. So was this an educational learning experience, with some motivation? I think not. What happened was that a requirement was met, a log was kept of attendees, and everyone left quickly to get back to doing their regular job.

Security in this particular case was seen as a burden for the employees; it took away from their normal duties — interrupted their work flow — so no one really paid attention. Had the trainer been more attuned to the audience, he would have seen that some brought office work to the briefing and worked throughout it, paying little attention to what was actually going on. Next, a review of the presentation indicated that the same presentation was given every year — no changes or updates, no new information that could have made the employees want to know more. It was a poor presentation, but the trainer didn't realize it!

This brings up a major and somewhat critical point: Is the presentation meant to be a learning experience or just a briefing? Note that we use the word *briefing* here because in the preceding example the point was to *lecture* the attendees on their required security responsibilities and no training, awareness, or motivation ever took place! If it is just a briefing, why not just write it down and send a copy to each employee? The same result would occur. The document would be tossed away or filed without the recipient reading it. Were it a valid learning experience, the employees would have questions, comments, or realize some mind-provoking thought, and they would carry away a positive message that could help them, their fellow employees, and the organization as a whole down the road because the security message was received, understood, and filed away in their memories for future action.

Make every presentation a learning experience. You don't want to lecture, but rather interact with the employees. Whether you are on the podium giving a formal or semiformal presentation or if you just talk with the employee in the parking lot or hallway, every action you take and do should be positive from the employee's viewpoint.

The basic "meet and greet" is a prime example of gaining employee support to the program. Stand at or near the door to the training area and greet employees by name when they enter; say a word or two to them. Pass among them as they are getting seated. Don't stand off to the side or at the podium looking at them, reading your notes, and preparing the visuals (you should have done this much earlier). Never be standoffish, but engage them continually. You want to be friendly, semi- or informal, and relaxed as they enter. This comfort level is conveyed to them, and they, in turn, reciprocate with their feelings and movements and are more likely to become better engaged in the give-and-take of the presentation.

At other times, ensure you don't spend all day hiding out in the office. Move throughout the organization on a daily basis, meeting and greeting employees in the hallways, at the lunch or break room, and before, during, and immediately after work. Let them know you're available any time to assist them. These are occasions for the more informal type of security education engagements:

"Good morning, Jim. You're in early."

"Hi. Yeah, I've got to get this stuff done quickly and over to the production department. Thought I'd get an early start before the others come in and the phone starts ringing."

"So, how busy is it?" as we walked down the hallway toward his office.

"Well, the program manager — Stu — is pushing to get it out, and I've got to pull some stuff from the files, consolidate it, make copies, and get it to production quick so they can move on it. I expect to revise a few areas of the document, but fortunately I've got a printer free down the hall this time of the morning."

"Okay, Jim, I'll leave you to it. Oh, by the way, is this the prototype production design?"

"Yep. Why?"

"I'm just thinking. This could really turn us around if it goes, and we beat the competition by perhaps a couple years. Maybe you ought to be sure your drafts are put into the destruction bag to be destroyed later today, and get some controls on the documents so we know nobody will copy them. You recall the case in the paper about two or three months ago about the Ferber-Highling company losing a new concept product worth several million dollars to another company because they accidentally put the stuff into the regular trash instead of their destruction burn room."

"Hey, good thought; I didn't realize that. I'd probably forget. Thanks."

Another good deed, another positive security message delivered, and it only took a walk down the hall to accomplish the mission. Every action causes a reaction. A good action on your part provided a good reaction on Jim's part. Everyone wins because some subtle motivation was included in your informal talk.

I like unofficial security education, and so should you. Meeting and talking informally — one on one, as it were, or with small groups — is exceptionally effective. You're still in your security role, but on a lower visibility plane. You can more easily demonstrate your desire to help, to assist, to support other employees with a win-win situation. Remember, every action creates a reaction, so make the reaction positive.

At lunch or break times, use the company cafeteria and break rooms to your advantage. Take lunch and breaks at different times — even 15 minutes will make a huge difference — and meet with different employees by sitting at different tables. Don't pick the empty table, but get with others. *If the conversation stops when you sit down, you definitely have an image problem.* It might be with a particular group, but it also might be that you are perceived differently because you are from the security office. Don't leave, but make small talk, avoiding any thoughts of interjecting security concerns into the discussion — unless someone asks you a specific question. You want the other employees to like and support the security staff, not fear and distrust your motives.

Keep a bunch of pencils or pens with a security slogan on them in your pocket. Make these different from others that you may have. Pass them around saying, "Hey, just got these in; what do you think of the slogan on them? I think it's okay, but don't really know."

Sure you started a conversation, but you also could have just pulled one or two pens out of your pocket and jotted something down (a reminder to your self about something to do) and then passed the pencil/pen on without comment.

What happened is that you have created an icebreaker. You put something forward without any expectation of a specific return. It's up to the other person to respond, or do nothing. Typically, after the person looks at the pen and the slogan, he or she will ask, "Got any more?" and bingo, you've just broken the ice as a nice guy and have been accepted into the group for at least a short period of time.

On the way back to the office from lunch, drop by a break room and, whether or not somebody is there, drop off a few of the pens/pencils. Leave them on the table; nothing else is required of you.

These are "gimmees," little security products that other employees can use. A security message or note is on the item, and it becomes a reminder to the person to think about security. A subtle but effective form of motivation will enter the person's mind every time she or he sees or uses the gimmee item. This is just one type of a gimmee item that can be used effectively to get a continuing security message across. In a later chapter, we'll cover some other types of product promotional materials.

You've read several examples of giving a learning experience; they weren't the traditionally known "briefing," but all the same, employees could take away a positive security message. The bottom line, then, is to *be helpful to all employees all the time.* You don't always get a second chance to positively demonstrate security, so be sure the first time is your best.

DO THE MINIMUM, OR MORE?

A question arises, "Must we do the minimum, or should we do more?" And if we do more, what should we do, how much, to what extent, and, finally, when do we stop? The answer is just several words long: Do more, always, as much as possible, and never stop! We must never stop, because we need to work with just about everybody. Security doesn't stop when a presentation is finished, when a question is answered, or when you leave for the day.

Types of Employees

You can never stop motivating employees because you can't control the minds and emotions of your coworkers. You have all types of employees in your organization. These include employees who are self-motivated to support your program, and then there are others. The self-motivated aren't usually problem types unless they go overboard with security, but they are so few and far between, they needn't be discussed here. What you may become concerned with are the other types. These include the

- lazy
- angry
- snobby
- complainers

- unmotivated
- overly sensitive
- uncooperative
- smart alecks

- know-it-alls
- not team players
- overly ambitious
- negative influencers

Truly good security education means that you have to work to convince people to get behind the program and your ideas, and then you must support them and make the program work for everyone's benefit. It's hard, yes, but it needs to be done.

When you deal with the types of employees listed, usually coming to the point early and with specifics helps immensely. Use illustrations, facts, and examples that can hit close to home for them. As an example, I had a situation arise at an offsite location. The security presentations were good because they were tailored to the employees, mostly computer technicians, programmers, and analysts. The computer personnel had a lot of computer materials and reports of a sensitive nature for the organization and those they supported. They also had the raw data on computer tapes and other files that could be easily copied and removed. I got some feedback that indicated the presentations were good, but something bothered the local site security representative, a feeling that all might not be well. The employees weren't really careless or uncaring, but they were perhaps too relaxed. They were team players relative to the job at hand, but they were somewhat uncooperative in other matters, ambitious to get ahead and succeed — both in getting promotions and financially — but nothing could be pinned down.

Less than two weeks after the annual refresher presentations were given, the morning paper indicated an FBI sting had gone down at another company just across the parking lot. In the sting, the FBI undercover agents had purchased for a half million dollars sensitive computer files.

By time I got to the office a half-hour later, I had several telephone calls voicing concerns: "Could it happen to us?" "What are we doing to protect our sensitive computer data?" and "Could you come out and talk to us?" A busy week loomed for me, but the incident increased security awareness and positive formal and informal presentations and discussions boosted morale to a new high. Employees were concerned — for themselves, for others, for the data they worked with — and their wanting more advice and assistance was the best news of the week.

Employees who gave lip service to security, the uncooperative who made life difficult for others outside their work group, and even the lazy, complainers, and nonteam players realized that industrial or economic espionage could hit close to home. This realization got them to become team players and more supportive of the security program. Down the road, a number of these employees made valid suggestions for upgrading security procedures to better protect the data (and, I suspect, their jobs) by instituting stricter internal controls, more frequent security presentations, and requesting a security representative to frequently sit in at staff meetings.

A positive work atmosphere was developed and sustained where everybody felt good about security and themselves. For the individual teams within the work areas, a definite strengthening developed. This is important because when security solutions are embraced by all, the support within a team unit rises and becomes more supported by the members themselves. Further, continued productive communications within and between teams, in addition to senior management, will become more effective.

This brings us back to the previous comment that you need to convince people to get behind the program and support them in order to make the program work. The sustained work atmosphere, the "feel good" relationship between everyone, and the positive tone given because of a strengthened security program also establish and improve rapport with others outside the team.

As a security educator, you are outside the various teams within your organization. By establishing and improving your rapport with others, they accept you, your advice, and your assistance and more willingly allow you to enter into their world. In a formal environment, you have a coat and tie and a given vocabulary. When meeting with teams, though, lose the coat and tie, if appropriate, and change your language structure and mannerisms to better fit in with the audience. Here, a relationship can be strengthened, as can the acceptance of your message via how it is communicated in the careful selection of vocabulary that they can easily relate to and accept.

What all this does is build on any given presentation and the manner in which it is being given. The impact of the presentation and its acceptance is what is of importance; you can have a good presentation developed, but the impact can be low or average if the presentation isn't properly accepted by your audience. So look at the audience and their aspects of human behavior.

UNDERSTANDING HUMAN BEHAVIOR

When properly motivated with a good presentation, the understanding of human behavior will have great benefits. You bring out the best in the audience; they want to accept your message and any motivators supplied. They will do this because the have a desire to develop and share essential security work skills and ethics for the betterment of everyone.

In developing and giving a presentation, your people skills become important, and the audience is acutely aware of whether you have them or not. In preparing for any audience, consider how you work with others in a variety of situations.

Take the view of a customer in a store; see how the clerks and salespeople act on your requests. Are they really helpful, do they simply give lip service, do they seem distracted by other matters, or what? Now transfer what you have learned to your own audience. Are you really helping them? Are you just giving them lip service? Are you considering numerous other issues while in their presence and not giving them your full attention? Your visible presence, mannerisms, attitude, and demeanor from the time they walk into the room and see you until the time they leave will be colored by what you do. They will carry that impression with them for days or even weeks, regardless of whether you made an excellent impression or a very poor impression on them.

A problem here is that not everyone is a team player. You will need to rely heavily on your people skills when meeting with a nonteam player. These people are usually classified as loners, but in reality, many are self-driven and project oriented to the point that when you enter the scene, it is disruptive to their thought processes and it disturbs them to the point that they step back and want out of the limelight — hence the loner label that is attached to the individual.

ESTABLISH RAPPORT AND BUILD TRUST

By building trust and a rapport, you improve morale and employee loyalty. Through motivational techniques, you can influence and inspire employees to perform better in the workplace while, at the same time, considering the security aspects of their job. When mistakes are made (by you or others), what do you do? Point them out, or try to resolve them in the best manner possible without doing further harm or hurting individual feelings.

You need to be accepted by your peers and also by those not associated with you. Being accepted means proving trustworthiness in all things that you do. Go by the book; don't cut corners to get the job done. And when something arises, refer to the book instead of telling an individual "I think . . ." or something else. If you can't answer the question completely, give the person a partial answer and follow it with the statement that you will check on the matter specifically and get right back to the person when you know more. *And mean it*! When you get back to the person, explain why something is done a certain way, how it benefits the employee and the organization, and how doing it wrong can create a further or much larger problem. Never take the superior attitude, but use an even ground for discussions and explanations.

The worst a person can encounter is the security trainer or manager who replies to a question with the authority of an "expert" and merely states "because it's in the book; the manual says do it this way, *period*!" With this attitude, the security manager has lost a potential adherent and will never be looked on as being helpful in the future, but rather will be viewed as a troublesome person who is out to make life miserable for all employees. If you can't foster relationships with others and keep them motivated in a positive vein, then security, security education, training, and awareness are not the areas you should be in.

Gaining respect from the boss, coworkers, and subordinates only comes with a good understanding of human behavior, the building of rapport, which leads to trust with others, and effective communication. With this respect, you can do much more with the security education program, gain program acceptance throughout the organization, and have a great program that is viable and creates a win-win situation for everyone.

DIFFICULT AND ANGRY PEOPLE

This is the downside of security; every organization has one or several people that in no way can be easily motivated. It may be because of a perceived grudge against them (recently or in the distant past), their mindset is not typical of the average employee, or for a number of other reasons. Your problem — and greater concern — is how to defuse potential situations that can arise in the course of day-to-day activities. Many times you can pinpoint a hidden message in the actions, movements, or abilities of difficult employees and can then find a way to calmly discuss a subject or specific item. The mannerisms in which they stand and move their arms and legs are tied to their voice. The voice tone and quality itself, in addition to facial muscular movement can provide clues to the level of their anger, resentment, or personal distaste for another individual, group of individuals, or a duty or requirement they are expected to perform. These are problems that do not easily go away; they tend to build and fester, and perhaps you just can't fathom why.

It may well be that the individual's character makeup, coupled with his or her distant background environment, has a great deal to do with the problem at hand. Nevertheless, make a concerted effort to get through to the person in a positive manner. If the individual is not receptive to positive enforcement and empowerment through a variety of motivational means, then perhaps it is better for all concerned — especially when it may involve potential security infractions or degradation to the program — that the individual be moved on to another environment outside your organization.

One of the difficult types of individuals frequently found within the larger, long-term organization is the know-it-all. After all, the individual has been with the organization for many years, held numerous positions, and is accepted throughout the organization as a person who can answer just about any general question or else can direct an individual where to go for the answer. The know-it-all is just that — a self-centered individual who claims to have a finger in every pie (or did at one time) and thus becomes a self-styled expert to which you should defer. Your security training program is not for the know-it-all; after all, this individual "*grew up with security, has many years in the organization, and certainly knows more than you!*"

This individual will pick at your suggestions and new security criteria, finding fault with everything that is different from what this person perceives as his or her own "expert" knowledge of security or a given security concern. He may subtly or directly attack policy and procedural guidelines, nit-pick words, or reinterpret anything to make your life more difficult. At the same time, as you defend what is right, this person will continue doing everything his way. The bottom line is that such individuals really don't want to change or truly support the security program, but would rather create an environment of internal discord.

"Your security education and training program is not for me," the know-it-all might say, "because I grew up with the program, saw the changes, and realize that you don't know the history of the program." Does this mean that the adjustment might be difficult? Sure. Surmountable? Possibly. But will you be able to overcome those objections with time and patience? Of course.

The need for the security educator to look, act, and be professional now comes into play. More than ever, the professionalism of security and its representatives must be at the forefront of everything that is accomplished in order to get the know-it-all to go along with the latest program. Subtle discussions, continual motivation, and the willingness to discuss specifics and their interpretations will probably play a major role in turning around this attitude toward the new security program.

The need to overcome traditional reactions and criticism follows in due course. The level of security professionalism must be evident in your dealings with this type of individual. "It won't work" or "it's been done before and wasn't right then, and won't be right now" are typical statements from the know-it-all. Countering this criticism is somewhat difficult, but the worst mistake a security educator can make is to reply that it must be done "because it's in the policy (regulation), and it's required of all employees." This in itself will tend to set the know-it-all off with a negative reaction, causing the person to become more difficult and angry at *you*, and then at the program, for "not understanding."

Finally, there are people that are just plain disliked by others. They, in turn, dislike these people and expand their dislikes to what other people do, attempt to do, or direct. These individuals take out their frustrations and perceived (or true) slights against individuals who represent senior authority, who seem to dictate policy or procedures or determine, via the training mode, what is the best way to do something and why.

Like the know-it-all, getting through to disliked or angry employees and gaining their trust and acceptance will require some of the most difficult security education moves that you will ever make. These employees want their ideas and thoughts to be accepted by all, but they are unwilling to accept yours, and this makes life difficult for all concerned. Handling these individuals will be a continual uphill battle, but it can be won. The motivation must be "customized" to their situation, and this is usually the best approach to make.

Sensitive, unhappy, and negative people are also, at times, frustrating to deal with, but a discussion of problem barriers, usually through one-on-one conversations or in small groups, can get your message through to them. These touchy people will take whatever you say, even the most general statements, and view it personally. Be the natural optimist; introduce positive change into negative situations and redirect their negativism to a better view of the situation and the overall environment.

All of these situations are examples of motivating others for everyone's success. The need to support the leader in team situations is necessary to a successful action being taken. By using an optimistic atmosphere, you keep people feeling good about themselves and others, which further motivates them to support the security education program. Motivating rather than immobilizing is what must happen. Never stop the process, but keep things fresh and expand on them. This keeps people on track and can produce meaningful results for the security program.

HOT POTATOES

As a security educator and trainer, you will come across certain types of conflicts and tough situations, some related to the types of people previously discussed and others that don't fall within any given type of individual or behavior category. Avoid "hot potato" words and phrases. Some deal with jokes, ethnicity, or background, and others refer to items within your organizational corporate culture. All call for low-key conflict resolution. Office politics, gossip, and game playing within the organization can create initial conflicts and situations that are easily dealt with. They may not directly relate to security, but if allowed to continue, they can impinge on the quality and level of security within an organization. Hot potato issues must be carefully monitored and stopped at the earliest possible time.

If the need to disagree arises — and it will — disagree agreeably. Don't become so strong in your opinions or statements that the other person takes it as a personal affront, but be reasonable in your response. Pause and think before you disagree, but do it with understanding and affectability.

Within these areas, don't react too fast to a question or problem or situation. Be thoughtful and consider a reasonable response. You must totally understand the message you received in order for your reply to be totally understandable and reasonable to the receiver of your message.

Thoughtful reasoning in your discussions expands your role as an individual who takes time to listen and cares about what is being said. This actually helps to maintain a level of morale for the security program. It is a subtle morale builder, but it can work.

The downside is the educator or trainer who sidesteps a problem, situation, or question and avoids making a response.

ARE YOU A COMMUNICATOR?

What has been happening all along with these various types of individuals is your use of dynamic skills when talking with these individuals. You are a communicator; you must be a communicator in order to get your security message across to everyone. Some of the skills required include the following:

- Establishing limits

- Saying no — even under pressure

- Making requests — not issuing orders

- Using listening skills to get the right information and absorbing all that's being said

- Persuading people to get behind reasonable ideas to reach new goals

- Avoiding sending the wrong message via verbal or other means

These items evolve to the adequacy of the communication skills used by the security educator and trainer. *Dynamic* is a word that is thrown around a lot, but being dynamic is necessary in order to be effective. Communication skills are developed, not inbred as some might hazard to think. The educator must establish limits to what is accomplished, what is "given" in the give and take of conversation or training, and the point of saying "no" at times becomes a necessity.

Even under pressure, the word *no* must be forceful, but never given in an antagonistic manner. You are making requests of your people, not issuing orders. The moment the listener perceives it as an order, conflict is a potential outcome;

the order may be accepted, but grudgingly and with resentment. When making a request — not an order — be sure listening skills are brought into play. This includes obtaining the right information, interpreting it correctly, pausing and considering your answer before giving it, and interpreting the tone and quality of the speaker. Absorb all that is being said; to do otherwise is to negate or reduce the impact and actual content of the speaker. Thus, persuasion is necessary, and only good communication skills will ensure that this happens.

If a single or multiple listeners react with subtle hostility, indifference, or further criticism, then your communication is fraught with potential danger down the road. You must persuade people to get behind your ideas and message in order to reach the security goals that have been set. To accomplish this goal, avoid sending the wrong message. Never react too fast to a question or comment, be thoughtful in developing your response, and consider how that response will be accepted by a given listener.

The previous discussion concerns a variety of impediments to good security education. These impediments fall from a varied tree. There is a lot of "stuff" out there, and some of it can be tied to the false assumption of knowledge. Because you have different types of people in your organization, they will express different attitudes and views toward security. You need to address their concerns and their lack of concern in varying situations.

ASSUMPTION OF KNOWLEDGE

The authors, like you, have observed or been involved with a wide variety of individuals over a period of time who, after continual exposure to information, have stated on numerous occasions that they (or their immediate office) never have any problems with security. However, this doesn't mean that they really and truly understand and know the knowledge factors — especially when they relate to overall security policy and procedures.

They may abide by the rules or are only concerned about security and its effects when it directly impinges on what they can and cannot do (or get away with) at any given time. Those most affected by this assumption of knowledge fall into those groups previously discussed: the know-it-all ("Don't tell me how to do my job. I've been doing this for 10 [or 15 or 20] years"); the "overly educated" and, thus, the more superior individual; the argumentative person; and, most definitely, the nit-picker or interpreter of words. Each and every one of these types can be found in any medium- or large-sized organization.

Only time, consideration of their views and attitudes, and a slow application of motivation coupled with specific examples will lead them down the correct path in properly supporting the overall security program. Security education, training, motivation, and awareness will be a continual struggle for the educator until that person "sees the light," and realizes that you are right, and their attitude changes for the better.

Now there comes the last person of concern — the "somewhat important" or the person who has "just too much to do and can't be bothered to come to you." He (or she, although it is most often a he) *expects* you to come to him when he has a problem. The concern from your end is that you don't know when such people have a specific problem, because they have much more important things to do than to call down to the security office for assistance. They expect you to "just know" when they need assistance.

It's not that security doesn't necessarily mean anything to them or that it is an impediment to getting their job completed in a timely manner, but rather they feel an importance for themselves and their work more than they do the effect of negative security on work accomplishment. Most likely if you stick your head in their office and ask if they have any problems or need some help, the response is likely to be, "Where were you last week?" Then, and again, "I'm busy, I've got a hot project to complete" can be a second response and the request is that you should get back with them *when they are finished.*

All this leads to the core of the problem: People who have an assumption of knowledge feel that security interferes with their job! They want you to be helpful all the time, but not when it might interfere with what they are doing. A conundrum? Yes. Is there a solution? Yes.

Be available; set a time period each week to stop by, ask what specific security areas they have a concern with and how you might be able to help. Infer that there are probably others that may have the same problem and, with their help, you can more specifically identify areas of concern. Ask for their help in formulating a response. From this meeting, a short 15- to 30-minute training and awareness session that will benefit everyone is possible, thanks to their careful insight about a potential problem that wasn't previously brought to your attention. Of course, let others know of their vital assistance in identifying these areas of security concern. While setting a time period each week to visit is great, let them know they don't have to wait for you to stop by. Tell them to just pick up the telephone and call or come by your office — you'll be available to meet their needs.

What have you just done? You used subtle motivation to bring these employees around to your view by requesting their assistance in identifying one or more security areas that need improvement, and they may be pivotal in developing something that will help a lot of other employees. They are now looking at security from your viewpoint. Because they are work oriented, they perceive that helping you makes them look better and streamlines the work for others, so it becomes a win-win situation for them. It is also a win-win situation for you and others.

EMPLOYEE JOB FUNCTIONS

The security manager must be able to relate to employee job functions and responsibilities on a daily basis. The employee must see and understand a correlation between security requirements and the end result, which is the motivation to do what is right all the time in supporting the security program.

Remember, the basic training and education for any employee falls under four headings:

- Initial

- Refresher

- Foreign Travel

- Termination

Beyond this, you become creative in what is given, based on how it will apply to the application of security rules and procedures in terms of employee job functions.

The training and education must be a learning experience, something that can be absorbed easily and taken away to be used on the job. Never lecture in these sessions.

Government Security Concerns

Government, just like private-sector organizations, strives to protect sensitive information. Government uses a classification system to identify such information and then uses various policies and procedures to implement and maintain the protection of such information. Heads of government, and then the heads of various government agencies, departments, divisions, and offices, develop general then specific programs and procedures to protect the information entrusted to their care. One of the items included in the policy and procedures at every level is the education and training of all employees and ensuring that employees receive a quality level of education and training as may be required to do the following:

- Provide necessary knowledge and information to enable a quality level of performance of various security functions

- Promote an understanding of information and computer security program policies and requirements and their importance to the overall security of the nation

- Install and maintain a continuing awareness of security requirements and the threat to the organization and the government

- Assist in promoting a high degree of motivation for all to support the varying security program goals

All personnel of an organization who have, will have, or are about to have access to government-classified or otherwise sensitive information or who may be in a position to obtain — even inadvertently — access to classified or sensitive information must be provided with an initial orientation to the overall security program. The initial orientation — a briefing some will call it — is intended to produce a basic understanding of the nature of classified or sensitive information and the importance of its protection, to place employees on notice as to their roles and responsibilities within the program, and to alert employees as to what to do with the information as it comes into their possession in one manner or another.

Initial Security Training

In terms of employee roles and responsibilities, the education and training of wholly new employees, much less those employees who have access to these types of information over time will vary (for roles and responsibilities at middle and senior levels within an organization vary):

- Who are the senior organizational officials and security personnel, and what are their general responsibilities as concerns security?

- What are the responsibilities of the organization's employees who either create or handle classified information?

- Who should be contacted about questions or concerns regarding any security matter?

Classification Elements

Where classified information is specifically involved, the elements for classifying and declassifying information must be understood:

- What is classified information, and why is it important to protect it?

- What are the government classification levels, and what damage criteria are associated with each level?

- What are the types of classification markings that will be used, and why is it important that they be properly applied?

- What are the general requirements and methods for declassification information?

- What are the procedures for challenging the classification status of information?

Safeguarding

Once an organization has classified information, it must be protected, which means there will have to be security and education relative to the various elements in order for the information to be properly safeguarded:

- What are the proper procedures for the safeguarding of classified information?

- What constitutes a compromise of classified information, and what are the penalties associated with compromises?

- What are the general conditions and restrictions for access to classified information?

- What should a person do when it is believed that safeguarding standards have been violated?

- What steps should be taken in an emergency evacuation situation relative to the protection of classified information?

- What are the appropriate policies and procedures for the transmission of classified information?

The security office must address all members of the organization who are not cleared for access to classified information. These individuals must also be included in the security education program if they will be working in any situations where inadvertent access to classified information might occur or if they will have access to unclassified or sensitive information that might be of value to others. These individuals should be provided with a brief explanation of the nature and importance of classified information and the actions they should take if they discover classified information that is unsecured, not an apparent security vulnerability, or if they believe they have been contacted by an individual attempting to gain access to such information.

Individuals who would normally be included in such a presentation include janitorial staff and other cleaners, security guard force personnel, various administrative staffers, finance and budgeting personnel, part-time individuals, facility engineers and outside maintenance, and general workers who have frequent access.

Original Classification

Governments and their various organizations also realize that individuals in positions that require performance of specified roles in the security program must be provided with security education and training that is of sufficient quality to ensure the proper performance of their duties. The education and training should be provided before, concurrent with, or as soon as possible after an individual assumes duties that have a direct security impact.

Individuals who are original classifiers of information must be provided training that, at a minimum, addresses the following:

- What is the difference between an original and derivative classification?

- Who can classify information originally?

- What are the standards that an original classifier must meet in order to properly classify information?

- What are the prohibitions and limitations on classifying information?

- What are the basic markings that must appear on all classified information?

- What are the general standards and procedures for declassification of classified information?

- What are the requirements and standards for creating, maintaining, and publishing security classification guides?

Declassification

At times, the declassification of information is in the hands of someone other than the original classifiers. The security education and training that must be provided to these declassification authorities must include the following:

- What are the standards, methods, and procedures for declassifying information?

- What are the standards for creating and using declassification guides?

- What is contained in the organization's declassification plan?

- What are the organization's responsibilities for the establishment and maintenance of a declassification database?

Derivative Classification

Besides original and derivative classifiers and declassifiers, there also are those derivative classifiers, security personnel, and others who may be specifically designated as responsible for derivate classification, as well as some classification management officers, security specialists, or other personnel whose duties significantly impact and involve the management and oversight of classified information. These people must receive training, to include the following:

- What are the original and derivative classification processes and standards applicable to each?

- What are the proper and complete classification markings to be applied to classified information?

- What are the authorities, methods, and processes for downgrading and declassifying information?

- What are the methods, for the proper use, storage, reproduction, transmission, dissemination, and destruction of classified information?

- What are the requirements for creating and updating classification and declassification guides?

- What are the requirements for controlling access to classified information?

- What are the procedures for investigating and reporting instances of actual or potential compromise of classified information and the penalties that may be associated with the violation of established security policies and procedures?

- What are the requirements for creating, maintaining, and terminating any special access programs and the mechanisms for monitoring such programs?

- What are the procedures for the secure use, certification, and accreditation of information technology (IT) systems and networks that use, process, store, reproduce, or transmit classified information?

- What are the requirements for oversight of the security program, including self-inspections?

Security education and training in other areas is also expected and should be customized and tailored to the subject area involved and the individuals receiving the training. Areas of concern include those who work with IT systems; travel to foreign countries; travel to other national areas wherein the potential for loss or inadvertent disclosure is possible; threats to classified information; escorts or the hand-carrying of classified materials; conferences, meetings, and symposia; and clubs, associations, or societies where like-minded individuals gather for semisocial reasons.

SELF-EVALUATION THROUGH A PRACTICAL EXERCISE

Now comes a short practical exercise for you. The following is a problem for which you have to come up with a potential solution. It involves determining the security education and training needs for an employee of your organization. You must decide what type of education and training you will provide the employee at several points in his career — the employment life cycle.

Problem Background

Given an outline description of an individual's employment history, you need to identify the Security Education Awareness and Training (SEAT) needs at four specified career milestones. Focus on each career milestone to determine what type of education and training is necessary, then move to the next milestone in the employee's career. When finished, you should have laid out — in at least outline form — what your concerns are, what the employee needs to know, and how you are to present the information to him. After completion, you may also perform a self-critique of each milestone. In doing so, look at your solution in terms of adequacy, considering the TEAM framework, quality of tailoring, and avoidance of unwarranted assumptions about prior knowledge.

Some possible solutions are presented immediately following, but please don't look at them until after you have completed the exercise.

Your Problem Tasks

Specific tasks for the employment life cycle:

1. Review the employment history for Mr. Doist (Figure 5.1).

2. Starting with the first milestone, identify the various TEAM needs for Mr. Doist. You should be able to justify each task identified. As you move to the following milestones, make reasonable assumptions about any security education and training that Mr. Doist would have received in the past.

3. Determine how you will properly tailor the quality of your information and materials to fit what Mr. Doist needs to know for his job.

4. Outline your solution for each milestone.

5. For references, consider your own security policies and procedures, as well as what types of training and education are required, and refer to all sections of this book up to this point.

- *Milestone 1.* Hired by your organization. Mr. Doist will be working on a government contract and receives a security clearance at the Secret level. He will require access to North Atlantic Treaty Organization (NATO) information in order to perform job duties.

- *Milestone 2.* Promotion. Mr. Doist takes on additional responsibilities, which include overseeing the day-to-day work of two new programmers.

EMPLOYMENT BACKGROUND

for Mr. John R. Doist, Jr.

Employment History Summary

NAME: John R. Doist, Jr.

Mar 1999	Computer Programmer
Sep 2001	Computer Analyst (upward mobility program)
Feb 2002	Computer Analyst (Program & Analyst Br)
Jul 2003	Computer Analyst (Mil Opns Br)
Jul 2004	Acting Branch Chief for Military Operations
Sep 2004	Will resign to go into private industry

Figure 5.1. *Employment history for Mr. Doist.*

His clearance is upgraded to Top Secret. He is to be detailed on a half-day basis to assist a special access program office for the next four months.

- *Milestone 3.* In July 2003, Mr. Doist transfers to the military operations branch and goes into the midlevel management program, which will allow him to better address issues of employee professional training and the identification of others who will assume additional duties — such as those of an office IT security manager, document control, and custodial responsibilities. Mr. Doist will himself have an additional duty as branch security manager.

- *Milestone 4.* In July 2004, Mr. Doist becomes the acting branch chief and has 35 personnel working under him. He tends to concentrate all his time on improving computer applications and getting the required work accomplished in short order. Mr. Doist's considerable computer abilities make him one of the organizational computer experts, and he essentially lives computers. He get jobs done on or before any suspense date and, as a hard driver, pushes his people to excel in their computer projects and meet or beat suspense dates. He has announced that he will be resigning in September to begin working for a government contractor.

Solution Considerations

In selecting the various security education and training requirements at each milestone, make sure you have determined each specific training need in terms of the following:

- Will the training and education be — to the extent possible — a continuing influence during the employment life cycle?

- Will they cover all regulatory training and education requirements?

You cannot view these as the only responsibilities. Take these requirements — and more — and tie them to the TEAM goals in ensuring a viable program.

Everyone within the organization must understand the promotion of security as a job responsibility. Ensure that, as a security educator, you don't fall into the fallacy of the assumption of knowledge. Consider the following in developing the methods of training, awareness, and motivation for Mr. Doist and others who will be attending any presentation you would give:

- Advise personnel of the adverse effects to national security that can result from the unauthorized disclosure of classified information.

- Indoctrinate personnel in the principles, criteria, and procedures for classification, downgrading, declassification, marking, control and accountability, storage, destruction, and transmission of classified information. Alert them to the strict prohibitions against the improper use and abuse of the classification system.

- Familiarize personnel with the procedures for challenging classification decisions believed to be improper.

- Familiarize personnel with security requirements unique to their particular job assignments.

- Inform personnel of the techniques employed by foreign intelligence activities in attempting to obtain classified information and make them aware of their responsibility to report such attempts.

- Advise personnel of penalties for engaging in espionage activities.

- Advise personnel of the strict prohibition against discussing classified information over an unsecured telephone or in any other manner that permits interception by unauthorized persons.

- Inform personnel of the penalties for violation or disregard of provisions of this regulation.

- Instruct personnel that individuals having knowledge, possession, or control of classified information must determine, *before* dissemination of this information, that the recipient has been cleared for access, needs the information in order to perform official duties, and can properly protect/store the information.

SUMMARY

You need to get to know all employees in the organization. When the organization is large, get to know employees by their segment type, team, or division within the organization; for smaller organizations, get to know them individually. Either way, a review of their job functions, management expectations, and the organizational goals at their level is important, as each relates to the security goals of the organization. What do they do and what is expected of them? Is it the same or different, and if so, why?

You need to be aware of various personality types so you can determine how training, education, awareness, and motivation can be most effective in promoting and encouraging effective security awareness and compliance.

Determine how the security policy and procedures *and TEAM* goals mesh together. Identify fallacies that are impediments to Security Education, Awareness, and Training, and tie employee job functions to SEAT methodologies and training.

Understand the people types, as some lead to potential problems for implementing effective security education and following the requirements. Whether or not these are potential problems, the behavior and attitudes of various types of people can influence others. You need to identify each type and concentrate on using positive influences and motivation methods to keep them from working against you, openly or otherwise..

6

Motivation: Getting People to Do Things

People are complicated creatures. Motivating them to perform their roles in security programs is a complicated business, too, and sometimes a very frustrating one. Just figuring out why people are acting the way they are can leave you scratching your head. In this chapter and the next couple of chapters, we're going to help you eliminate some of the head scratching and frustration. We're not promising miracles or to make your life easy. (Our magic wand's in the repair shop.) But we'll try to provide you with some ideas and ways of looking at motivation that you can use as you work on your motivation efforts.

The nice part is that all of us have tons of experience motivating people. We've been doing it literally all our lives. When you were a baby, you motivated your mom and dad to give you a bottle. You motivated your neighbors to buy Girl Scout cookies or tickets for the basketball league raffle. You motivated that cute girl or guy in high school to ask you for a date or say yes when you asked. And you motivated your employer to hire you. We're involved in motivating people and being motivated by others in lots of ways every day. We've got loads of experience. What most of us don't have is a set of tools — theories or models — to help us think about and understand what's going on and apply what we've learned through experience in unfamiliar situations. We're going to try to fix that.

CHOICES AND EFFORT

Way back when, we defined *motivation* as working to raise the probability that people will make choices that are positive in terms of our security program and to increase the amount of effort they devote to security performance. Notice that there are two types of things we want to influence: choices and effort. We want people to make choices that have positive results for security: perform a security task rather than let it slide, protect the asset rather than leave it at risk, keep the sensitive information to themselves rather than blab it, or report the suspicious activity rather than ignore it. At other times, we'll be trying to influence the amount of effort people invest in performing security functions: to do a task properly rather than shoddily or very well rather than just okay.

In both cases, people are making decisions. We make decisions about what we're going to do all day, every day. Some of our decision making is so routine and decisions are made so quickly that we don't even realize we're doing it. This includes things like deciding to put on your shoes in the morning, stir the creamer in your coffee, put on your ID badge when you get to work, and close the door behind you when you leave the office. Other times, the decision process is more involved, takes more time, and is something we consciously think about: deciding to buy orange juice rather than grape juice in the grocery store, closing and locking the safe when you leave your desk for a few minutes rather than leaving it open, or memorizing your new network password rather than writing it down, for example. You make decisions about level of effort all the time, too: how much time and effort you're going to devote to filling out that monthly report, writing that employee performance appraisal, inspecting your perimeter lighting, or examining a visitor's ID. We need to look for ways to positively influence these decisions when they affect the security program.

MOTIVATION PROBLEMS IN SECURITY

When people in the security business think about motivation, they seem to automatically think of problems — common problems that all of us have faced now and again and that seem to be particularly widespread in security. Since you're probably going to be thinking about them anyway, let's talk about them before we go any further.

The first problem is the perception of security as a threat and the desire — and sometimes active effort — to avoid any involvement with it. The security officer walks into the purchasing office and somebody says, "Uh-oh! Look who's here! I wonder who's in trouble this time." This may be a joke, but it has a serious issue behind it. We'll talk more about this avoidance business in a little while, but we'd like to get you thinking about it now. Just where did it come from? Were these employees born with an inherited fear of getting in trouble if they got involved with security? Think about it.

Another common problem is the strong aversion among Americans to getting someone else in trouble. We despise finks, rats, snitches, tattle-tales, informers, stoolies, and squealers. So along comes the security officer and tells us we're supposed to report suspicious activities on the part of our coworkers. Yeah, right! And we're supposed to let security know if we see situations in which assets are being put at risk. Okay, but wait a minute. Somebody's responsible for that, and they're going to be in trouble over it. This natural reluctance to inform on others is something that people who work in the personnel security side of our business have struggled with for years. But it's something that all of us need to keep in mind as we work with our organization's population.

The third problem is that security is viewed as an impediment to mission accomplishment. This one is particularly damaging when it affects managers, whom we have to rely on to make sure security is a reality in their organizations and to allocate the proper resources of people's time to make it happen. "If my people didn't have to spend so much time locking and unlocking things, they could build more widgets!" "These people are potential customers, but security says I can't give them the details of our proprietary software!" "I need this new employee at work *now*, not in six months when her security clearance finally comes through!" "What do you mean I can't talk about the new laser guidance system with that Chinese physicist? He might have some good ideas for us!" The first step we have to take when we encounter someone like this is to admit to ourselves and the other person a painful but obvious truth: Security *does* (in most cases) degrade operating efficiency, if only a little bit. It may hurt to admit that, but if we don't, our credibility drops to near absolute zero and we are written off by managers as mindless drones who don't understand the real world of our organization. Security doesn't produce widgets, sell products, get employees on the job faster, or promote the sharing of ideas among researchers. That's reality. We have our work cut out for us to demonstrate to management and others in the workforce that, even so, security makes a valuable contribution to the health and well-being of the organization, its people, and, in certain areas, the nation.

The final problem is the view that security is for somebody else to do. This problem pops up in two forms. The first is the infamous "it's not my job" syndrome. Question: "Why didn't you tell us somebody had backed into the fence and tore a four foot hole in it?" Answer: "Hey, that's not my job! I'm a vehicle mechanic, not a security guard!" There can be many reasons for such an attitude, but we'd like to suggest one. Remember when we talked about the damaging effects of giving rule-based answers?

The second form this problem takes infests management. It's seeing exemption from security rules as a status symbol. Sometimes this exemption is actually embodied in the organization's security rules. Other times, managers simply give themselves the exemption: They consider themselves exempt from the rules because they're too busy and important to be bothered with them. This problem is dangerous because it's catching. Middle managers see that top managers are exempt from the rules and decide they are too. Employees see that middle managers are exempt and want to be exempt too. Let's just deal with this one here.

In the first case, where the organization's security directives actually provide for the exemptions, the solution is simple but maybe not easy: Eliminate the exemptions. You may be shaking your head right now, thinking that we've just lost our minds. "Tell the CEO he has to follow the rules? You gotta be kidding me!" Well, maybe that's not as off the wall as it sounds. Let us give you a real-world example.

One of the authors was once assigned as chief of security for a large military installation. As he was studying the post-security regulation, he noted that it required everyone to wear a security badge while in the operating areas of the installation — everybody, that is, except the commander, deputy commander, and civilian executive assistant (the top-ranking civilian employee on post). The regulation specifically said that they were not required to wear badges. The author couldn't see any good reason for the exemption and asked some members of his staff who had been around a few days longer than forever. The reply was always the same: "It's always been that way." Because he thought the exemption might be sending the wrong signals to the employees and didn't have sense enough to be cautious, he decided to discuss it with the post commander — a gruff, abrasive full colonel serving in a general officer's slot. He brought the subject up during his next meeting with the colonel. The commander's reaction? "That's ridiculous! Get that [badge exemption] out of there! Where the ———'s my badge?"

If you run across the second version of this problem, where people are granting themselves the exemptions, the best solution is to get top management involved. Doable? Sometimes. Maybe more often than we think. Consider another example from the military world. A security office was giving its annual security presentations to all military personnel and civilian employees. There were sessions scheduled over a three-week period. At a staff meeting late in the second week, the commanding general mentioned that he'd attended one of the presentations and thought it was interesting and thought provoking. He asked the attendees at the meeting what they'd thought of it. The attendees — all generals, colonels, and high-priced civilian managers — sat silently, looking faintly uncomfortable. Not one had attended any of the presentations. They were all "too busy" to find the time or "too important" to be bothered. The general told them he'd probably be asking the same question at the next week's meeting, and he hoped he'd hear some comments from each of them. It probably goes without saying that there was 100% attendance by top management at the next day's presentation.

That's enough about problems. We just wanted to make sure you knew we understood some of the tough situations you probably face in your real world. Now let's move on to some real-world ideas for handling the motivation component of your security education program.

7

Motivation: Some Theories with Practical Applications

We promised you we'd give you some theories and models to work with, and now you're going to get them. These items have been stolen from the fields of motivational psychology and organizational behavior. If you study these theories in college courses, you'll find that some of them get awfully complicated as the experts and researchers tuck in all sorts of *ifs*, *ands*, and *buts*. We've stripped them down to the basics so they'll be easier to understand and put to work. For each theory and model, we'll give you a few ideas about how you might find them useful. Keep in mind that the purpose of these theories and models is to give you tools for understanding what's happening on the motivation side of your security program and figuring out possibilities for what to do about it. We've found these tools valuable in our own work, and we hope you will, too.

First, let us remind you of something we discussed in an earlier chapter that is vitally important to what we're going to be working with here. It's the basic truth that people react to their *perceptions*, not to reality. Consider this scenario: I'm getting ready for my morning walk. The weather forecast the night before predicted subfreezing temperatures. I look out the window and it looks cold out. (How does the weather "look cold"? I don't know; it just does.) I perceive that it's cold out and act accordingly by putting on my heavy coat, wooly gloves, and funny-looking ski cap. I react to my perception. Then I go outside and find out that its 56 degrees. That's reality. One of your employees perceives that a particular task is too hard and therefore avoids doing it. The task is actually fairly easy, but the employee reacted to her perception of it. A security guard is making rounds and looks at a door. It's closed and he perceives that it's locked. Why? Because it's *always* locked when it's closed. He doesn't bother trying the knob. The door is actually unlocked, but he reacted to his perception. An employee perceives that he'll get in trouble if he lets security know about a mistake he's made in a security task. So he doesn't report it. He reacted to his perception.

There's a particular type of perception that's particularly important in motivation: expectation. An *expectation* is a person's perception of what's going to happen in the future. I turn on the faucet; my expectation is that water will come out. I do a good job working on a security task; my expectation is that my boss won't care. (Sound familiar?) I carefully lock my office when I leave; my expectation is that I will get in trouble for leaving it open. And so on. Like other kinds of perceptions, expectations can be 100% accurate or totally out in left field. They can match reality exactly or be purely imaginary. Whatever the case, perceptions are what people use to make decisions about their behavior.

Now let's look at some of the theories and models we've been bragging about. We'll start with a theory developed by one of the authors for a course he used to teach.

THE LADDER OF INVOLVEMENT IN SECURITY

An attitude is a general feeling about something. We can have attitudes about all sorts of things: green vegetables, political correctness, dogs, television news, Korean-Americans, reading, apartment living, computer technology, and on and on. We form attitudes based on our own experiences or on the experiences and opinions shared with us by others — including our friends and family, coworkers, and the authors of books, news reports, and opinion pieces in the media. We may admit that there's an exception or two, while still keeping our basic attitude. And attitudes can change.

We said in the first chapter that we were going to focus on performance, but we can't ignore attitudes. People in your organization have attitudes toward security in general, your organization's security program, your security staff and security force, and specific security requirements. These attitudes form a baseline for motivation. If someone's attitude is positive, it's easier to motivate that person to take specific steps to support the program. If he or she has a negative attitude toward the program, your motivation chore will be much more difficult.

As we try to motivate specific people or groups, we want to try to understand their attitudes. We don't have to accept or like these attitudes, just understand them. We're still perfectly free to think their negative attitude toward us or the security program is misguided, wrong, stupid, or ridiculous, and we don't have to like it. But understanding a person's attitude will give us a place to start as we work on motivating the person. It's sort of like a military commander analyzing the terrain on a battlefield. He doesn't have to like it and he may not be able to do much to change it, but he needs to understand it in order to work out his tactics.

People's attitudes toward security in general and your organization's security program in particular tend to fall into one of six categories, which we've put on what we call our ladder of involvement in security.

- Ownership

- Participation

- Compliance

- Apathy

- Avoidance

- Subversion

It's just a gimmick we've found useful for figuring out where people are coming from when they encounter a security program. We'll start our discussion at the bottom — with the negative — and work our way up.

- *Subversion.* People on this rung of the ladder deliberately and willfully try to make your security program break. This includes the traditional "bad guys": the pilfering employee, the guy who sells classified information to an espionage agent, the woman who passes along trade secrets to a competitor to try to get a good job with the other company, the terrorist, and so on. But this category also includes the people who think they're too important to bother with your security rules, the people who think your security requirements are stupid and deliberately ignore them, and the people who break the rules because they're disgruntled and want to satisfy a grudge they have against the organization. These people can do just as much harm to the organization as the ones we've traditionally considered threats.

- *Avoidance.* People on this rung view security as inherently dangerous. In their eyes, nothing good ever happens to anyone by being involved with security; it only gets people in trouble. So, being human, they do everything they can to keep from getting involved. They turn a blind eye to the need to apply security measures. If they see a situation that puts assets at risk, they ignore it. They go out of their way to avoid any sort of contact with the security staff.

- *Apathy.* These people just don't care one way or another about security. They don't think it makes any difference. They may not believe the threat exists, or they may not think your security program is a worthwhile countermeasure to the threat. They just don't care. They'll follow the rules if they think they'll get in trouble if they don't. But that's it. They won't go one fraction of an inch beyond that. If they don't think they'll get in trouble, they won't bother with the security stuff at all.

- *Compliance.* People with this attitude will do exactly what they're told to do in the security program. Period. They'll carefully comply with the rules, but if something's not specifically covered by the rules, they'll act like it's not their problem. If they're criticized for this approach, they'll bristle and get defensive. They'll tell you they're very careful about following the rules and they can't be expected to be security experts and handle situations you haven't covered in the rules.

- *Participation.* Folks on this rung believe that security, your security program, and your program's specific requirements make sense and contribute something worthwhile to the organization. They're quite willing to cooperate, to follow the rules carefully, to go a step beyond the requirements when they see it's necessary, and to make a suggestion for improvement to the program when they think of one.

- *Ownership.* Here, people have assumed responsibility for the security program. It's not your program, the company's program, or the agency's program. It's *their* program. They don't view the security staff as having ownership of the security program. It's their program, and the security staff is there to advise and assist them in making it work. This is the ideal situation, particularly if you find it in your management ranks. These people are willing to devote whatever time, attention, and resources are necessary to make security work well because it's an integral part of their responsibilities. They're willing to invest in the security program because they own it.

We hope these attitudes sound familiar to you. You've probably run across at least most of them. In a good, solid security program, you'll probably find

most of the organization's population clustered at the compliance and participation levels. Some employees will likely be down around the apathy and avoidance levels. If you're lucky, there will be a few up on the ownership rung.
Unfortunately, you'll find a very small number down at the subversion level.

Another issue to consider is that it used to be that when you were dealing
with new employees, particularly those new to the working world, you were
dealing with blank slates. These employees didn't have preformed attitudes
about security, because they'd had little or no experience with it and probably
hadn't paid much attention to what they may have heard about it. You had a
golden opportunity to start them off right and help them form positive attitudes toward your program. That situation is changing rapidly. With all the
news coverage of homeland security since September 11, 2001, and increased
security efforts to curb violence in schools, people entering the workforce are
much more likely to have already formed opinions and attitudes about the
subject. For example, one of the authors was chatting with a kid in the
neighborhood, a high school student. You'd have expected that the teenager
wouldn't have thought much about security at all. But the conversation happened to turn to security, and it became immediately obvious that this kid had
formed a definite attitude about it: It was stupid as far as he was concerned.
His high school had instituted a number of security procedures to ward off violence in the school. In his view, the procedures were poorly thought out, badly
implemented, and almost completely ineffective. Unfortunately, if his description of them was accurate, he was entirely right. (Want an example? Locker
searches for weapons and other prohibited items were done at regularly scheduled intervals, which every kid in the school had easily figured out.) The student
had already generalized from that experience that security programs in general
were probably equally useless. In dealing with new employees, we need to be
alert for these preformed attitudes.

So what do we do? Naturally, we'd like to move people up the rungs of the
ladder if we can. Failing that, we should at least try to get some understanding
of where they are so we can understand how difficult (or how easy) it may be
to motivate them when it comes to specifics. In changing attitudes, probably
the strongest influence is firsthand experience. It probably won't happen
overnight. It may be a slow and gradual process. But if people repeatedly find
that their experiences run counter to the perceptions underlying their attitude,
the attitude will likely start to change.

One of the authors had an attitude about pit bulls: They were vicious, dangerous dogs. He'd never met a pit bull, but he'd formed the attitude from hearing

horror stories about vicious pit bulls that were aired on the TV news and the reality shows. Then, on one of his morning walks, he met Thea, a 47-pound, ugly-as-sin, frighteningly mean-looking pit bull. He reacted to her as dictated by his attitude, keeping a careful distance and a wary eye on the dog. But the guy walking Thea was a pleasant fellow who usually stopped to chat. After several instances of Thea nuzzling and licking the author's hand, begging to be petted, the author's attitude changed. The biggest danger Thea posed was that she'd knock him over as she put her feet on his chest to give him a big doggie kiss on the nose. Now he believes that pit bulls — like any other breed of dog — are vicious and dangerous only if they're raised to be vicious and dangerous.

Here are a couple of tips about working to change attitudes. First, have patience. As we said, attitudes often change slowly and gradually. Take every sign of progress in the right direction as a victory. And keep working at it. You may have a whole pile of firsthand and secondhand experiences to shovel out of the way.

Also, as you work to change attitudes, realize that experiences that are dramatically different from the person's perceptions will probably be seen as aberrations or one-time happenings, and the attitude will still hold firm. Let's say a person is on the avoidance rung. She believes that nothing good ever happens to anyone if they get involved with the security program and that the security office is staffed by hard-nosed, grim-faced people whose goal is to get others in trouble for breaking the rules. One day she finds herself in a situation where she cannot avoid contacting the security office. When she makes her report, she encounters Fred — a jovial guy, positively exuding a we're-here-to-help-you attitude — who thanks her several times for bringing the matter to his attention. Her reaction is, "Gee, what's that guy doing in the security office? I wonder if he's for real?" Next she runs across Donna, another member of the security team, who is reasonably pleasant but all business, rather helpful, and obviously interested in making the program work. If this employee runs across enough "Donnas," she will probably start thinking differently about the security staff. She may put a hand up on that next rung of the ladder.

A SIMPLE MOTIVATION MODEL

When you think of motivation, it's helpful to think of it as having three elements: a task, an objective, and a consequence.

Task → Objective → Consequence

The *task* is just what we've been calling a "task" all along: something you need the performer to do. It may be a positive action, like locking the cash drawer, or it may be to avoid doing something, like not revealing confidential information about a hospital patient. In either case, a prerequisite to motivating the person is to establish the task, meaning to make sure the person knows that he or she is expected to do it.

The *objective* is what results when the task is successfully accomplished. With negative tasks, that's usually pretty simple: you didn't do what was prohibited. Dealing with positive tasks is where we run into trouble. One of the most common problems in employee management is setting performance objectives. There has to be a clear and unambiguous understanding between the manager and the employee over what the objectives are. This holds true for us in security, too. If our motivation efforts aren't going to fall apart, we have to make sure that people know just what we expect of them — what success looks like. If you're dealing with a performance problem and have done a front-end analysis, this issue should be taken care of, except for making sure it's clearly communicated to the employee. In other cases, you may have to do some hard thinking about what you mean by "attaining the objective" and how to communicate it to the performers.

As you work on establishing the objective, be careful to distinguish results from methods, and make a decision about which is important. In some cases, there's only one right way to do a task. Maybe it's the only possible way to get it done, or maybe it's specified by a law, directive, or corporate policy. In other cases, though, there may be two, three, or dozens of ways to achieve the needed result. It may not matter *how* the person does the task as long as the needed result is obtained. If so, you want to state the objective in terms of the result itself, not how the person goes about achieving it.

A consequence is something that will or will not happen *depending on whether the objective is achieved.* The last part of that sentence is the kicker. The performer has to perceive that a reward or a punishment will come along based on whether he or she achieves the objective. We'll talk more about this in a subsequent section. For now, remember that the person has to perceive that achieving the objective or failing to do so will have either a positive or a negative consequence and that the objective is the trigger for the consequence.

POSITIVE AND NEGATIVE MOTIVATION

There are two basic styles of motivation: positive motivation and negative motivation. In *positive motivation*, a person is led to expect a positive consequence for achieving the objective. This is often called a reward or an incentive. *Negative motivation* is, of course, the flip side of that coin, where the person is made to perceive that failing to achieve the objective will bring a negative consequence — a punishment or disincentive.

Actually, there's a third style of motivation, for which we've adopted a highly technical term: *carrot-and-stick*. This comes from getting a mule to move forward. You dangle a carrot in front of the mule, hoping he'll step forward to get it, but keep a stick in your other hand to whomp him upside the head if he doesn't. Using the carrot-and-stick style, you provide incentives for success, accompanied by disincentives for failure. You present both at once, applied to the same task and objective.

Though simple ideas, these motivation methods need to be thought about carefully. Which styles of motivation are being used in your security program right now? Think about the question before you answer. When we asked this question of students in our classes, many of them told us they used carrot-and-stick or all three types. But then we'd ask them to tell us about the positive side of their effort. What positive consequences did people in their organization actually *receive* when they achieved security objectives? That's when things often got uncomfortable, because many times the students couldn't come up with an answer. It turned out that there simply weren't any rewards floating around, just punishment for failure or breaking the rules.

We've found that too many security programs rely almost completely on negative motivation. What's the problem with that? The problem is that purely negative motivation is the least reliable of the three styles. Behavioral psychologists and organizational behavior experts have warned us about that time and time again, but the security profession, in large part, hasn't heeded these warnings. The basic problem with negative motivation is that you're never quite sure what it's going to do: motivate people to (1) follow the rules or (2) not get caught breaking them. Are people going to try to achieve the objective or keep you from finding out about their failures? Are they going to do the job right or cover up the wrong? With negative motivation, you just don't know. Depending on the people and the situation, things could go either way.

Positive motivation, the experts tell us, is much more reliable. People seem less likely to cheat to get a reward than to cheat to avoid a punishment. That seems to match up with our experience. Think back to your school days. Who was more likely to cheat on an exam: the B students who wanted *A*s or the kids who were trying to avoid failing the test? Using the carrot-and-stick approach gives us the power of both positive and negative motivation working together.

Let's get something straight. We are *not* saying you shouldn't use negative motivation in your security program. Negative motivation can be useful and powerful. It definitely has a place. But using *only* negative motivation in your security program is an iffy business that can leave you with huge holes in your motivation effort.

EXPECTANCY THEORY

One of the most popular and powerful models of motivation is called expectancy theory. It originated from the work in the 1960s of an organizational behavior expert, Victor Vroom. Since then, people have added refinements and extensions. You'll sometimes see it called V-I-E theory.

The "V-I-E" stands for valence, instrumentality, and expectancy. These are the three factors that the theory tells us determine the force of a motivation attempt. They're the perceptions that people consider as they decide what to do about the task we've set for them.

Valence is the perceived value (positive or negative) of the consequence to a specific performer in a specific situation. *Instrumentality* is the person's perception of the probability that achieving the objective (or failing to achieve it) will actually result in the promised (or threatened) consequence. *Expectancy* is the performer's perception of the probability of successfully achieving the objective. Wrapped up in these fancy terms are some simple but useful issues to think about, including a lot of possibilities that might not otherwise occur to us.

VALENCE

The concept of valence reminds us that different consequences (incentives and disincentives) have different perceived values for different people in different situations. The first part of that idea is another way of putting that old saying from the 1960s, "Different strokes for different folks." Obviously, the people in our organizations have a wide variety of needs, desires, preferences, outlooks, and personalities. The more we know about them, the more chance we have of picking consequences that will have maximum force in motivating these employees. Now, you're not going to be able to dig into the minds of every individual in the workforce, but there are tools you can use to make accurate generalizations about groups. (We'll look at one of them, the hierarchy of needs, in a little while.) With people you work with regularly, you might be able, with some thought and imagination, to do some specific tailoring to individuals. For instance, we generally regard public praise as a more powerful motivator than private praise. But if you know an employee is shy and hates to be in the spotlight, you'll want to avoid public praise with that person.

We'd like to squelch one misconception that seems to have clouded some people's thinking about motivation. That's the notion that money is the most powerful — or even the only — reward that motivates people. If you think about it for more than three seconds, you realize that's not true at all, but we've run across a number of security managers who felt at a real disadvantage in their motivation efforts because they weren't in a position to hand out cash rewards. Money is *one* motivator, of course, but it's far from the only one, and if it's not available, we simply use something else. Depending on who we're trying to motivate and the situation the person happens to be in, money may not even be the most powerful motivator to use.

When dealing with cash awards, we've got a suggestion for you. The award may be a performance award for someone on your security force, a cash award for an adopted suggestion, or a special award for a particularly fine piece of work in performing a security task, among others. Cash awards are wonderful motivators in many cases and sometimes can be made even more powerful with a bit of creative thinking. You do this by tying the award to something you know the person has been wanting. The award becomes not just a few extra dollars in the bank account, but rather a means of acquiring some desired object — sort of a double whammy. You've increased its valence.

Back in medieval times, one of the authors wanted to get himself a personal computer — one of those nifty little Commodore 64s that had just come out. He really wanted it, but he hesitated to spend the money that he and his family could put to other, more "sensible" uses. It so happened that he was chosen to receive a performance award. His supervisor knew about his lust for a computer and realized that the amount of the award was just about the cost of the C-64. When he presented the award, he made an off-hand comment: "Well, maybe now you can get that computer you've been whining about." With that comment, the supervisor magically transformed the award from an abstract dollar amount on a check into the means of getting something the recipient had been longing for. More powerful? You bet!

Publicizing an award — monetary or otherwise — may also increase its perceived value to the employee by giving him or her some public recognition. This has another benefit, too, which we'll see in a minute.

So far, these are the commonsense steps you'd probably take anyway, theory or no theory. We've found that the real power of the valence idea lies in the second half: finding or creating *situations* in which the consequence has a greater perceived value. We're going to give you some examples of doing this with an incentive that a lot of people dismiss as not worth much, but which, in the proper circumstances, can be surprisingly powerful: a word of praise. We like to use praise for examples because it has one terrific advantage: it doesn't cost a cent.

Someone does a particularly good job in performing his or her security responsibilities — maybe in some specific, critical situation or maybe overall. You want to reward him or her, but all you have to offer is a word of praise. How can you make sure it has maximum valence? Let's think about some possibilities:

1. *Praise the person in front of his or her coworkers.* Most people value public praise more than private praise. Maybe you do it at an all-hands meeting, or just sitting around a cafeteria table.

2. *Put the praise in writing.* To most people in modern American society, the written word has a higher perceived value than the spoken word. Send the person a note (*not* e-mail, which is perceived to have the same permanence as speech). Or write a formal letter.

3. *Praise the person in front of his or her supervisor.* If you're offering oral praise, do it when the boss is within hearing. If you're putting it in writing, send the note or letter through the boss or — even better — *to* the supervisor. This last method has a double whammy. It gets the praise to the person while keeping the supervisor in the loop, and it gives the supervisor a motivational nudge to support the positive behavior. If you're going to send written praise about a person's general security performance to or through an employee's supervisor, here's a suggestion. Do it just before the time for the person's periodic performance appraisal or efficiency report. This adds just a touch more valence, because the person will probably see the praise as a potential influence on the evaluation.

INSTRUMENTALITY

When you come right down to it, instrumentality is a function of the credibility of your motivation program. It's making sure your folks believe they'll really be rewarded for doing a good job and that there will really be negative consequences if they fail. At the basis of creating and maintaining credibility is a simple but sometimes forgotten rule: Never promise (or threaten) what you can't deliver.

Keep in mind that what will influence people in the organization are their perceptions of your program. We need not only to follow our rule about promises and threats, but to make sure people know we are doing so. For positive motivation, that's pretty straightforward: you do everything you can to make sure people hear or read about rewards for good security performance. Have the rewards announced at a meeting, or put a short blurb in the company or agency newsletter. However you do it, make sure employees know that good things really do happen to people who take security seriously.

With negative motivation, the situation gets a little trickier. There may well be legal constraints on publicizing punishments meted out to people. You want to be sure to check with your legal and employee relations staffs before you try to impact legal consequences. And there's another problem. Publicizing negative consequences may promote the dangerous misconception that getting involved with security always ends up getting a person in trouble. If you do decide to publicize punishments, make sure rewards get equal time.

EXPECTANCY

Expectancy reminds us that people won't try to do the impossible. The amount of real effort they'll put into a task depends partly on their perception of the probability of success. If someone sees a task as really hard and figures he or she probably won't be able to do it acceptably, he or she isn't going to put a whole lot of effort into it.

My favorite example is my memory of trying to teach my older son to tie his shoes. That looks like — and *is* — a complex task for a little guy. Things started out fine, with the kid willing to learn. But then he tried it a couple of times after I'd shown him how, and ended up with a couple of tangled messes. As we tried again, I saw him putting less and less effort into it. Finally, with a wail of "It's too hard!" he quit trying altogether. Expectancy had dwindled to zero.

So how do we promote expectancy and the perception that security tasks aren't really as hard, time-consuming, or burdensome as people might think? Here are some suggestions:

1. *Quit telling people how hard a task is.* This is particularly applicable when you're trying to motivate people to learn how to do something. How many times have you heard an instructor say something like, "Now this is really hard/complicated/tricky, so you better pay close attention!"? Although this may motivate some people to pay close attention, it's almost certain to motivate others to tune out, figuring they probably won't be able to get it right anyway.

2. *Find ways to create a perception that the task isn't as hard as it looks.* Here's an example, again from the classroom. An instructor was teaching a class how to mark classified government documents to show the source or sources of the information's classification. The agency's regulation had several long and complicated paragraphs on the subject, and it was commonly seen as a complicated and tricky task. The instructor started out by saying, "What you put on the 'Classified by' line is the answer to one simple question: 'What told you this stuff was classified?'" Every time, the reaction of the class was dramatic. You could see surprise and a measure of disbelief on most of the faces. They were anxious to see if the process could really be that simple, and they were willing to give some effort into learning how to do it right.

3. *Give people a life preserver.* Make people understand that they're not going to fail, because if they run into problems the security staff will be there to give them a hand. One security officer was teaching a group how to implement a new security procedure. Before she started, she wrote a phone number in huge numerals on the blackboard. It was the security office's main number. She never mentioned it until the end of the class, by which time people had either written it down or perhaps memorized it. When she finished her presentation, she told her listeners that the phone number was the immediate solution to any problems they ran into with the procedure.

4. *Use job aids.* We'll be talking later in the book about a performance enhancement tool known as a *job aid.* When we do, remember *expectancy!* You'll see how job aids can reassure people that they can do the job 100% right, every time.

HIERARCHY OF NEEDS

Back in the late 1960s, psychologist Abraham Maslow constructed a model of motivation called the *hierarchy of needs.* Basically, Maslow proposed that there are several types of human needs that people are motivated to satisfy and that these levels sit one on top of the other, in a hierarchy:

- Self-actualization needs

- Ego needs

- Social needs

- Security needs

- Physiological needs

Quickly, here's what each level is. *Physiological needs* are the basic physical needs such as warmth, air, food, and water. *Security needs* are concerned with being able to feel safe: free from danger, fear of loss, and so on. These needs are satisfied by such things as living in a safe neighborhood, having enough money to get by on, and so forth. *Social needs* include the need for affection and the desire to feel like part of a group. *Ego needs* consist of the need for self-respect and the need for respect from others. *Self-actualization needs* are sort of nebulous, perhaps best described by the recruiting slogan, "Be all that you can be."

This may not seem to have much to do with our motivation efforts, but there's one aspect to this model that we might find useful. Maslow contended that lower needs on the hierarchy are *pre-potent*. That means that, until a person's needs on one level are satisfied, those needs are the person's main concern, and the person is not going to pay a whole lot of attention to the needs above them in the hierarchy. Once those needs are satisfied, the person moves on up to focus on the next higher level. Makes sense. Maybe thinking about needs from this perspective can help us pick and choose rewards that have greater valence for particular employees and avoid stepping on our own toes. Let's look at some examples.

A new part-time security manager was appointed in one branch of a large corporation. She was an engineer who had just transferred to that location from another corporate operation in a distant part of the country. She was also much younger than the location's other security managers. At one of the monthly security manager meetings, the corporate security director singled her out for praise for her effective handling of a complex situation in her organization. Unfortunately, he added, "I wish we could count on everyone to handle things like that!" One of his staff noticed that the engineer looked distinctly uncomfortable. She was very much aware that her colleagues — all long-time coworkers and almost a generation older — considered her the new kid on the block and an outsider. She'd been having a tough time breaking through the barriers and making friends. She was focused on fulfilling her social needs. The oblivious security director had contributed to setting her even further apart while trying to fulfill an ego need. A little more understanding of her situation might have led him to offer the same praise, but with a different twist. Perhaps he could have said, "We have a fine bunch of security managers here, and I'm glad to see it looks like you're going to fit right in!"

The hierarchy of needs can also help us in choosing higher-valence rewards for specific people. For example, we tend to think of monetary rewards as automatically the strongest motivators, but this is not necessarily true. If someone is financially comfortable and his or her safety needs have been satisfied, the person has probably moved beyond physiological and security needs to a focus on social or ego needs. Recognition may be a more effective motivator for this person than cash.

A BOTTOM LINE OR TWO

What much of this boils down to is that the more you know about what makes the people you're trying to motivate tick, the better job you can do of motivating them. Watch out for security education programs that rely exclusively (or almost exclusively) on the notoriously unreliable negative motivation. And keep the V-I-E theory in mind as you plan your motivation efforts or try to figure out what's going on with unmotivated employees. Over the years, we've found it a very effective tool for dealing with tough motivation issues.

8

Planning an Awareness Program

Within this chapter, we will be looking at the various objectives of security awareness and the impediments to an effective awareness program. We will explore the elements of the planning process, defining the audience, determining audience needs, articulating specific performance objectives, identifying your research support, and getting management on your side, and we'll take a look at selecting delivery systems or media that can go with a security presentation. Finally, we will present an overview of the planning process.

THE OBJECTIVES OF SECURITY AWARENESS

Security awareness, as the term is commonly used in government and industry, is essential security education for members of employee populations that has immediate or practical application to the workplace and beyond. It suggests an awareness of possible risk, danger, or real threats to life, safety, or valued assets that will be translated into action or behaviors that address those risks and threats. Another dimension of security education is professional-level training for employees who perform specific security functions (full- or part-time) as members of a security workforce. When we admit, however, that everyone needs security awareness as well as a dose of how-to training tailored to incorporate sound security practices into their specific job, the distinction between awareness and training becomes blurred.

Security awareness usually, but not always, implies the existence of an adversary such as a foreign intelligence service, a terrorist organization, or a criminal agent. Thus, one task for a security educator is to instill "awareness" of the credibility of threat or of adversarial interests that are intent upon theft, espionage,

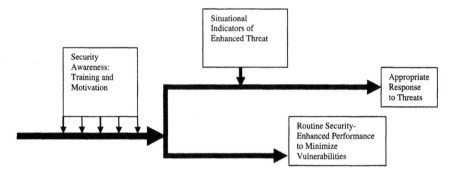

Figure 8.1. *The figure indicates that security awareness as an educational experience is not a one-time thing, but a continuing program of communication between the educator and the employee. The process is geared to produce behavioral change that addresses both vulnerabilities and threats. More will be said about these abstract concepts later.*

or damage. Once the educator is able to impress the employee audience with the reality of the threat or danger, at least two additional tasks remain: People must be informed about how to recognize indicators of risk or danger and how to react to these indicators.

But if, in fact, the educator wants to change or modify behavior (performance), another formidable task presents itself. Employees must be *motivated* to do the right thing at the right time once they recognize indicators or situations that should cause them to spring into action. They have got to *want* to do the right thing whether out of a sense of self-preservation, national loyalty, or genuine concern for others.

Security awareness is therefore focused and narrow in scope, but nevertheless it has elements of motivation and training. One might see it in terms of a stimulus-response model (as shown in Figure 8.1), in which the educator provides a treatment that results in (1) routine behaviors that minimize vulnerabilities in the workplace and (2) appropriate action given the recognition of indicators of enhanced threat. The emphasis here is on performance or behavior because, as argued earlier in this volume, the *terminal* objective of any security education is not simply to enhance understanding or impart relevant facts and information, but to empower people to act at appropriate times and in appropriate ways.

IMPEDIMENTS TO AN EFFECTIVE AWARENESS PROGRAM

Unfortunately, changing the way people think and act is never easy. Much stands in the way of a successful educational or awareness program as it might be gauged by the testing of performance objectives. Some of the obstacles that stand in the way of effective learning are in the minds of our intended audiences even before they hear what we have to say. These differ from one setting or audience to the next. In the first decade of the 21st century, the international terrorist threat has a reality for the American public which was never equaled by our concern about foreign intelligence agents. Nevertheless, the educator must acknowledge that each of the following presents a potential barrier to learning and each needs to be addressed head-on where it appears to exist.

The Pollyanna Syndrome or the "It Can't Happen Here" Mentality

This mind-set is usually based on the premise that because no damaging event or security breach has happened before in an organization, it is unlikely to happen in the future. Whether it is a mail bomb, theft of proprietary information, hostage taking, or computer crime — these are calamities that happen to other people and not to me. Consequently, little serious thought is given to what to do if any of these events should occur.

Low Credibility of Security Professionals

This problem is created when the security staff fail to live up to expectations of confidentiality, truthfulness, and competence — particularly when an employee is faced with a personal problem that should be addressed through counseling and employee assistance programs, and with sensitivity about privacy issues and personal reputation. The callous watchdog style of so many security officials in years past, unfortunately, has poisoned the air for many firms and agencies. In such cases, new generations of security professionals must work hard to establish a positive image.

Perception of the Disappearing Threat

Security educators in the 1990s and later whose programs were geared to the prevention of espionage have had to contend with the fact that perceptions of the foreign intelligence threat have radically changed. Without the monolithic Soviet adversary, security educators were hard-pressed to argue that critical information was still at risk. However, the continuing frequency of espionage cases associated with a variety of foreign entities in recent years — Cuba, China, Saudi Arabia, South Korea — has redefined the foreign intelligence threat and made it credible.

The View That Security Is Not Related to the Mission of the Organization

Several years ago, a senior official in the Pentagon declared that security was like "barnacles on the ship of state." Obviously the official was frustrated by delays brought about by a security review process. In recent years, more enlightened commanders and executives have come to realize that security practices are mission-essential functions, and without them the goals of their organizations will be in jeopardy. In any agency or firm, visible management support is critical to a successful program of security education. Members of your audience take their cues from management. If management thinks that security procedures are a nuisance or imposed by a mindless higher authority, this will be the prevalent attitude.

ELEMENTS OF THE PLANNING PROCESS

There is a logical process for planning a successful security awareness program, but the exact sequence of actions may not be critical. The first three elements identified next represent decisions that must be made before later decisions can be made regarding the delivery of training and education.

For the sake of discussion, mentally assume the role of a newly appointed security educator who is tasked to plan and implement a security awareness program for a target audience. At some point, early in the process, you must define or clearly identify that training audience and what the members of that audience need to learn. Flowing from this step should be decisions about educational objectives as discussed earlier. We urge that this be done in a formal sense and clearly articulated so that there is no ambiguity about the limits or scope of the educational effort. Next, we cannot assume that just because we have been hired to do a job, our efforts have unqualified management support. Our interaction with management may well be where the education program begins; and if our program fails at this level, it is in danger of failing below the management level. Having taken the previous step, we can then work on the development of a communications strategy. We will say more about each of these decisions or planning actions in the following paragraphs.

1. Define the Audience

Often the membership of your audience is defined for you (e.g., every employee in the organization or agency). But as an educator, you need to know much more about their characteristics and where they are located, both organizationally and geographically. Factors such as average age, gender, educational level, and physical dispersion have implications for the content of your message and how that information is delivered.

Possibly the best source of data for defining an employee audience is the human resources office. The educator also needs to ask about the distribution of employees on several demographic variables. Think of each of the following variables as having a set of categories and the percentage of your audience falling into each category:

- Age

- Gender

- Education achieved

- Grade or rank

- Position titles or occupational roles

- Physical location

- Turnover in employment

- Access to and responsibility for safeguarding critical assets

The relationships among demographic variables can also be valuable information. In a multifacility organization, the fact that senior engineers are located at remote facilities and younger information technology (IT) staff at another may influence decisions about how you plan your program.

2. Determine Audience Needs

What members of the audience *don't* know about security and why it is important represents their needs in an educational sense. Demographic characteristics (age, gender, education) tell us little about what a person thinks and believes. Psychological or attitudinal variables, as opposed to demographic characteristics, are much more difficult to determine. They are related to both understanding and motivations. Ideally, as a security educator coming into a new position, you would like to know the extent to which your employees have a knowledge of basic security principles and practices. Audience needs, which may lead to decisions about learning objectives, can be interpreted as meaning what people need to know to minimize vulnerabilities in the workplace and to create an environment in which employees know what to do when confronted with danger signs. It is possible that you have more than one audience with distinctly different characteristics and needs.

There are basically two ways to determine audience needs: (1) direct questioning and (2) observations or some measure of actual behavior. It is unlikely that the security educator will have the time or resources to engage in an extensive interview of audience members or to undertake a systematic survey of the population. People are increasingly resistant to survey research, because we so frequently are surveyed about a wide variety of issues. However, some security educators have done minisurveys of their employee populations with success. A minisurvey involves a small sample (possibly 40 to 50 individuals) that is randomly drawn from a much larger employee population. Respondents are assured anonymity, but techniques such as a follow-up memo are employed to assure a high response rate. In this method of assessing employee basic knowledge, the number of questionnaire items is limited and focused. A multiple-choice format minimizes the time and effort it takes to respond. Repeating the same survey questionnaire using a new random sample of the same population, after a number of months during which your educational program has been active, will allow you to see whether the program is successful in terms of conveying information to the audience.

There is a similar method of assessing the level of employee knowledge that both gathers information about audience needs and promotes interest in the subject of security. This is a *security quiz*, which stimulates interest and debate among employees who might not have given the subject serious thought. A security quiz itself is an educational tool as well as a fact-finding device, especially when it is accompanied by a follow-up memo with the correct answers and comments. An example of a security quiz related to the foreign intelligence threat, used some years ago in the Department of Defense, is found at the end of this chapter.[1]

The questions in this example, which focus on the status of personnel holding government security clearances, are now somewhat out of date;

---

1. Department of Defense Security Institute, *Security Awareness Bulletin*, Number 2-90, Richmond, VA.

however, they illustrate how a security educator might identify areas of confusion or doubt in the minds of members of the audience. Responses to quizzes of this type are normally anonymous and are therefore not seen as intrusive or threatening. Unlike the minisurvey, a quiz should be distributed to all members of the audience; no sample is drawn. But like the minisurvey, the length of the quiz must be kept short to avoid appearing burdensome and time consuming. Participation in the quiz is strictly voluntary. Because a random sample is not used, the educator cannot assume that the resulting responses accurately represent the thinking of the entire employee population.

The second strategy for determining educational needs is to track events in the organization that reveal general deficiencies in understanding, motivation, or training. These could include frequency of reported security breaches, unauthorized access to restricted areas, theft or vandalism, information systems misuse by employees, failure to report change of status, lost or damaged materials, accidents and injuries, use of illegal substances, or violence in the workplace. Your time on the job will, of course, reveal underlying weaknesses or commonly held misconceptions among the employee population.

3. Articulate Specific Performance Objectives

In planning their work, modern educators think in terms of performance objectives, and in light of these objectives they design both content and optimal methods for delivering or providing that content to their audiences, whether that audience is composed of students in the formal sense, employee populations, or members of the general public. The idea here is, simply, once the education or training is delivered, members of the audience or target population will perform in desirable ways not seen before. The authors of this volume take the position that if the education has no visible or objectively measurable impact on the performance of its recipients, the objectives have not been met. Some might argue that if students can pass a written test following a course of training, this is evidence enough of the favorable impact of the educational experience. However, it is not certain that newly acquired knowledge is so easily translated into positive behaviors.

For the most part, performance objects will be based on your assessment of audience needs and in turn will result in the content and direction of the training and education that follows. However, for the educator, it's never that simple. Other factors may and should impact on your educational program. Government or corporate policy may mandate that certain types of content or educational materials be incorporated into your program regardless of your personal estimation of audience needs. External threat assessments or organizational security assessments will also influence your training program. Management may also have its own ideas of what should or should not be included in your communications. Whether or not you agree with what might be called external input, it cannot be ignored and must be accommodated. Part of your role as a professional security educator is that you are a spokesperson for the organization and represent the overall interests of that organization. You are not an independent agent answering to some higher calling.

As argued earlier in this chapter, it is not enough to just change attitudes or motivations, such as producing a sense of reality about the threat to valued assets. Success has got to be realized in behavior and performance. The main question is, what are the specific desired end effects of the educational activity that is to follow? As discussed earlier, the reference point for an educational program is the set of clearly articulated performance objectives that have been developed from an assessment of audience needs and requirements.

When writing a performance objective, think of it as a clause that follows the open statement, "After receiving this educational experience, the employee will. . . ." The next part of the sentence will begin with an action verb, but a verb that denotes not an intellectual or motivational quality but a behavioral activity. Instead of *understand, perceive,* or *be familiar with,* use verbs like *employ, report, identify,* or *apply.* Another aspect of performance objectives is that as desired outcomes of education, behaviors must be measurable or observable in some way so as to verify that the effect has actually taken place.

The method for employing performance objectives in education is simple:

1. Determine and state exactly what the performance goal or goals are for members of your audience in terms of actions or behavior. This will be the outcome of the training, if successful.

2. In developing your communication, briefing text, or training instrument, address the performance objectives. Use an example to illustrate the desired objective.

3. Test every part of the content or message against the objective. Does the content of the message directly address the objective or are you providing information that is just nice to know? Unfortunately, the time allotted to security education in any organization is so restricted that there is little time to allow for anything that is not right on target. If content does not meet the test, it will have to be cut.

4. Lastly, as a test of the effectiveness of your educational program, we should be able to observe or measure change in the specific performance identified in the objective. Referring again to Figure 8.1, the educator should undertake some benchmark data collection or observations prior to the start of the educational program and compare these with the final outcomes.

Although objectives may vary with the purpose of an educational or training program, it is essential that the educator explicitly identify and clearly articulate what they are, if not post them on the wall, so that everything that is done — every resource or time commitment that is made — can be justified by one or more of these stated objectives. Here are a few examples of security awareness objectives that presumably result from a successful educational program. All of these reflect new behaviors or behavioral modification. Employees will do the following:

- Identify and respond to indicators of imminent threat or danger
- Apply adequate safeguards to valued assets on a routine basis
- Report security violations and infractions
- Identify and act on reportable violations and infractions
- Identify and act on security-relevant anomalies
- Apply threat countermeasures given situational conditions
- Alert coworkers and supervisors regarding vulnerabilities
- Follow prescribed safeguarding practices
- Avoid sharing sensitive information in social settings

In summary, advocates of the use of performance objectives cite three important benefits:

- They help the educator with regard to organization, conciseness, and efficiency.
- They help the receiver by alerting the employee to the job-related implications of what the educator is providing.
- They help the training or educational evaluator by comparing stated goals with measurable outcomes.

4. Identify Your Resource Support

It hardly needs to be said that planning must take into account what you have to work with — budget, staff members, and support from other sectors of the organization. Is there funding for the purchase or rental of educational materials and media products, travel for the purpose of networking with other security educators, and training funds? These questions need to be addressed in regard to program planning. Another question, related to resource support, may have a significant effect on planning: How much release time will be allowed to members of the employee population for educational activities? All too often, security educators prepare a lengthy briefing for new employees only to find that they are allotted only 20 minutes on the new employee orientation schedule or are told by management that annual refresher briefings are to last no more than half an hour.

Limited resource support is often compensated by the ability of educators to help each other out and to network through professional associations that are open to both government and private-sector security professionals. At least three organizations offer local assistance, depending on the specific location. Several of these chapters maintain lending libraries of videos and other media products. They sponsor annual briefings and security awareness events.

1. National Classification Management Society (NCMS): The NCMS has 29 local chapters operating in the United States. Its activities are geared to the goal of protecting classified and sensitive information in government and industry (www.classmgmt.com).

2. ASIS International: The American Society for Industrial Security (ASIS), with more than 200 chapters worldwide, has a much broader scope of interest, including physical protection, antiterrorism, and access control.

3. Industrial Security Awareness Councils (ISACs) meet regularly at many U.S. urban centers. These meetings are open to both government and private-sector professionals. There is no central organization, but information about local ISACs can usually be obtained from regional offices of the Defense Security Service or from field offices of the Federal Bureau of Investigation.

5. Get Management on Your Side

The importance of a supportive relationship between the security educator and the organization's management team cannot be overstressed. Failure to convince executives of the benefits of a viable security education program and the need to see security as an essential component of the organization's mission could handicap any program that you might undertake. Good advice on how to sell security to management is difficult to find. However, a Department of Energy working paper on security education provides six recommendations.[2] The following is an abstract of that publication.

Know Your Program

Until you know your own program thoroughly, your management will not take your requests for support seriously. Conduct a self-assessment of your program. Identify problem areas where management support is most needed. Prioritize needs so that limited resources may be most efficiently used to correct the most devastating problems. When seeking management support, you should be able to speak with authority and confidence and be able to answer nearly any question posed to you. This is extremely important in presenting a positive professional image.

Establish an Image: Positive and Visible

Traditionally, management and employees alike have had a less than positive view of security. A visible program can develop a positive image, raise employee morale, and encourage involvement and support from the general employee population and management as well. Make a regular contribution to the organizational newsletter or start your own newsletter. Establish a recognition program for employees and assist the local security effort and include management in the recognition program. Avoid negative messages like "failure to comply." View security as a service and employees as customers.

Keep Management Informed

Establish a working relationship with your supervisor. Identify management reporting and communication mechanisms, and contribute information on the

---

2. Oak Ridge Institute for Science and Education (ORISE), "A System for Gaining Management Support for Your Security Education Program," Oak Ridge, TN November 1992.

security education program activities. If you participate or attend a workshop, conference, or seminar, prepare a written summary of the information presented. As much as possible, provide information within your established chain of command. Demonstrate an awareness of the concerns of the overall organization rather than tunnel vision regarding the security program.

Communicate with Management: Speak Their Language

Balance negative information with positive aspects to prevent management from perceiving your program (and you) as a problem child. Never forget the budget. Include cost information in your program proposals, and reflect anticipated return on investment from anything you propose. Effective methods of communicating with management involve the development of tools and data. Use presentation tools such as requirements charts, time studies, and flowcharts for making your case to management for additional support.

Develop Teamwork to Pool Site/Facility Resources

Compensate for limited resources and staffing by aligning your effort with those being made by other security-related programs in your organization that have similar requirements and responsibilities (e.g., safety, health, or quality). Outline benefits of a coordinated effort such as a reduction in labor hours, cost savings, and a reduction in time off the job for employees. Cooperative efforts and resulting cost savings will reinforce the image of the security program as an asset to the organization.

Join the Security Education Community

Get involved with professional organizations and cooperative groups of security educators faced with similar challenges. Their common purpose can provide a sense of unity and encourages interaction and the sharing of advice and products.[3] These groups frequently sponsor seminars and workshops that offer training opportunities for security staff members.

---

3. For Department of Energy security educators, the publication recommends the Training Resources and Data Exchange Security Education Special Interest Group (TRADE SE SIG) that meets annually.

6. Select Delivery Systems or Media

Chapter 9 discusses communication strategies, including the development of appropriate content (the message) and the scheduling of communications. This chapter on planning concludes by looking at alternative ways to deliver the security message to enhance awareness or to provide baseline training to employee populations. The selection of media for communicating a security message is determined by three major factors that have already been discussed in some detail:

1. *Performance objectives* and the complexity of the information necessary to satisfy each objective. Often the choice of media is determined by whether the message has a strong motivational content or focuses on how to do something.

2. *Audience characteristics and needs* refers to whether that audience is large or small, centralized or dispersed, its level of education, its age distribution, and its current level of understanding of security issues.

3. *Budget and resources* available to the educator to include facilities and technologies available for security education. Limited resources place considerable constraint on the work of the educator and seriously restrict choices for getting the message to the audience.

In a program to enhance security awareness, however, the larger question is which media or delivery systems to select and when. Because security education should be a continuing experience for members of a target audience and because specific methods are more appropriate as vehicles for different types of information, we recommend a multimedia approach that provides a variety of educational experiences for the recipients spaced over a period of time.

EVALUATING MEDIA OPTIONS

How security educators communicate with employee populations changes over time and with the availability of new educational technologies. The time-honored standup briefing is fast giving way to online systems that allow employees to choose the time and place to receive essential information and educational content. The latter is highly favored by management, which would prefer training time not to impact critical production time.

However, despite the advocates of newer technologies, we don't know enough about whether electronic media (to include Web-based delivery and online interactive briefings) have the same impact on the recipient as more traditional methods in terms of maintaining attention span, overall comprehension, and long-term retention. Different media or delivery systems are believed to work better for different categories of employees. Younger adults who have been brought up with home computers are believed to be more receptive to and comfortable with online education than their seniors. For some, an up front and personal contact with a security professional may make the most lasting impression.

The media options or communication methods listed in the first column of Table 8.1 are in current use to provide security awareness to employee populations. Each has its pros and cons, and each can be evaluated using a number of more objective criteria.

Although most of the statements in the following table are commonsense judgments, what we see here is an attempt to make cost-effective decisions about the selection of one medium or a mix of media for employment in a security awareness or educational program. Other factors might be added to this matrix that would weigh heavily in one organizational context or another. These could include existing talent and technical facilities for developing specific types of products or already established distribution systems that would require no additional cost.

What the security educator might pay careful attention to, however, is cost for providing essential awareness information per employee. With larger employee populations, a relatively costly electronic product (e.g., a Web-based interactive briefing) to which everyone can have easy access offers the greatest economy or bang for the buck. Decisions based on these criteria alone, however, have little to say about quality. Production quality and the effectiveness of any type of presentations or products for meeting performance objectives can make the difference between a lackluster and a highly successful program. For this reason, security educators need feedback from impartial observers and members of the target audience. Chapter 15 discusses how to evaluate security education program effectiveness.

AN OVERVIEW OF THE PLANNING PROCESS

The flowchart in Figure 8.2 portrays the planning elements discussed by showing a logical sequence of actions leading to actual implementation of a

Table 8.1 A Framework for Comparing Various Delivery Methods

Delivery Method	Development Cost/Recurring Delivery Cost	Appropriate Content	Potential Reach/Time Demands on Audience	Appropriate Audience
Conventional group briefings	Moderate cost with briefing aids; considerable investment in development time. Recurring cost low.	Initial indoctrination, basic concepts, and baseline security training.	Limited reach, confined to population at one location. Significant downtime demands on employee populations.	Limited in size and centralized at one or several locations.
One-on-one briefing	Low cost to develop and to deliver on a regular basis. Permits interaction with employee.	Initial indoctrination, basic concepts, and baseline security training.	Low reach, limited to one person at a time. Time demand on the individual not significant.	Limited in size with low personnel turnover. Access to security educator assumed.
Video productions	Extremely high to develop.* Low recurring cost assuming facility and equipment are available.	Training and awareness on special subjects. Threat awareness a frequent topic.	Limited reach, confined to population at one location. Significant downtime demands on employee populations.	Moderate in size at central location or at a limited number of locations.
Interactive CD training	Extremely high cost to develop.* Little or no recurring cost.	Initial indoctrination, basic concepts, and baseline security training.	Available to all with access to workstation. Can be received at convenient times.	Large audience that is widely dispersed.

Table 8.1   A Framework for Comparing Various Delivery Methods (continued)

Delivery Method	Development Cost/Recurring Delivery Cost	Appropriate Content	Potential Reach/Time Demands on Audience	Appropriate Audience
Web-based training modules and briefings	Moderate development costs. Little or no recurring cost once developed.	Initial indoctrination, basic concepts, and baseline security training.	Available to all with access to Internet. Can be received at convenient times.	Large audience that is widely dispersed.
Posters and related graphic displays	Low to moderate development costs. Low cost to deliver.	Motivational content; single ideas or concepts; excellent for reinforcement and reminders.	Limited to personnel at central locations. No demand on work time.	Audience centralized or at a limited number of locations.
Newsletters, pamphlets, and other printed materials	Low cost to develop and low to moderate cost to deliver to target audience.	Initial indoctrination, basic concepts, and baseline training. Useful for quick reference and reminders.	Unlimited access. Time demand negligible; can be read or studied at convenient times.	Widely dispersed as well as centrally located audiences.
Closed-Circuit Television	Low cost to develop and to deliver on recurring basis.	Initial indoctrination, basic concepts, baseline security training, and special topics.	Limited reach, confined to population at one location. Time demand moderate if presentation is repeated.	Centrally located audience in dispersed workspaces (used frequently on board ships).

* Both quality video production and CD training modules have extremely high development costs and are normally produced by larger organizations under contract. These products are then made available to a larger community.

The Planning Process

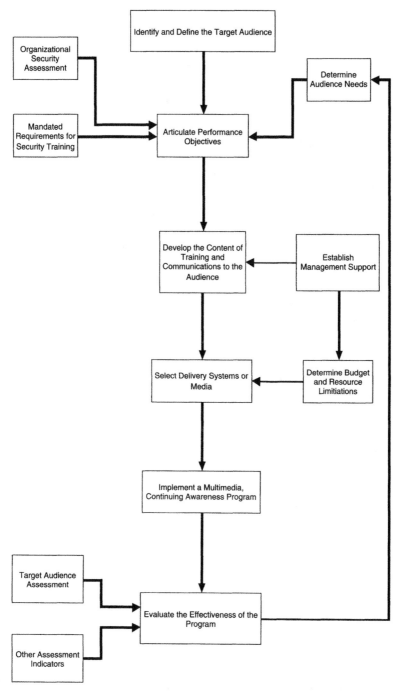

Figure 8.2. *This continuous flowchart depicts the planning elements showing the actions necessary to implement a security education plan with appropriate evaluation instruments.*

program plan with program evaluation that should be an essential component of any educational plan. It would be correct to interpret this as a continuous flow diagram in which performance objectives are under recurring review as a result of at least four factors: (1) the external threat and assessments of the vulnerabilities of the organization itself and its facilities, (2) governmental and other requirements and mandates related to employee training and education, (3) changes and refinements in the definition of the target audience, and (4) changes in the perception of audience needs as a result of feedback from the program evaluation process.

An ongoing pattern of support from management may not only influence budget and resources but may have some impact on the content of communication — one hopes in a positive sense. As new media are employed and the educational program unfolds, mechanisms should be in place for periodic evaluation by members of the target audience and by other assessment methods.

A SECURITY QUIZ FOR CLEARED PERSONNEL IN GOVERNMENT AND INDUSTRY[4]

Select the one best response from among the choices offered:

1. What statement best describes continuing evaluation?
   a. It is a method for measuring on-the-job productivity.
   b. It should ensure continuing suitability to hold a clearance.
   c. It is intended to replace the old procedure of background investigations.
   d. It requires that all cleared employees be under constant surveillance.

2. What is the reason that continuing evaluation for suitability to hold a clearance is necessary?
   a. Background investigations are inherently unreliable.
   b. People and their behaviors change over time with new conditions.
   c. The nature of the hostile intelligence threat changes over time.
   d. Periodic reinvestigations are being phased out as an economy measure.

3. Under current regulations and policy, when should a person holding a secret clearance report intended foreign travel for personal reasons?

---

4. The *Security Awareness Bulletin*, Number 2, 1990. A following issue of this periodical carried the correct or preferred answers with a discussion of each question.

a. All foreign travel must be reported in advance.

b. Only travel to designated countries must be reported.

c. With only a Secret clearance, no prior reporting is required.

d. All foreign travel except to neighboring countries must be reported.

4. If you see a coworker taking away classified material at the end of the workday, what should you say or do, if anything?

a. If that person has an appropriate clearance, you shouldn't question his or her actions.

b. Confront the individual immediately and demand an explanation.

c. Report your concern in confidence to your security officer immediately.

d. Make sure that the material is not personally accountable to you in case it is lost.

5. An employee who gets into financial difficulties and is subject to a garnishment of pay to cover debts:

a. Will have his or her clearance suspended until all debts are paid.

b. Is automatically considered a security risk.

c. Is required to submit to a polygraph examination.

d. Is potentially more vulnerable to a recruitment attempt for espionage.

6. You have seen a cleared coworker use an illegal drug at a social occasion and you make this fact known to a security officer. Under the best possible conditions, what should happen?

a. The coworker's clearance will be suspended immediately.

b. Nothing will happen unless drug addiction affects the individual's job performance.

c. An employee assistance program comes into effect; the clearance may be temporarily suspended based on other factors and information.

d. The employee will be given an initial warning and be required to report for regular drug testing.

7. You had the bad judgment to drive home after a cocktail party and get involved in a minor traffic accident. You were charged with a Driving Under the Influence (DUI) and your license is suspended. How is this likely to affect your clearance status?

a. You can expect to lose your clearance the next morning.

b. Nothing will happen.

c. Nothing will happen if you decide not to report the incident to security.

    d. It will depend on your personal history and the information on record pertinent to your continued suitability to hold a clearance.

8. At a contractors' convention, Boris Ivanovich introduces himself to you as a Bulgarian commercial representative and suggests that you get together sometime soon for a business chat. You have no professional interest in a meeting of this type, so what should you do?

    a. Politely decline and don't report the incident since you did not agree to meet him.

    b. Politely decline and report this contact immediately to your security officer.

    c. Agree to meet with him and see how things develop.

    d. Agree to meet with him and report the contact to your security officer.

9. Which of the following do you *not* need to report about yourself to the security office?

    a. Intent to travel to Romania.

    b. Marriage to a foreign national.

    c. Personal bankruptcy.

    d. Resignation due to a better offer from another firm or agency.

    e. Report all of the above.

10. Based on information reported in the media in the past 10 years, what is the most common motivation for involvement in espionage?

    a. Financial — a craving for money.

    b. Revenge against a system or government.

    c. Fear of disclosure of your lifestyle or illegal activities.

    d. Ideology or confused national loyalty.

9

Promoting Informed Awareness: Program Implementation

This chapter continues the discussion of program planning and the selection of delivery systems that we began in Chapter 8, and it addresses the choice of content for promoting informed awareness in an employee audience and the development of a communication strategy. This chapter also offers an approach to the scheduling of educational events, based on the premise that awareness programs should be a continuing educational experience for the workforce in which messages and themes are renewed and reinforced over time.

THE QUESTION OF CONTENT

What to say and how to say it is the overriding issue in the educational program. There are at least three guiding factors in making this decision. The most important of these, as discussed in the previous chapter, is your predetermined performance objectives — what members of your audience should be able to do after hearing the message that they could not or would not have done before. The focus of anything said to your audience should be a direct response to one or more of your objectives. Another factor impacting on the choice of content is the selection of media for delivering the communication. Limitations as to *how* you can deliver the message may easily influence what you can say and how much you can say about any one subject. A third factor to consider is time — time permitted for direct communication with your audience and the amount of time that audience members can carve out of their schedules for education.

Keep in mind that security education for members of your employee population should be an enabling experience in which they are advised about the benefits of good security rather than a prescriptive experience in which they are warned about what they must or must not do according to some regulation or set of orders. Adopting the former approach will lead to a more receptive audience.

Elsewhere in this volume, we have urged the security educator to take on the role of a salesperson selling a valuable product: You truly believe that this is a great offer and that your mission in life is to convince potential customers that they should buy into it; this will be to your profit and to their lasting benefit. The "selling security" concept is a useful approach to baseline security education, which by analogy could be compared with marketing Campbell's Soup or the latest Toyota, but more closely parallels public service announcements and special advertising campaigns aimed at influencing the behavior of general audiences for the public good.

Several years ago, the director of marketing services for a leading advertising agency, speaking at a conference on security awareness, made the point that we could learn a great deal from the public service work of the Advertising Council. The Ad Council has become famous for its successful efforts to prevent forest fires (Smokey the Bear) and to increase funding for the United Negro College Fund. The speaker argued for "highly targeted" advertising campaigns that move beyond just awareness to persuasion in order to get people, for example, to report suspicious behavior in the workplace. Then he described this as nonproduct or public-issue advertising that can be a catalyst for change. The success of these advertising campaigns are attributed to their appeal to reason, emotion, and old-time values held in common by the listening audience.[1]

MAKING WELL-REASONED ARGUMENTS

Exactly what to say to an audience is a dilemma for many security professionals faced with the opportunity to deliver a live briefing. The following is a suggested approach; however, the same method may apply to other delivery media. The receivers of your communication could be doubting and irritated employees, who may have been required to attend an annual security briefing but who

---

1. This presentation was originally published in *Security Awareness in the 90's*, proceedings of a symposium held in Monterey, CA, in December 1990, and was reprinted as "The Role of Advertising in Promoting Security Awareness," by Robert Bailey, *Security Awareness Bulletin*, Issue 4-97, November 1997.

would rather get back to work. In such a situation, it's best not to apologize or indicate that you would rather be somewhere else as well. Adopt the selling security approach; you have to chance to give your listeners a sales pitch. Think of it this way — You have your foot in the door, and now it's your job to convince your potential customers that the time they have carved out of their workday to hear what you have to say has been worth it.

1. Establish a rapport with the audience by making an amusing remark, a joke, or an acknowledgment of your sense of what they may be feeling about security on the job. The psychological basis of rapport is common interest and common experience. But keep it positive and upbeat.

2. Describe the problem (or problems) with the implication that by working together you can overcome the problem. Confirm your commitment to the mission of the organization, and state that the role of security is to support that mission and to ensure its accomplishment. If the problem stems from an external interest, that threat or external interest should be identified along with its ultimate objectives.

3. People like stories. Provide a couple of true accounts of situations (in a similar organizational context) in which failure to address a problem in time led to serious consequences. There is hardly anything more interesting to an audience than the sins or negligence of someone else. This technique increases attention span and improves retention of the essential messages. In hearing a story, the listener is likely to project herself or himself into the role of the concerned coworker, the well-intentioned supervisor, or the observant and proactive employee who is vainly attempting to prevent a disaster.

4. Engage your audience. The advantage of promoting security awareness in a live setting is that it offers the opportunity for open dialog, new ideas from the audience, and questions and answers. Monologues on security often fall flat after 10 minutes; however, group discussions are difficult to control and can eat up valuable time. It this type of situation, the presentation skills of the educator are critical. Offer ideas to promote a safer, more secure working environment. Each idea or suggested measure should be accompanied with an explanation on why it has proven to be effective in preventing insecurities.

5. Provide guidance that is clearly job related. Offer and solicit solutions to the problems stated earlier. You may not be conscious of this fact, but near the conclusion of the time allotted for your briefing or training event, each audience member is listening for the bottom line. Each is asking the question, "What does all of this have to do with the work I do?" or "Exactly what will I be doing that I haven't done before?" One might hope that some are thinking, "How will this help me do my job in a way that will promote a safer or more secure working environment?" Your role is to help spell this out.

6. Make yourself available. Despite modern training technologies, some of the most effective security education is still one on one and face to face. People tend to worry about security issues that they would rather not voice in public. (Usually it is something that can be handled in a couple of minutes.) If you have established your personal relationship with each member of the audience, this should remove the impediments to personal encounters with your audience in which questions can be addressed in confidence. Thus, information about contacting you — location, hours, phone number, e-mail address — should be linked with your personal assurance of confidentiality.

SPECIAL ADVICE ABOUT THREAT BRIEFINGS

Many security awareness communications focus on establishing the reality of a specific threat (internal or external to the community) and defining appropriate responses to that threat. *Tips for Developing an Effective Threat Briefing,* which originally appeared in a 2000 report on foreign intelligence threat awareness programs in U.S. government agencies, is located at the end of this chapter. It represents the author's attempt (at that time, though still effective today) to describe for a security educator what should be present in an effective threat awareness briefing.[2] Although this advice pertains to a specific type of live presentation, several of the guidance points have application to other types of security awareness communications. A generic formula for organizing threat awareness briefings on a variety of subjects is reflected in the following ques-

---

2. Defense Personnel Security Research Center, *Foreign Intelligence Threat Awareness Programs: A Review.* February 1998, Monterey, CA, pp. C7–C18.

tions — which if answered in the course of the presentation will probably include everything that needs to be said.

- What asset is being threatened or targeted?
- Who or what is the source of threat or danger?
- How is the source endangering the asset?
- Why is the source doing this?
- What are the consequences for allowing this to happen?
- What vulnerabilities are present that place the asset at risk?
- What can we do to prevent the loss of the asset?

THE USE OF SECURITY AWARENESS PRODUCTS

To review a couple of points made earlier, the best security awareness program is one that could be described as a continuing educational experience (not based on a set of prescribed briefings), and to as great an extent as possible, that experience should be achieved by a variety of media. A multimedia program will by necessity draw on the large and growing inventory of awareness and educational products available in the educational community.

It is now possible to search the World Wide Web and locate a wide variety of training products — videos, interactive CDs, online courses, brochures, and special events — that address specific educational objectives. These products can fill the gaps in content to bolster your own efforts at direct communication, and they can be very motivational. Often a recognized expert, TV personality, or national figure can leave a greater lasting impression on your audience members than you might have had saying the same thing. But care must be exercised in your choice of products to use in your program. They can get out of date with changing events or policies. They can be inappropriate for specific audiences. They can miss the particular message that you would want to convey to the audience. With video products in particular, critical prescreening before their purchase and use is essential, and when used in conjunction with a live presentation, a short follow-up discussion is essential.

A comprehensive listing of product sources is beyond the scope of this book. However, here are a few examples of providers, all of which are accessible on the Web, that cover a variety of security issues:

The Defense Security Service DSS
www.dss.mil/training/perserec.htm

The DSS Training Academy Web site offers a product for baseline security education that is, at present, unique regarding its wealth of useful material and versatility. *The Customizable Security Guide* is a tool for security awareness any employee can use either as a quick reference or as a method of initial indoctrination to security in government and in the government contractor community. For the security educator, it provides background information on a wide range of subjects as well as a source for newsletter articles, briefings, or other educational products. The guide enables anyone with basic computer skills to develop briefings on a wide range of topics including information and personnel security, antiterrorism, and protection of sensitive but unclassified information.

The guide can also be tailored, edited, or supplemented by a security educator to meet unique organizational needs. For many government and corporate entities, it is becoming an official automated method of providing security awareness education for specific audiences. As the time of this writing, beta testing is under way for an automated briefing system that employees can receive at their own workstations. This briefing system is to be used with the guide and goes to specific chapters as the employee takes an interactive security quiz.

The Defense Information Systems Agency (DISA)
http://iase.disa.mil/eta/index.htm

DISA has taken the lead in government in the development of exportable training and awareness products on specific topics related to information assurance (IA) and information systems security. It currently offers more than 40 training and awareness products including Web-based training modules, CD-ROMs, and videos for distribution on request. These products are free of charge to the U.S. government and its contractor community. In addition to IA and information systems security, subjects include critical infrastructure protection, Web and database security, computer network defense, protection of sensitive but unclassified data, cell phone and fax vulnerabilities, and threats to intellectual property. The security educator can order all items from the Web site.

The Interagency OPSEC Support Staff (IOSS)
www.ioss.gov

OPSEC (Operations Security) focuses on vulnerabilities that occur when we fail to protect indicators associated with our planning, processing, or operations that in the hands of potential adversaries could be extremely harmful or damaging. In the post-9/11 era, the OPSEC analytic process of identifying, controlling, and protecting these indicators has become particularly relevant to homeland security and counterterrorism. IOSS produces and distributes videos, publications, and interactive training modules (on CD-ROM) on a wide range of topics related to OPSEC including OPSEC fundamentals, counterintelligence, the foreign intelligence threat, and antiterrorism. All products are free of charge to members of the U.S. national security community (government agencies and their supporting contractors). The organization also promotes an annual OPSEC conference and exhibition and other training events available to the security educator who needs to know more about this important subject.

All of these sources currently offer quantity products or source materials at low or no cost to the security educator, and even if you decide not to incorporate any of them into your program, they offer a wealth of basic information that you can quote or draw on for your own educational communications to the workforce. In our enterprise, we are always borrowing information and are constantly on the lookout for accurate and authoritative content. It is good practice, however, to give credit for information used from other sources in your own briefings, newsletters, and memoranda. If an intelligence agency or reputable government authority is cited as the source of the facts that you use, the credibility of what you are saying will be enhanced.

PUTTING THE PROGRAM TOGETHER

Assuming that you, the security educator, have developed materials or briefing plans, prepared special awareness presentations or events, and have identified various media products and training modules that address all specific performance objectives determined at an early planning stage, what do you have? You have pieces of an awareness program that need to be ordered and synchronized to achieve the maximum effect. This we can call a *communications strategy*. A strategy is a plan of action at the macro level. In strategic planning, each element is positioned or executed in the total context of all others with respect to a logical sequence and with a view to contingencies, resources, and relative benefits. It implies that there are a lot of decisions to be made about what should happen and when.

It also makes sense to see your program as a *communications* strategy, as there should be a two-way flow of information between the educator and audience members. The content of audience communication to you will take verbal and nonverbal forms. You need to know if your program is effective. One of your tasks should be to seek and solicit indicators of comprehension, cooperation, and evaluative feedback, positive and negative.

SCHEDULING OF COMMUNICATION EVENTS

One of the complicating facts of life that will impact on your planning process is that the audience keeps changing. New hires come on the scene who need initial indoctrination or basic awareness training. People who retire or who are transferred out of your organization may need an exit briefing or information about new or enhanced risks en route to their new assignment. People traveling to foreign locations require special travel or antiterrorism briefings. Even within the same organization, movement from one position to another with more critical or sensitive functions may necessitate enhanced awareness or training to match the level of risk. This means that over time, there needs to be programmed repetition. In larger organizations, the educator must track this dynamic movement through systematic contact with direct supervisors or with the human resource department.

The actual scheduling of communication events and other educational experiences and the frequency of these events reflect the dynamic nature of the audience: turnover, growth or downsizing, upward mobility, and travel requirements for members of that group. Whatever the situation, the scheduling of events should be mapped out for all to see. Schedules, such as the example shown at the end of this chapter, keep the security staff on track and serve as an excellent instrument for communicating with higher management about what you are doing. A *schedule of security education* is a hypothetical plan based on an actual format provided to the authors by the security manager of a leading information technology firm. It shows communications in each month by subject matter and method of transmission. A second table shows for each subject all communications scheduled, method transmission, the projected date, and the actual date of completion.

Scheduling a yearly program in advance by this method, even if the dates are tentative, allows the security educator to validate that the program satisfies the following criteria:

- Comprehensive coverage of topics and performance objectives during the year

- Reasonable periodicity of coverage of each topic

- Where possible, variation in the method of delivery of content in each topical area

- Variation over time in the use of several delivery methods

- Reasonable advance time for the planning of briefings, written products, and the ordering or purchase of educational products

- A documentation of events and resource requirements to support the program

MAKING RISK-MANAGEMENT DECISIONS

How much security education and awareness is enough? This is a corollary of the often asked question, "How much security is enough?" There is no simple answer to these questions, but in recent years a methodology, *risk-management decision making*, has been developed to guide program managers in functional areas where the range of possibilities and the freedom to be innovative are clearly not limited by regulation or policy. The application of risk-management methodology to the planning and delivery of security education makes sense because these programs concern the judicious use of resources to confront or minimize risk.

According to a senior security official at a major intelligence agency, risk management is "the guiding philosophy of modern security programs. It is going to be our new way of doing business and will be with us for years to come."[3] In contrast to risk management, risk avoidance is doing everything possible and as much as you can to prevent loss or damage with reference to the degree of risk present. It is not difficult to argue that a total risk avoidance policy is wasteful and probably counterproductive, particularly when it comes to promoting security awareness. If there should be little or no risk of loss, there is hardly any point in pouring money into an educational program to prevent that loss. You may end up only irritating your audiences.

But we are rarely faced with a black or white situation — it is a matter of degree, and this is where the methodology of risk management can help. The objective is to make good risk-management decisions that will result in the most effective and efficient use of time and resources. Educators are prime candidates for embracing a more systematic approach to decision making and the allocation of scarce resources. There are a number of reasons for this. Historically,

---

3. Gail S. Howell, "The Challenges of Risk Management," *Security Awareness Bulletin*, Issue 3-97, September 1997, pp. 3–4.

although budgets have been limited, security educators have had an austere discretionary freedom to get the job done. Minimum standards about how to conduct security awareness programs are increasingly open to interpretation, and budgets are often negotiable with management (when management is on the side of security education).

Security educators have had to make tough decisions in the past, and in an unsystematic way they have followed the principle of placing resources where they think these resources would do the most good. As one security specialist stated, "This is what we have always done, but we have not called it that." Security educators have tended to place the effort and resources where they think these resources are needed most. But the methodology of risk management calls for a more deliberate, systematic approach to decision making than the educated guess or common sense. It dictates that we do only what is justified as the result of a systematic assessment of the degree of risk in a situation.

Risk-management decision making for security programs is a five step process:[4]

1. Assess the value of the asset that might represent a potential target for adversarial interests. (What would be the consequences of the loss of that asset?)

2. Identify and characterize the magnitude of the threat to that asset at its physical location.

3. Analyze the vulnerability associated with the asset. For the security educator, identify the human vulnerabilities of employees given the responsibility for safeguarding the asset.

4. Assess the risk. Risk is based on an estimate of the value of the asset, the magnitude of the threat, and the vulnerabilities present.

$$Risk = Loss\ impact \times (Threat \times Vulnerabilities)$$

5. Identify the cost of possible security countermeasures and tradeoffs. For the educator, this would be the cost of all the actions and communications undertaken to enhance awareness.

---

4. For a more detailed discussion of risk management methodology see Edward J. Jopeck, "The Risk Assessment: Five Steps to Better Risk Management Decisions," *Security Awareness Bulletin*, Issue 3-97, September 1997, pp. 5-15. Also recommended is the comprehensive book, *Risk Management for Security Professionals*, available from Elsevier.

For our purposes, any program or element in that program, because it is aimed at neutralizing a threat or reducing a vulnerability, should be considered an extremely important security countermeasure.

A tradeoff can be explained this way: For any one educational effort, how much reduction in risk would be enjoyed with each additional expenditure for the same type of effort? Conversely, how much additional risk would be incurred as a result of inaction? It would be ideal if we could come up with a quantitative measurement for each factor that determines risk. However, this is extremely difficult to do, particularly where we may not have accurate knowledge of the level of situational threat. It may be sufficient to assign low, medium, and high designations to each factor (loss impact, threat, and vulnerabilities) and from this make a reasonable determination of relative risk. Note that if any factor is nil or negligible, the level of risk will be negligible as well. This would be an argument against allocating time, money, and effort into employee education aimed at protecting that asset as opposed to other assets or security objectives that may be more highly valued.

Whether you make decisions about elements in your awareness program based on risk-management or cost-effectiveness procedures, it is important to have a rational and defendable basis for making those decisions — decisions that you are able to justify to yourself and to management. Risk management offers a method for deciding among options for the expenditure of resources for the accomplishment of specific performance objectives or for the use of specific delivery systems in a communication strategy.

In a subsequent chapter, we will discuss program evaluation: How can we possibly know whether the various programmatic decisions — discussed here and in Chapter 8 — have led to an effective program? What are the measures of success?

TIPS FOR DEVELOPING AN EFFECTIVE THREAT BRIEFING[5]

The following is advice for the security educator who is tasked with the development and delivery of a foreign intelligence threat briefing. There are 10 topical areas that, if correctly handled, may make the difference between a well-

---

5. From the *Security Awareness Bulletin*, Issue 1-98, April 1998. An earlier version of this guidance first appeared in "Foreign Intelligence Threat Awareness Programs: A Review," prepared for the National Counterintelligence Policy Board by the Defense Personnel Security Research Center, Monterey, CA, February 1998.

received, effective presentation and one which misses the mark. And it could be worse than missing the mark. A briefing that is viewed as out of date, inaccurate, or not relevant to the mission of the organization undermines the credibility of security countermeasures programs.

Several of these general topics focus on what we call the *nontraditional threat*. This central idea might form the theme of an up-to-date threat briefing in which the presenter compares how Americans perceived the foreign threat in the 1960s and 1970s with how we see it today (in the post–Cold War era) in terms of sources, targeted information, and modus operandi. If you plan to prepare a threat briefing, these topics and parts of the discussion included here might serve as a basic structure for the presentation. Of course, one would want to tailor any briefing to meet the needs of a particular audience, based on local and organizational priorities.

SOURCES OF THE THREAT (WHERE IS IT COMING FROM?)

We can easily make the case that the adversarial threat is more complex now than that frequently described in threat advisories during the Cold War era. Gone is the bipolar world of free versus communist or Soviet-bloc countries. Although the Russians and their intelligence services remain a significant threat, we must recognize that there are now a multitude of nations, commercial organizations, and non-national entities that pose a threat to our national and industrial assets. In situations that involve economic competition, even national-level organizations of what we consider to be friendly nations can actively attempt to acquire U.S. commercial information and technology by illicit methods. The complexity of the adversarial threat must be sketched out with an emphasis on the fact that many foreign national and non-national adversarial interests are involved.

This presents a more sophisticated worldview for members of the employee population to grasp and appreciate. The contemporary intelligence threat has proven to include drug cartels, international crime organizations, terrorist groups, and revolutionary organizations, as well as freelance former agents of now-defunct Eastern bloc intelligence services. Both classified and unclassified authoritative U.S. government sources have identified several of the most aggressive adversarial countries that target, in particular, U.S. critical technology, both dual-use and advanced technologies having direct military application. Suggested points to cover include the following:

- Examples of countries involved in intelligence operations against U.S. interests

- Case example(s) of "friendly" countries involved in intelligence operations against U.S. interests

- Examples of nonstate entities targeting U.S. interests

- Examples of threats to U.S. information from nonstate entities such as organized crime or international terrorist organizations

TYPES OF INFORMATION BEING TARGETED: WHAT ARE THEY AFTER?

Within the past few years it has become clear that threat awareness briefings must include a discussion of targeted information that goes beyond formally classified U.S. government information. Adversarial interests now target advanced technology and a variety of other unclassified information including private-sector proprietary information, OPSEC indicators, economic information, and information on advanced research.

The targeting of U.S. critical technology is, in fact, the most important shift in the nature of the foreign intelligence threat in recent years. This includes both dual use (microcircuitry, communications technology, and advanced software) and technologies that have direct application to military weapon systems. Various methods are used by adversarial interests to gain this information for both military and economic advantage to the detriment of the United States. These include illegal export, outright theft of data and source codes by foreign employees, the foreign purchase of U.S. firms, and the hiring of U.S. experts by foreign companies.

Whereas we remain primarily concerned about the protection of U.S. government information, adversarial interests place an increasing priority on advanced technology having military significance and dual use. This information is usually unclassified but is protected by export controls. There is also the question of safeguarding the proprietary information of U.S. firms, which if lost to foreign competitors, represents a threat to the viability of our economy.

Briefers should consult the current FBI National Security Threat List (NSTL) for high-priority issues and other sources that list advanced technologies that are believed to be high on the collection lists of international competitors who might stop at nothing to obtain this information. Here are some points to cover:

- Review of high-priority targets (e.g., based on NSTL)
- Recent cases of espionage where critical technologies have been targeted
- Review of specific technologies that have been targeted and evidence of this
- Outline of the shift of focus by adversarial interests to militarily significant technology
- Example of dual-use technology and its military application

THE INSIDER THREAT AND VOLUNTEER SPIES: WHO IS REALLY HURTING US THE MOST?

One of the most important facts about contemporary espionage to convey to employee populations is that most of the cases fall into the category of volunteer spying. The crime is, more often than not, self-initiated. Even by the early 1980s it was clear that volunteer espionage was becoming a more dominant pattern than foreign agent recruitment of vulnerable U.S. citizens. Since then, about three-fourths of the espionage cases have fallen into this category.

Regrettably, there is a tendency in threat awareness information, particularly that provided by counterintelligence elements, to focus on external forces (foreign intelligence services and their agents) as the principal instigators of espionage and the cause of the loss of classified information. While intelligence services and *modus operandi* are an important component of the problem, the security educator would be well advised to address foreign agent involvement in the context of the human vulnerabilities and (often) initial actions of those having access.

Recruitment is certainly not out of the picture, particularly in the international marketplace where the lure of large "consultancy fees" may lead an engineer or executive to illicitly share proprietary information. But in those few instances involving the loss of classified government information, recruitment for espionage has meant the recruitment of U.S. citizens by other U.S. citizens having access.

These disconcerting facts have important implications for threat awareness and security education. We need to present these issues to our audiences: Why would supposedly trusted employees and service members voluntarily betray an essential trust? What deterrents should be put in place to minimize the possibility of this happening? And how can the problems of apparently distressed or confused employees be addressed before they go to the extreme of doing something self-destructive? Here are some points to cover:

- Appropriate balance in the focus on employee vulnerability versus external agents and services

- Review of frequency and causes of volunteer espionage

- Identification of presumed motivations and vulnerabilities of known offenders

- Use of specific case studies to illustrate the predatory activities of foreign intelligence organizations responding to initial contacts by U.S. citizens

MODUS OPERANDI OF FOREIGN INTELLIGENCE AGENTS, SERVICES, AND COLLECTORS THAT TARGET U.S. PEOPLE: HOW ARE THEY DOING THIS TO US?

Whereas in years past much was said about steps in the recruitment process, blackmail, and sexual entrapment (which even then was rare or nonexistent except outside of the United States), recent history indicates that the contemporary emphasis should be on elicitation for information and ethnic targeting. As stated previously, there is no indication that foreign adversaries or international economic competitors have abandoned recruitment based primarily on the offer of financial incentive. However, the recent history of espionage strongly suggests that overt recruitment of U.S. citizens for espionage is rare, and where recruitment has been successful, it has been undertaken by U.S. citizens recruiting other U.S. people who are susceptible.

Aggressive elicitation for information combined with misrepresentation of identity or interests especially in the international commercial arena is said to be very prevalent at this time. U.S. representatives who have access to any privileged information should be informed of common elicitation strategies and have a clear idea in their own mind about off-limit subject matter for discussion with foreign representatives or even with people believed to be domestic competitors or professional colleagues. This level of awareness is particularly important prior to overseas travel or attendance at international conferences.

The targeting of individuals based on common culture is a significant but sensitive problem and should be addressed somewhere in a security awareness program. One way to handle this is to discuss two or three cases of recent espionage in which a foreign intelligence service had obviously attempted to manipulate a U.S. citizen having access to privileged information by appealing to the individual's cultural linkages and emotional attachments. It is important, however, to present a balanced picture of the problem and not zero in on one group. It is important also not to imply that members of any cultural or religious community, who are also U.S. citizens, might be any less loyal than any other citizens. Here are some points to cover:

- Description of various types of adversarial agents: moles, sleepers, undercover, and so forth

- Definition of elicitation for information and use of hypothetical or real examples

- Definition and case study examples of ethnic targeting

- Disclaimer of any implied lack of loyalty by any cultural or religious group

- Reminder of the limits of work-related discussion with foreign representatives and others not authorized access to privileged information

PERSONNEL SECURITY INDICATORS AND VULNERABILITIES: WHY DO PEOPLE BETRAY A TRUST?

Recent studies of why people get involved in espionage lead to the conclusion that we need to be in tune with the people around us, particularly if our coworkers, like ourselves, have been entrusted with sensitive or classified information. We cannot allow serious signs of emotional or psychological distress to remain unaddressed. The new executive order on personnel security in fact calls our attention to the need to refer troubled personnel to the employee assistance program (EAP) for reasons including substance abuse and severe financial difficulties. The reporting of coworker behavior, which might indicate impairment of judgment, should be seen as supportive, in the interest of that person, and possibly a moral/ethical responsibility. Vulnerabilities of any type must be addressed before they become a security issue.

There is also the issue of coworker and supervisory responsibility for reporting of suspicious and negligent behavior, which may indicate that classified information is not being appropriately safeguarded, might be vulnerable to compromise, or, at the extreme, espionage may be involved. Examples of suspicious behavior should be described as well as the preferred method of reporting in confidence to a security or counterintelligence (CI) professional. Here are some points to cover:

- Review of indicators of possible espionage on the job

- Vulnerability indicators that demand intervention by concerned coworkers

- Discussion of employee responsibilities under personnel security programs

- Description of available employee assistance programs for referral of personnel with serious problems

THE TECHNICAL AND NON-HUMINT[6] THREAT: HOW HAVE NEW TECHNOLOGIES MADE US MORE VULNERABLE?

At one time, coverage of other than the HUMINT threat was referred to as "the multidiscipline threat" — an awkward term at best. In our threat awareness programs, we need to look at modus operandi of various types, both HUMINT and SIGINT, or any other method by which potential adversaries are known to be particularly successful. This would include a discussion of (1) the interception of nonencrypted telephonic communications (voice, fax, and data), (2) the penetration of restricted government and corporate computer networks by hackers after sensitive data, and (3) the greatly increased use of technical surveillance devices. These three methods are believed to be the most productive of targeted information for adversarial services and organizations. Here are some points to cover:

- Discuss the intelligence targeting of unencrypted voice, fax, and data communications

- Review the current threat to restricted information systems and computer networks posed by hackers

---

6. HUMINT, SIGINT, and IMINT are acronyms, commonly used in the intelligence community, meaning *human intelligence* activities, *signals intelligence* collection, and *imagery* (photo) *intelligence.*

- Review the technical threat and reasonable countermeasures used to minimize electronic eavesdropping

- Review and define other non-HUMINT intelligence collection methods (IMINT, SIGINT, etc.)

CONSEQUENCES OF ESPIONAGE FOR THE NATION: HOW MUCH HAS ESPIONAGE HURT THE NATION?

One of the misconceptions held even by loyal and trustworthy employees is that espionage is some sort of white-collar crime that might mean some paper or accounting losses to government, but not more. In the past we have been unable to portray the extent of damage partly because the extent or nature of the damage itself is highly classified. Falling back on statements from leading law-enforcement officers such as "The damage from this case is beyond calculation" is not particularly helpful to the cleared employee.

Our audiences need to know something concrete about the magnitude and nature of the loss to our national community. It might be in millions of dollars or numbers of lives, but even in an unclassified mode it is often possible to be more specific. To present the argument that espionage has done real and costly damage to the nation, it may be useful to use case examples with authoritative estimates of damage assessment. Here are some points to cover:

- Specifics about damage or potential damage from recent espionage cases, quoting media or open sources

- Concrete information from classified or nonopen official sources about damage incurred by the loss of information

- Types of damage possible from espionage: loss of life, intelligence systems, diplomatic negotiating strength

CONSEQUENCES OF ESPIONAGE FOR THE OFFENDER, FAMILY, AND FRIENDS: HOW DOES ESPIONAGE IMPACT THE PEOPLE DIRECTLY INVOLVED IN IT?

At the personal level the consequences of espionage are comparably destructive. In the past, official guidance has mandated that everyone be informed of the statutory penalties for espionage or for conspiring to divulge national security information. Though no more than a brief reference to the U.S. Code, Title 18 might be useful, audience members must be informed that involvement in espionage activities, especially where serious damage is incurred, has led to life sentences. Using specific case studies and video interviews, audiences come to understand the need to be aware of the intense personal suffering inflicted on friends and family members and that the offenders have essentially ruined their own lives.

A related theme under personal consequence is the certainty of eventual detection of this crime. Several cases have come to light and have been prosecuted as a result of confidential sources, defections of former intelligence officers, or the availability of foreign intelligence service files following the reunification of Germany. Here are some points to cover:

- Using case examples, with video support in live briefings, if feasible, portray the level of despair and suffering by persons directly or indirectly involved with espionage.

- Cite case studies that illustrate the severity of imprisonment in serious cases.

- Stress the facts that offenders have no realistic hope of getting away with the crime in the long run and that serious penalties follow.

SPECIAL VULNERABILITIES DURING FOREIGN TRAVEL: WHY ARE TRAVELERS TO FOREIGN LOCATIONS EVEN MORE VULNERABLE?

Although U.S. personnel who travel to or through foreign locations should be provided with pretrip information on special threats and dangers in the areas they plan to visit, general threat awareness should include basic information about the unique vulnerabilities which U.S. personnel are likely to encounter. In general, U.S. travelers are subject to a wide variety of covert monitoring, technical surveillance techniques, and searches of luggage and personal effects. This may take place en route or in hotels. Technical advances in communications and microcircuitry have made it increasingly easier for foreign intelligence services to monitor all travelers through their areas of jurisdiction.

In addition, U.S. representatives may be subject to intensive and aggressive elicitation and, in extreme cases, provocation and harassment. Travelers to higher-risk areas should be advised not to place themselves in vulnerable situations by engaging in black market activity, illegal currency exchange, substance abuse, illicit sexual activity, or politically sensitive activity. Here are some points to cover:

- Discussion of technical surveillance measures directed at U.S. citizens abroad

- Examples of the targeting of U.S. official personnel, even in "friendly" countries

- Examples of covert search and theft or compromise of classified or proprietary materials while en route or at hotels

- General guidelines for the U.S. traveler at a foreign location to counter espionage threat

MAKING A GOOD BRIEFING INTO A GREAT BRIEFING

The topics previously addressed have to do with content and how to discuss that content in the course of a formal presentation. There is, of course, much more to a successful briefing than the subject matter and facts. The quality of any briefing is related to presentation skills, briefing aids, and the personality of the presenter. These issues are outside the scope of this article; however, more can be said about how we as communicators relate to and establish rapport with the audience by what we say.

The objectives here are to improve audience attention span; to help extend the long-term retention of principal ideas, concepts, and arguments; and to elevate motivation for supportive performance on the job by recipients of the message.

Appeal Directly to Employee Interests

All too often in the past, threat briefings were padded with "nice to know" details about the structure and staffing of foreign intelligence services, the intrigue of espionage, and spy craft technologies. The unanswered question for the employee was, "What does all of this mean to me?"

In recent years, security educators have become increasingly focused on clearly defined performance objectives before they write or develop a product or briefing. This is one way to keep a briefing concise and on target and the audience attentive. Furthermore, there is a good argument for spelling out performance objectives right up front to the employees so that they are conscious of how this information is supposed to impact their professional and even private lives.

It is often said that employees of different generational groups respond differently to motivational content. For example, that senior members of our workforce (who formed their political and community loyalties during and just after World War II) are more likely to respond to patriotic symbolism than are baby-boomers. Whatever the truth of this argument, each threat-awareness communication should attempt to include motivational content to activate the recipients of your message. If members of the Me Generation need an appeal to self-interest or money to get them motivated and interested, that is doable in an awareness presentation. The idea here is that a threat briefing should not simply conclude with information about the foreign intelligence threat. As mentioned earlier, some focus on expectancy of employee response to the threat should not be missing. They are waiting to hear: "This is what you can do, and this is why you want to do it."

Use Current and Up-to-Date Information

We are all sensitive to dated material that occasionally pops up in videos, annual briefings, or written pieces about the threat. After the Cold War was over, references to the Soviet Union or the KGB in threat briefings could evoke snickers from an audience and sometimes ruin the credibility of a presentation. Negative feedback also results from the frequent telling of "old" espionage stories. The author has overheard comments like, "If they talk about the Walker case again, I'm going to walk out." "Have you got any new cases we can tell our folks about?" At the other extreme are security educators who make it a point to plug into their refresher or threat awareness briefing information about the very latest cases. This is a powerful attention grabber for the audience who think they are getting the latest inside information.

Compliment, Don't Demean, Your Target Audience

The question often arising in these awareness efforts is, "Who is the target audience and who are we trying to reach with this message?" Is it the potential spy? No. We are unlikely to make an impression on the potential offender who for one reason or another is not listening and seems compelled to do something self-destructive regardless of security training. Actually these people are few in number, despite the tremendous damage that they do.

The population that we want to reach and to activate is composed of the vast numbers of essentially loyal, patriotic, and reliable employees and service members. However, their problems sometimes include indifference to what is going on around them, cynicism about security programs, and fear about getting involved in personal issues. These are the attitudes and behavior we would like to change or modify if at all possible.

Consequently, the audience must be addressed as a population of loyal and otherwise responsible individuals. Threats and signs of the "watch-dog — we're out to get cha" mentality, if expressed by the educator, are sure turn-offs. In general, each message, briefing, or written communication should be clearly tailored to meet the needs of a particular audience as defined by organizational identity, occupation, educational level, age, or geographic context.

Make the Threat as Real as Possible to Your Audience

The use of recent espionage case studies or even real examples of how information was compromised (or successfully protected) can illustrate many of the themes mentioned in other topic areas.[7] Each case offers its own lessons to be learned. Case studies (any good stories for that matter) also maintain audience attention and provide evidence that espionage and trust betrayal are not otherworldly phenomena. But care must be used not to glamorize or romanticize espionage as an intriguing spy story. Two good arguments that can be established by this method include (1) offenders not only risk causing great damage to their nation but invariably suffer great personal consequences including lengthy imprisonment, and (2) detection and apprehension is almost inevitable due to the use of confidential sources and advanced counterintelligence methods.

Furthermore, the selection of cases to be covered should be made on the basis of currency and commonality with the target audience situation. The discussion of older cases — Bell, Boyce and Lee, or Walker — is by now of questionable value because employees are literally tired of hearing about "the same old cases." On the other hand, a discussion of the latest espionage events (cited in public media sources) will earn a favorable response.

Reinforce Your Own Credibility

The establishment of the credibility of a threat awareness message is essential to ensuring that members of the employee population will pay attention and

---

7. For information about recent events, see *Recent Espionage Cases*, a training product posted on the DSS Web site.

meet the kinds of performance objectives we are aiming at. Credibility, of course, means that the receiver of the message believes that the source of the information is objective and reliable and that the message itself is accurate. Consequently, the crediting of courses such as intelligence organizations, particularly in the presentation of facts that might otherwise sound conjectural, is a very advisable practice.

The question of whether threat briefings should be classified or not often arises. The arguments in favor are these: Much more can be said in detail to support an important argument if the communicator is allowed to include classified information. Because we can mention sources and methods in a classified context, the overall message will be more convincing. And in the area of counterintelligence, much of the important information that cleared employees should know about the threat is either classified or designated for official use only (FOUO). In addition, for many people, the mere fact that a piece of information is classified lends credibility and importance to it and to the entire presentation or product.

Although the latter argument is not by itself a valid justification for the inclusion of classified material (consistent with the principle of need-to-know), the need for quality should prevail as the deciding factor. That extra effort at developing and delivering a classified presentation on the foreign threat, when it is at all feasible, argues strongly for doing it.

But Don't Make It Too Long

Even the best of audiences have a limited attention span. Some studies have indicated that it is something like 15 minutes on any given subject without a break. After that point, minds start to wander. Admittedly, in the time normally allowed for a formal presentation, it would be possible to cover only a few of the topics mentioned here in any depth. There are, of course, other delivery systems for getting the message across and often the opportunity to modularize a comprehensive presentation on threat awareness.

In summary, success with this type of briefing, possibly more so than with other security awareness presentations, depends on careful planning. This must include a thoughtful consideration of educational objectives, the use of timely and credible information, and sensitivity to the fact that your audience members want to hear something that is directly applicable to how they perform their mission and even live their lives. (See Tables 9.1 and 9.2.)

Table 9.1   The Scheduling of Awareness Communications and Educational Events: A Hypothetical Example

Education Subject	Method of Transmittal
January 2002	
Foreign intelligence threat	Company online bulletin board
Security procedures	Security staff briefing
Information security	Company newsletter article
New employee briefing	Presentation by security staff
Cyber crime	Brown-bag lunchtime video
February 2002	
Information systems security	E-mail (notice to all system end users)
Reporting responsibilities	Special articles on security
Terrorist threat awareness	Company online bulletin board
New badge procedures	Company newsletter article
March 2002	
Foreign intelligence threat	FBI ANSIR briefing
Safeguarding classified material	Poster; special articles on security
Operations security	Brown-bag video; IOSS video
NISPOM update	Company online bulletin board
April 2002	
Counter-espionage	Brown-bag video: NCIX video
Reporting responsibilities	Departmental meetings
Terrorist threat awareness	Company online bulletin board
Foreign travel briefing	Security staff briefing
May 2002	
Safeguarding classified materials	Special articles on security
Information systems security	E-mail notice to all system end users
Annual refresher briefing	Security staff briefing
Operations security	Brown-bag video: IOSS video
Security in the news	Company online bulletin board

Table 9.1 The Scheduling of Awareness Communications and Educational Events: A Hypothetical Example (continued)

Education Subject	Method of Transmittal
June 2002	
Reporting responsibilities	Special articles on security
Terrorist threat awareness	Poster
Foreign intelligence threat	FBI ANSIR briefing
Personnel security	Brown-bag video: *As Others See You*
July 2002	
Information security	Company online bulletin board
Operations security	Brown-bag video: IOSS video
New employee briefing	Presentation by security staff
Safeguarding classified materials	Special articles on security
Company badge policy	E-mail reminder to all employees
August 2002	
Annual refresher briefing	Security staff
Reporting responsibilities	Company newsletter article
Terrorist threat awareness	Special guest speaker
Security week open meeting	Lunchtime events to be announced
Security week	Lobby displays and posters
September 2002	
Foreign intelligence threat	Company online bulletin board
Operations security	Departmental meetings
Safeguarding classified materials	Special articles on security
Foreign travel update	Company newsletter article
Protecting critical technology	Brown-bag lunchtime video
October 2002	
Reporting responsibilities	Company online bulletin board
Terrorist threat awareness	Special articles on security
Counterintelligence	Brown-bag lunchtime video; NCIX video
Information systems security	Poster

Table 9.1   The Scheduling of Awareness Communications and Educational Events: A Hypothetical Example (continued)

Education Subject	Method of Transmittal
November 2002	
Operations security	Special articles on security
New badge policy	Company newsletter article
Security in the news	Company online bulletin board
Foreign intelligence threat	Brown-bag lunchtime video
December 2002	
NISPOM update	Special articles on security
Safeguarding classified materials	Company online bulletin board
Terrorist threat awareness	Company newsletter article
Foreign travel briefing	Security staff
January 2003	
New employee briefing	Security staff
Operations security	Brown-bag lunchtime video: IOSS video
Foreign intelligence threat	FBI ANSIR briefing
Information systems security	Company online bulletin board
Access control	Special articles on security

Method of Transmission

Security in the news: A compilation of news articles on counterintelligence and security

Company bulletin board: Online bulletin board containing security advisories

Security staff briefings in auditorium, live presentations with PowerPoint slides

FBI ANSIR briefings by guest agents in auditorium

Brown-bag lunchtime video in auditorium

Company newsletter article (internal hard-copy distribution)

Special articles on security, downloaded or reprinted from various publications

Table 9.2 The Scheduling of Awareness Events by Subject: A Hypothetical Example

Education Subject	Method of Transmittal	Projected Completion Date	Actual Completion Date
Foreign intelligence threat	Online bulletin board FBI ANSIR briefing FBI ANSIR briefing Online bulletin board Lunchtime video FBI ANSIR briefing	January 2002 March 2002 June 2002 September 2002 November 2002 January 2003	January 2002 March 2002
Information systems security	E-mail notice E-mail notice Poster Online bulletin board	February 2002 May 2002 October 2002 January 2003	February 2003
Information security	Newsletter article Online bulletin board	January 2002 July 2002	January 2002
Operations security	Lunchtime video Lunchtime video Lunchtime video Departmental meetings Special security article Lunchtime video	March 2002 May 2002 July 2002 September 2002 November 2002 January 2003	March 2002

Table 9.2 The Scheduling of Awareness Events by Subject: A Hypothetical Example (continued)

Education Subject	Method of Transmittal	Projected Completion Date	Actual Completion Date
Reporting responsibilities	Special article Departmental meetings Special article Company newsletter Online bulletin board	February 2002 April 2002 June 2002 August 2002 October 2002	February 2002
Terrorist threat awareness	Online bulletin board Online bulletin board Poster Special guest speaker Special security article Newsletter article	February 2002 April 2002 June 2002 August 2002 October 2002 December 2002	February 2002
Badge procedures access control	Newsletter article E-mail to all employees Newsletter article Special security article	February 2002 July 2002 November 2002 January 2003	February 2002
Safeguarding classified materials	Poster; special security article Special security article Special security article Special security article Online bulletin board	March 2002 May 2002 July 2002 September 2002 December 2002	March 2002

Table 9.2 The Scheduling of Awareness Events by Subject: A Hypothetical Example (continued)

Education Subject	Method of Transmittal	Projected Completion Date	Actual Completion Date
New employee briefing	Security staff Security staff Security staff	January 2002 July 2002 January 2003	February 2002
NISPOM update	Online bulletin board Special security article	March 2002 December 2002	March 2002
Annual refresher briefing	Security staff presentation Security staff presentation	May 2002 August 2002	
Counterintelligence	Lunchtime video Lunchtime video	April 2002 October 2002	
Foreign travel	Security staff presentation Newsletter article Security staff presentation	April 2002 September 2002 December 2002	
Protecting critical technology	Lunchtime video	September 2002	
Security procedures	Security staff briefing	January 2002	January 2002
Cyber crime	Lunchtime video	January 2002	January 2002
Security in the news	Online bulletin board Online bulletin board	May 2002 November 2002	
Personnel security	Lunchtime video Open meeting Displays, posters	June 2002 August 2002 August 2002	

10

Practical Exercise for Promoting an Informed Awareness

Given the background for a specific target audience, a description of the immediate threat and awareness concerns, and a library of materials with potential use in an awareness activity, identify the particulars that would be used to construct an awareness presentation to address the varied security educational concerns. Your solution should include a description of presentation strategies and an identification of selected materials (with intended means of use). After the exercise section, the authors have included some thoughts and considerations that are appropriate for this situation, as well as ideas that can be used in other presentations down the road to make the presentation and its impact more meaningful to employees. The following is a basic description of your target audience, the immediate threat, and other possible awareness concerns.

TARGET AUDIENCE

The organization is a subelement of the Defense Ballistic Space Communications Command [DBSCC] and is located approximately nine miles from your current location. It is on the fourth to sixth floors of a twelve-floor commercial office building. A contract guard force is used for security. The guard force consists of two individuals manning the entrance/visitor control desk at the fourth floor and one individual who makes rounds throughout each shift. Access to the fifth and sixth floors are by a ID card reader with a pin number required. Closed circuit television (CCTV) cameras cover the fourth floor lobby and the access portals on the other floors. There is a two-level parking lot under the building with access available to anyone.

Your audience consists of 275 government military and civilian personnel and 180 contractors who work on site. They are mostly scientists, engineers, computer programmers and analysts; these are specialized "techies" who love their work. Employee turnover is relatively low. There is the usual mix of administrative personnel in the lower grades, which consists of 50 people. All personnel have a security clearance, ranging from Confidential to Top Secret. A number of contractor personnel are heavily engaged in working with sensitive contractor developed information that is necessary to the success of the project. Employee time with the organization ranges from six months to 18 years.

The organization is concerned with the design, development, and use of state-of-the-art technology (beyond that of other nations). The organization uses new and innovative methodologies and theories in the development of communication systems, both hand-held and office-type units, and these methods will involve satellite linkage. A lot of computer-based modeling of component configuration is performed. A fair amount of classified and contractor-sensitive data are generated, and most of these data are maintained in office files throughout the organization.

The contractor, Albo Electronic Specialties, is a specialized high-technology company that is closely involved with computer programs, communications, and advanced electronic design and development. Because Albo is critical to project development, its own onsite security manager works closely with the government security manager. Both are included in the overall security awareness program, each concentrating on his or her own employees in terms of the security education program. Albo proprietary information is onsite in a huge volume to support a larger amount of its contract.

A great deal of computer-based modeling of electronic systems and component configuration is performed. Work hours are 0700 to 1630 daily. Many employees may put in one to two hours of uncompensated overtime every evening or take work home. Numerous employees also come in on weekends for uninterrupted work.

VULNERABILITIES NOTED

There is an older alarm system with false alarm problems, and you have an aging security force. The security force personnel are friendly with employees, recognize them by face, and do not always check their ID badges. Although employees generally follow security rules, you note that a somewhat relaxed attitude is prevalent among many in terms of following security procedures to the letter. After all, they are in a protected area with controlled access and everyone has a clearance.

THREAT CONCERNS

Locally, random street crime is on the rise. Several offices in your office building have been robbed of computers, cash, and other easily salable items. Car thefts are somewhat frequent, along with robberies of individuals, during the evening hours within several blocks of your building.

No specific international-type threats have been identified that can be tied to any specific countries, but you are aware from newspapers and magazine articles that economic espionage is on the rise, and communications is an area that has an enormous potential for this form of activity. A local FBI threat briefing indicates the superior design technology in the area of communication technical advances makes the organization a viable target for commercial espionage or other exploitation.

OTHER CONSIDERATIONS

Most of the initial daily development and design work is considered Sensitive Unclassified, but when fully developed, the end products and various backup reference manuals may be Confidential or Secret. End products are for military/ other government applications with possible commercial use in 10 to 15 years.

Employees received their annual refresher briefing eight months ago and are aware of security in this regard, but they are not overly concerned. (After all, the computer disks and other papers are locked up at night and a security guard force is on the premises all the time.)

Office area cleanup is performed by a local contract company that handles the entire building. Cleanup hours are between 4 pm and midnight. The cleaning crew consists of 12 people and two supervisors who move between the floors to monitor and check on their employees. Daily trash is taken to an outside dumpster where it is removed each morning by the company. Crew personnel may be rotated with those on other floors of the building when there are not enough employees to fill out the contracted number of 12.

Security concerns over the past two years have identified other vulnerabilities from annual security audits. The physical security level is believed to be adequate.

You are new on the job. What should you do and how should you start to set up an effective security education program for your organization?

PREPARING FOR AN EFFECTIVE SECURITY EDUCATION PROGRAM

Performance objective: State what the training outcome — the bottom line — is expected to be.

Ask yourself the following questions: What are the employee needs, concerns, and requirements? Is there a threat? If so, where is it from? Is it real, potential, or possibly imagined? How does the threat apply in this training situation? What is its importance? Are the threats possible, but not specifically identified? If not, what is the basis for them? How will you best get your message across to all the employees?

- What type of presentation will you use: lecture, group discussions give and take, video, handouts, or a mix of these?
- Why are you using this type of presentation method(s)?
- What information will you use in the presentation to emphasize each strategy, and will that information make a difference to the attendees?

In your presentation development, take the following steps:

- Identify the security education concerns, indicating the main points to be covered.
- Describe the presentation strategies and *why* they were selected.
- Identify what selected materials will be used and their means of use.

Now, *outline* an awareness presentation to identify the security education concern. Indicate the main points and at least one subpoint under each. Specifically identify each presentation strategy to be used, why it has been selected, and why it will best impart the presentation message for effectiveness. If you cannot delineate the *why* of each selection in terms of the strategy, review the chapter materials.

If you are a government security manager, view this project in terms of your position and responsibility. If you are from the private sector (a government contractor or not), consider your own employee needs and requirements; then, if you determine that some specific/general areas overlap in the training, determine who will present, how, and why. You may want to present both cases together (a close interaction of government and contractor presentors to both government and contractor employees). What are the advantages and disadvantages of presenting as a team? Once you have completed the problem, ask for comments about the problem and your solution.

The problem presented is probably like no other you have faced in the recent past. Thinking and analytical judgment become very important. Problem analysis includes understanding employee needs, wants, and desires, but it also requires linear thinking and logically presenting a plan that is effective in terms of what your audience will take away from the presentation.

Think about communication skills and practices, design, development of systems, and other factors in the subject area to be presented. What are the personnel needs, wants, and desires in terms of security education and methods to be used to obtain employee acceptance?

Suppose you determine that the use of "technical design" — using state-of-the-art technology (beyond that of other nations) with new and innovative methodologies — looks to be a factor in your presentation. This is what the employees are engaged in on a daily basis. You need to relate to this area as you consider the presentation materials.

What about computer-based modeling of electronic systems/components? If this is being used within the organization, it must be addressed from a security viewpoint and you must then endeavor to demonstrate with examples how security can be impacted if this data were to be lost.

From a security educator's view, consider what the employees need to perform their assigned job functions. You should have an employee group makeup — a profile — in your mind as you explain the specifics of the presentation. This will ensure that the presentation is properly tailored to meet the employees' needs and wants and gives them the best value for their time.

Specify the local threat when threat is being discussed in the presentation. Pull appropriate information from current newspapers or magazines to ensure that your data are current and add realism to the subject matter. You should, in these instances, be able to identify several mission-critical items that relate to potential threat.

Review the items you developed for this scenario:

- Did you identify the employee concerns?
- Did you use a variety of presentation strategies instead of just one?

- Did you identify specific materials to be used and determine how to make their means of use effective?

- Have you considered using a presentation "outline sheet" for the attendees to fill in and take back to their offices? This is a wonderful way of reinforcing the information presented and, at the same time, providing a reference handout for attendees to keep.

Other considerations for completion of your outline include the following:

- Look at resources you don't currently have, but will be able to obtain in a reasonable period of time for the attendees. What will the impact of the lack of these resources have on the presentation?

- Look at the various motivation methods you have selected for use, determine the actual effectiveness, and think of ways to restructure the presentation (if necessary) to include as many of the TEAM elements (training, education, awareness, and motivation) as possible in the training.

- Remember that your credibility will be closely aligned with the preceding items in terms of the approach(es) to be used.

- Consider whether or not you put *too much* into the presentation; remember the KISS principle (Keeping it simple). On the other hand, avoid limiting the presentation too severely.

- Think about whether you took into account the meaning of the acronym "TEAM" when you were structuring the presentation.

At this point, you should have developed a well-thought-out presentation outline, considered the various presentation methods to be used, and looked at any handouts or other aids for your intended audiences. You seem ready to go. Now consider the effect of the information on your audience. What you say, what they hear, and how they interpret your statements may well be different from what you wanted or intended. So analyze the outline and what you will say for each point. Is there a possibility of misinterpretation of the information? If so, reevaluate the information, change the context, specify instead of generalize, ensure the discussion materials reflect any current policy or procedures in effect, and think about how the materials will impact each person's day-to-day job functions if putting something — like a new or revised procedure — into use.

Now consider the topic content or issues that must be resolved and how can you best resolve them through the presentation. Solutions can cover such subject area concerns as the following:

- Safety
- Crime prevention (local police representative)
- Newsletter articles and flyers
- Escorts to the parking lot at night

- Espionage
- "Gimmees"
- Handouts/job aids
- Taking work home

Also consider the use of guest speakers:

- Security consultant from outside
- Police/FBI
- Videos with subject matter expert
- Crime statistics
- Classroom demo of good/bad aspects of the subject

SOME IDEAS OF MERIT

You have come a long way now in considering just about every aspect of the presentation and its potential impact on your audience. But there may be some items you haven't thought completely through, have misinterpreted, or have misrepresented in the presentation. The following list provides some further background ideas, questions, and comments relative to information strategies that could assist you in developing your presentation strategies. Think about how the information can be related to threats, vulnerabilities, local and internal problems, general security awareness, possible speakers to use and further build on, ways to pass on policy concerns, and so on. From the immediate viewpoint of various threats and potential vulnerabilities that you — and a country — may face, what could you be doing, or doing more in depth, to ensure that all security concerns are addressed on a continuing basis?

- To best identify all possible security risks, screen your security blotter and reports, reports of investigation, rumors that may relate to security and that have a potential for causing security concerns or problems, and local police for crime statistics and types of crime in your area. Then collate this information into a chart, and add to it on a continuing basis to determine trends, areas that have not been addressed, groups or types of people that may be posing problems, and so on.

- Provide your security managers *and* other management supervisors at various levels, via a pamphlet or newsletter, information about the latest security statistics, concerns, and problem areas. Ask for their assistance in identifying other areas of concern or problems that they perceive from their day-to-day duties. They see and hear things that are not necessarily brought to your attention. The same concern or problem from different areas of the organization may indicate a potential trend that needs to be addressed.

- Attend various organizational management meetings, and be prepared to provide a few positive security tips and hints that may make security efforts — and the managers' jobs — run smoother. Ask for their input to further emphasize security concerns and your desire to assist at even an informal level.

- Use guest speakers for specialized topics that everyone can relate to, such as local crime prevention, identity theft, car theft, personal safety outside the organization building, or robbery.

- For local threats, consider law enforcement agencies and the FBI. For a larger threat, contact the FBI for presentations.

- Recognize individuals by presenting them with a token of appreciation for their support of the security program or their input that helped to solve a problem or potential concern.

- Have on your person some business cards that include your name, telephone number, and e-mail address. If you have a hotline set up, include the number on your card.

- Ensure that when people transfer or leave the organization, all security checks are completed. This should include turning in keys, deleting password access, returning ID and courier cards, accounting for property, and so on. The policy for exit procedures is typically never included in a security presentation, but it should be whenever appropriate.

- When an individual is leaving, especially if the person has been fired or is leaving under a cloud, ensure that management immediately terminates all of the individual's computer access, even though it may be a couple weeks before the person actually leaves. This is an important item when providing presentations to middle and senior management, and it should be highlighted at least quarterly.

- Ensure all people know that you are available to provide on-the-spot assistance — *all* the time.

- In the area of information technology (IT), specialized speakers from outside the organization make for a better presentation, as they are viewed with greater objectivity by an audience, especially when it comes to IT security concerns and practices.

- Use advertising concept techniques to get the security message across in a few short words (and pictures): posters, handouts, cards, flyers, short organization bulletin items, and so on. The same can be used to "advertise" your forthcoming presentation and develop a wider audience participation and interest.

- Meet and greet people at every possible occasion, and that includes when they first arrive for your presentation. Don't be aloof or doing "busywork," but take the time to meet and greet as attendees arrive.

- Use current newspaper/magazine articles to expand and amplify your message. Use these alternate sources to show examples of the greater threat.

- Discuss safety awareness with current procedures for safety protection. Use a video or have a security skit.

- Consider the attendee's security responsibilities in terms of reporting potential or actual threats and vulnerabilities. Whom do the attendees contact? How do they make contact? Security educators tend to state when, how, and why, but we don't motivate our listeners to follow through with the responsibilities. Many times, a report is made only when a person sees a detrimental impact to his or her well-being and job.

- Laptop and desktop computer issues, including theft, unauthorized access, password protection and frequency of password changes, and the Internet are always popular. Consider how you can fit this topic area into every presentation.

- Discuss employee responsibilities regarding trash. What is its sensitivity and value to someone? How should it be destroyed? How should it be protected until it is destroyed? There is a general need to alert employees to what the organization is doing and their responsibility to consider that even trash must be protected up to a certain point. Use examples and demonstrations; cite recent events that can demonstrate the importance of this area of security.

- Use procedural presentations, basing them on individuals and their duties, job functions, the sensitivity of the information they work with on a daily basis, and what to do when sensitive information is not properly protected.

- Alert employees to the fact that security is a 24/7 job, so there are always after-hour inspections and spot checks of the office areas.

11

Training and Education: Going One Step Beyond

THE STEP BEYOND TRAINING

When we took our quick look at the TEAM model for security education, we saw that what we would call "training" is what we do to make people able to perform their roles in our security program. And in looking at performance problem solving, we saw that training (or some alternative) was usually the right intervention if we found a skill, knowledge, or information shortfall. But we also saw there was another, odd component of the program — *education*. Training, you'll recall, helps people with the who, what, where, when, and how of a task or set of tasks. Education goes one step beyond that and deals with the whys.

Too many times, the education component of security education gets the short end of the stick. We're busy. Our time is valuable. We gotta get people trained. Educating them would be nice, but that sort of thing takes a lot of time, which we don't have. We're busy and the people in our organization are busy, and "nice-to-haves" just don't happen in the security business.

In this chapter, we'd like to help you kick two ideas in the head. The first is that educating people is something you do only in formal settings, with classes and textbooks. The second is that education is kind of a nebulous thing that really doesn't have much payoff in the real world of a day-to-day security program. We'd like to suggest that education can take many hours or a few seconds, depending on how much time you have to do it and how much needs to be done. We'd like to show you how educating your workforce can have a real, positive impact on the quality of the employees' participation in the security program.

RULE-BASED RESPONSES

We have a bad habit in the security education field. This habit doesn't just affect those who work in security, of course, but it seems to be more of a problem for us than it is for people who work in other fields. When people ask us a question about a rule or requirement that starts with "why," we too often give them what's called a "rule-based" response. We might answer, for example: "Because the regulation says so, that's why." "Because it's company policy." "Because that's the rule." "Because it's in the Standard Operating Procedures (SOP)." Get the picture?

So what's the problem with that? To understand one problem with that, let's dig back into ancient history, to when we were teenagers. Remember the one question that used to set your parents' teeth on edge more than any other? It was when they told you to do something and you replied, "Why?" Now think about that answer they used to give you that you resented so much: "Because I said so, that's why!" We didn't get the answer we thought we deserved as soon-to-be adults. We got a rule-based answer. The psychologists who do something called transactional analysis will tell you that we're seeing what they call a parent-child transaction. That's something adults — and teenagers — tend to resent.

So what does that have to do with security? Think about it. Is the security staffer who answers the "why" question with "because it's in the company hand-book" really doing something so different from the "because I said so" reply? Maybe not. Maybe this sort of thing helps, just a little bit, to promote the neg-ative, adversarial relationship that sometimes crops up between a security staff and the rest of the people in the organization. People resent being hit over the head with the security rule book rather than being given a proper, meaningful answer when they have a question about why. Our job isn't making nice-nice with people; it's protecting our organization's assets. If we really believe that everyone in the organization has a role to play in the security program, our program's going to be much better off if we can build a good, cooperative working relationship with each employee. A good working relationship is but a small step as a way to enhance employee support for the overall security program.

We can hear you now: "They really don't want an answer! They're just being obstructionists! Every time you tell them to do something, they start with the *why* stuff!" For some people in your organization, that's true. Some people just don't want to cooperate. They may have reasons, or they may just be naturally pig-headed. But is everyone? Are some of those "why" questions honest, inter-ested, concerned ones? How can you be sure which is which? We suggest that every question someone in your organization asks — even a "why" question —

deserves a good, meaningful answer. You're not going to have time to go into long explanations or philosophical discussions, but the people deserve to be given the best answer you have time for and one that makes them feel their question has been received and answered respectfully. Here's something else. You know those annoying people who never take what you say at face value without whining about "why"? Instead of telling them that it's in the rules, try explaining the rule to them a few times and see what happens. In many cases you'll find that they stop asking. If they didn't really want an explanation and were just questioning you to get your goat, they'll get tired of failing. They may even start feeling a little guilty about being such equine posteriors when they're being treated so respectfully by you.

Rule-based responses can have another negative effect on the security program. It happens when people who have asked an honest question about the reasons behind some requirement get a rule-based answer and try to understand what happened. Remember, please, that people react to their perceptions of reality and base their attitudes and understandings on their perceptions. When they ask a question about the reasons for a requirement and get a rule-based answer, logic might suggest to them that there are one of three reasons why that happened:

1. *The person who was asked doesn't know the answer.* That's not going to leave a good impression of the qualifications of the security staff, if they can't even answer a simple question about their own program. How likely would the person be to seek out someone like that for advice on a security issue?

2. *The person doesn't think my part in the program is important enough to deserve a proper answer.* We tend to spend a lot of time trying to convince people that their roles in the security program are important. But do we also send them subtle signals that they're not worth the time and bother to answer a question?

3. *There is no good reason behind the rule.* Here we're promoting the all-too-common misperception that security rules really don't have much to do with the real world. "If there was really a reason for this, she'd know what it is; if she knew what it is, she'd tell me. Therefore, this is one more of those silly security rules somebody dreamed up and all us poor people in the real world are supposed to follow." This is an attitude you want to eliminate, not unconsciously promote.

You avoid these potential boobytraps, of course, by taking a minute (or maybe just a few seconds) to provide a good answer. But what if you don't know the answer? Simple. Say so. Tell the person you really haven't thought about that, but you'll check into it. Give the answer the next time you see the person. Maybe even give the person a call with the answer, if you have time. The individual will probably appreciate the courtesy and perhaps be taken somewhat aback that you thought he or she was important enough to the program to bother. We'd hate to tell you the number of times we've done this and gotten a response along the lines of "Geez, nobody ever bothered explaining that before. Thanks."

Is this the education stuff we were talking about? Absolutely! Every time employees ask a member of the security staff, a supervisor, or anyone else about the reasons behind security requirements, they're handing the person an opportunity to educate them. And an opportunity, like a mind, is a terrible thing to waste. Making it a habit among the security staff to try their best to explain requirements when asked is one way to make sure these opportunities aren't lost. Now, we hope you see how the education component of security education can be easily worked into day-to-day interactions with the population, taking maybe only a few seconds to have real payoff.

MAKING AND TAKING TIME

Time? Sure, educating others about reasons behind security decisions takes some time, but maybe not much and maybe time you can spare. One savvy old security pro, Mr. C., made it a habit to go to the employee cafeteria for lunch at the busiest time every day. Things were crowded and you had to search for a seat. He'd find one at a table with people from one of the operating activities, ask to join them, and introduce himself. Quite often, someone would see a golden opportunity to ask about some security issue that had been bothering him. Mr. C. would then, between mouthfuls, spend a few minutes educating a table full of folks on the reasons for that particular requirement. It turned out to be time well spent, and it had an added payoff. Quite often, someone would come into the security office and ask to see Mr. C. It would be someone who had been at one of those tables, had now run across a security problem, and was looking for a friendly face to talk it over with. Quite often, Mr. C. would bring the person to someone else in the office, saying something like, "Don, this is Ellen Jones. She thinks there might be a problem with the access control system in Building 9. I thought maybe you could help her out." For Ellen Jones,

Mr. C. was the means of finding a way to bring up a problem in a nonthreatening environment. For the security staff, he was the means of getting people to let security know about problems before they became disasters.

POSITIVE EFFECTS

So far, we've been talking about using a type of education method to avoid negative effects. Now let's turn to the positive effects that educating your population can have on your program. One of the most important effects is that education promotes intelligent participation in the program rather than just blind obedience to the rules. An educated population may be able to bring their own intelligence, experience, and understanding to bear in making sure your program works. This can be very important, particularly in two situations.

Back a few years, one of the authors was working at a large military installation with a lot of highly classified research activity. As he was working on his part of the security program, he'd sometimes run across problems that were not covered by the regulations put out by headquarters. So he'd call the headquarters staff and ask about it. Sometimes the answer was preceded by a sort of standard comment: "You can't possibly write a regulation to cover every possible circumstance." To him, that sounded like a cop-out: a weak excuse for having left something out. A few years later, he ended up working at the higher headquarters himself and learned how true that old saying was. If your security program is a complex one (as most of them are) and operates in a changing environment (as most of them do), having people who are able to react intelligently in situations that the rules don't exactly cover can be a lifesaver. To do this, they have to understand what the rules are trying to accomplish, not just what the rules are.

Naturally, when people run across a situation that your security guidelines don't seem to handle, you want them bringing it to your attention so you can bring your professional expertise into play. But to do that, they need to recognize that such a situation exists; and to do that, they need to know what the requirement is trying to accomplish.

Intelligent participation of your workforce becomes particularly critical when new situations arise or circumstances change in the organization. The people in your operating activities will often know about these developments before the security staff does — simply because these events were planned or are happening in their own work environment. If these changes are going to have an impact on your security program, you'll want the workforce to let you know about them right up front and to do something intelligent about them until you can respond. Taking action requires an understanding of how the program fits together. Back when computers were giant monsters who lived only in large, carefully climate-controlled rooms of their own, one security officer got a call from one of his organization's data processing managers. The man wanted to know if the security officer was interested in the fact that they were going to be installing remote terminals, hooked up to the giant mainframe, in all the warehouse areas. The security officer, unfortunately rather typical for that long-ago time, asked what a remote terminal was. If the data systems manager hadn't understood the reasons behind the security rules governing the computer room and hadn't recognized that these new gadgets were going to dramatically change the vulnerability of the data being protected, there would have been major problems ahead. In another case, a shipping department employee noticed that there had been some changes in how one of the approved carriers was handling the shipments of one of his company's most sensitive products. Following the security rules in effect, the items would still have been consigned to the same shipper in the same way. But the employee understood the reason for specifying that particular shipper and shipping method, and he alerted the security department. Each of us can relate a number of instances like this, where a member of a workforce who understood what a specific security procedure was trying to accomplish tipped us off when circumstances within the department had changed to the point that the security goal was no longer being met. Without an understanding of the reasons behind the rules, these people would have gone on blindly following the rules, even though the rules had stopped working.

Paying attention to education can also pay off in worthwhile suggestions from the workforce. Keep in mind that the people in your organization's operating elements are closer to the action than you can possibly be. They work in their particular operating environment every day, so naturally they're more intimately familiar with it than the security staff is, which has to deal with the whole organization. This means that you as a security educator know more about security than they do, and they know more about their work situation than you do. Putting those two minds together can be a powerful influence on improving your program. Often, just getting the benefit of a fresh look at the situation is valuable.

We used to teach in a course on information security — dealing with classified government information. Many of our students had worked with classified information for some time but had never attended a formal course of instruction on the program. We'd work with them to make sure they understood the reasons behind the requirements. Many of them had never heard of that approach; they'd just been told the rules and followed them. As the course went on, the students would start to think about how the requirements were applied in their real world. And many times, they'd start working out how those requirements could be applied more intelligently and effectively, so the purposes behind them could be more reliably accomplished. In a number of instances, the students would come to us with ideas about how the current rules could be reworked to accomplish their purposes better. We loved the questions that started out: "I was wondering, why couldn't you just . . . ?" We knew there was a good chance that we were going to hear a good idea for simplifying and streamlining the system. Not always, but more times than you'd imagine.

EDUCATION AND MOTIVATION

The third positive effect of security education is its influence on motivation. How much time and effort are you willing to devote to something that's "Mickey Mouse," "administrative busywork," "just a bunch of red tape," or "bureaucratic nonsense" when you have other things to do that you know have a payoff in the real world? The more successful security educators are at convincing people in our organizations that our security programs make sense and serve valid purposes, the easier it will be to motivate them to devote the proper amount of time, effort, and attention to them.

One large industrial facility had warehouses where lots of high-dollar-value components were stored. They were kept in sturdy, built-in containers secured by expensive padlocks. The people who worked in the warehouses would have many of these containers open at once as they filled orders from the assembly shops. One of the security rules was that, when a container was open, the padlock had to be locked back on the hasp. Naturally, this was to keep a potential thief from switching out the padlock for one of his own, to allow him to open the container later. The security staff regularly found padlocks hanging open on hasps. The security director sent flaming memos about the problem to warehouse management. Supervisors nagged at the workers and occasionally took some disciplinary action against offenders. But nothing really seemed to have enough of an effect on the problem. Then one day, one of the security staff noticed an open padlock and called it to the attention of a warehouseman. The guy happened to be a bit more outspoken than average. He shook his head. "You know, you security people really get me!" he began. "You really think somebody's going to steal that padlock when there's all this other expensive stuff around? Don't you have anything better to worry about?" The security specialist managed to swallow his irritation and thought about what he'd just heard. Was it really possible that the people in the warehouse didn't understand the reason for the rule — that they thought it was just a dumb requirement someone dreamed up? It wasn't only possible, it was fact. A few words explaining the switch-out business at the next supply division all-hands meeting brought a significant reduction in the problem. The employees in the warehouse had been given a chance — through a couple of minutes of education — to decide for themselves that the rule made sense, and they became significantly more conscientious about following it.

WHERE AND WHEN

When and where should this education take place? Lots of times and lots of places. If you're on the lookout for opportunities, you'll find lots of them. Here are a few assorted suggestions.

Meetings

One of the authors used to be chief of security for a large military logistics organization. The commander happened to be big on staff meetings. Every Thursday morning, all the directors, division chiefs, major branch chiefs, and staff office heads were corralled in the commander's big conference facility for a two-hour session. The principal managers would be scheduled for short presentations, then the commander would go around the room asking questions about his pet projects and asking the staff officers if they had anything to say. Our fearless security officer had an automatic response: "Nothing, sir!" For him, as for many of the others in the room, the object of the game was to get through a Thursday morning without being asked a tough question by the boss. Years later and (hopefully) a little wiser, he wanted to kick himself every time he thought of those Thursday mornings. For two years, every Thursday morning, he had an opportunity to educate the top management of the organization about security. And every Thursday morning, with the toughest people in the installation sitting there as a captive audience, he blew his chance. Please don't follow his bad example. Look for chances in meetings to put in a few words of explanation about security requirements. Ask for a few minutes at all-hands meetings or staff meetings to say a little about the security program.

Training Courses

If your organization conducts training for its employees, is security in the curriculum wherever it fits in, and does the security presentation aim at providing some education? One excellent opportunity is the training many organizations conduct for new supervisors. One security officer noted that his office had a two-hour block of instruction in a basic supervision course, which was spent reviewing rules for protecting proprietary information, laying out crime-prevention responsibilities, and running down the personnel security requirements. He carved out 20 minutes of that time to spend with the class in a general question-and-answer session. The results were very positive. He had a chance to educate an important audience as well as to get a firsthand idea of the level at which the security program was understood in the organization. New employee orientation programs are another possibility, but you have to be a bit cautious about using them. We'll be giving you a few ideas about that later on.

Questions and Answers

As we mentioned before, every time an employee asks a question of the security staff, you've got an opportunity to educate someone. Often just a sentence or two will do the trick. The key is to have every member of the security staff understand the value and importance of giving people good, meaningful answers whenever they have a question. They need to know that you, as their supervisor, consider education to be part of your job; that you know they're busy, but that they need to take time or make time to address employee concerns and answer questions.

Management by Walking (and Talking) Around

Some of the most effective security professionals we've ever encountered were the ones who were hardest to catch at their desks. They were the ones who were out in the area, seeing what was going on and talking to the people they counted on to make the security program work. As they chatted with people they looked for opportunities to drop in a few words of education about security — to make sure the employees understood why their roles in the program were important and why the rules they were asked to follow were important, too. Mr. C. — the guy from the cafeteria — is just one example. We can learn a lot just from talking to employees, and we can teach them a lot, too.

Publications

Does your organization have an employee newsletter? An in-house magazine? A World Wide Web site for employee news and announcements? How about starting a short, regular column about security issues? You might find someone on your security staff who's an aspiring author and would love to put something like this together. One caution: We've seen many cases where the security office in an organization has had a regular column in an in-house publication. Unfortunately, sometimes these have ended up being nothing more than announcements of new requirements or procedures or sermons about how important security is. Don't forget to take the chance to educate your readers while you're at it. How about a security questions-and-answers feature? You can use it to present facts and information, but also to educate the staff about why some security decisions are made. "But what if we don't get the kind of questions that lend themselves to 'education' answers?" Easy. Make some up. Experience shows that, if people see "why"-type questions being answered in a medium like this, they'll start posing some questions for you. And here's an odd suggestion: Is your workforce unionized? Does the union have a newsletter? If so, maybe the union would be willing to include a short security column. Unions are often quite interested in getting information to their members about management issues, and a column explaining security requirements might suit their needs and yours. You might want to ask your labor relations people about the idea. It's been done quite successfully in at least one case.

Security Training Sessions

You most likely conduct some sort of formal training in security for people in your organization — at least those with particular security responsibilities, like your security force. Don't forget to include some education along with the training. One security educator was asked by a colleague to sit in on a training session she was conducting and to offer suggestions. The visitor was impressed in one way and dismayed in another. The person conducting the training laid out the requirements very well, taught the people the required procedures, and stressed that it was important that they pay attention and be careful to do the job right. Everything was well organized and well presented. But there wasn't a single word of explanation of anything. The class paid attention and took notes, but the only questions were about one or two somewhat fuzzy areas. The visitor never got a sense that the people were really concerned about how to make the requirements work in their situations. Afterward, she complimented the trainer on the technical quality of the presentation. The woman sighed. "Yeah," she said. "They seem to pay attention, and I think they do learn all right. But then they get back on the job and we still have the same old problems. They just don't seem to think all this means anything." A few words of explanation of the reasons behind the rules would probably have helped those people understand that it really did mean something after all.

Suggestion Programs

Most organizations have some sort of suggestion program, with cash rewards or recognition offered to employees who suggest improvements. Many times, these suggestions are referred to the subject-matter experts — like the security staff — for evaluation and response. These programs offer one more chance to do a bit of educating. The person who made the suggestion was at least interested enough in the issue to write out a suggestion, even if he or she was mainly motivated by the hope of a reward. When responding to the suggestion, take time to provide a little explanation of the subject. Please don't ever let the response be that the current method is a regulatory requirement. Explain the reason for the requirement.

Surrogates

You can't be everywhere, or even everywhere someone might have a question to be answered or a misconception to be corrected. Try to find surrogates to help you out. The organizational psychology folks tell us that in every organization there are people who have what they call *informal power*. Formal power is what managers and supervisors have. Informal power is the kind of power other people in the organization have because they're particularly knowledgeable, considered especially smart, helpful, or influential, or are just well liked. Marketers call this sort of person an *opinion leader*, and that's just how we'd like them to act for our security program. Find out who these people are and put a little extra effort into educating them about security. Then when they hear a coworker grumbling about an apparently meaningless security requirement or questioning the need for some security task, your surrogate may step in with a word or two of explanation. The surrogate may also step in with a correction when he or she discovers a misunderstanding. People usually like to show off that extra bit of knowledge.

Educating your organization's population on the reasons behind your security requirements can pay off in intelligent support of your program's goals, worthwhile ideas for improvements to the program, and a more easily motivated workforce. It's relatively cheap in terms of time and effort. It needs to be a regular part of your security education efforts.

12

Planning to Train: Reader Exercise

This exercise will allow you, as the security educator, to become engaged in the actual development of an education and training session for your employees. Understanding the thought process, and then turning that process into action on your part allows for the full development of a training exercise from which your employees learn specific skills, understand rules and procedures applicable to the skills, and ensure the process is properly performed.

Given a detailed description of a performance problem in a security program, the reader will perform a basic front-end analysis, decide on an intervention strategy, and develop a "plan of attack" outline for the training. The exercise describes a skills/knowledge problem that is *not* amenable to job aiding.

Upon completion of this exercise, you should be able to do the following:

- Identify problems within a security program that result in poor employee understanding, interpretation, and performance of duties.

- Select one or more appropriate strategies to attack and defeat the problem.

- Develop an outline for job aids to assist employees (these aids must also educate and train them).

Problem: During the past two months, you have determined — by reviewing the files concerning 11 security infractions — that personnel are not aware of how to properly transmit or transport classified or company sensitive information within or outside your organization. Close review indicates the following:

1. Addressing is poor, wrong, or inconsistent with requirements and local procedures.

2. Material involved is mostly Confidential and Secret. Two incidents involved midlevel employees hand-carrying Secret documents to another organization site some eight miles away. Nongovernment personnel (contractors) have company sensitive documents that are subject to problems because of a lack of awareness concerning the protection of sensitive proprietary information.

3. The R&D directorate, concerned with advanced computer electronics and advanced design, is responsible for the majority of the incidents. The directorate has 164 personnel in four divisions.

4. Most clearances are at the Secret level.

5. Courier cards have been issued to selected senior government management personnel. Contractor staffers all have courier cards in this directorate.

6. The infractions can be broken down as follows: 45% involved midlevel employees, 19% senior personnel, 8% unknown, and the rest administrative support staff personnel. Both government and the private sector staffers have been responsible for these infractions.

7. Command mail courier personnel have Confidential and Secret clearances.

8. Employee turnover in the secretarial, courier, and mailroom areas are somewhat high as jobs are at the lower end of the spectrum.

The organization has more than 1500 employees, in three buildings at the main location, and 750 more people at several other sites (all within 20 miles). You are concerned about couriers, mail distribution, secretaries, and mid- and senior level employees. Within this employee group, the time frame for handling classified materials ranges from 0 (for new employees) to 15-plus years.

The boss has said to you, "Give them some training!" What will you do? Which strategies will you use, and why? Although job aids could possibly be developed for use, assume you do not have the resources to create such aids, what now?

On the following pages are possible solution areas for the problem addressed. These solution areas are highlighted with questions within to allow you to determine what can be, or should be, accomplished during the training session. Use hands-on training for the proper addressing and hand-carrying of the materials. Review the local security policy and procedures for the protection of information that will be hand-carried to ensure that all areas are covered.

- For government, you must address the controls for the in-house handling of classified material, wrapping, control, receipts, authorization to hand-carry (courier cards or letters), controls for hand-carrying outside the organization, and considerations relative to mailing versus hand-carrying (time, short distance, information sensitivity).

- For the private sector, address controls that may be applied to the sensitive information, to include proprietary data, such as who is authorized to have the information, who may authorize its release, any required confidentiality agreements to protect the information, courier card or letter, receipts, and wrapping of the materials.

- For hands-on training, what actual materials will be used? Envelopes (single or double wrap), type of sealing tape to be used, address labels (to organization on the outside with your return address; specific recipient identified on the inside), receipts (for the package, the receipt goes on outside; for specific document included in the package, the receipt goes inside with the document); who handles the document (authorized access to it).

- Will the envelopes have any specific control markings? ("Contains Sensitive Proprietary Information"; "To Be Opened Only by Addressee"; "Return to Sender [or Contact for Pickup] if Individual Unavailable.")

- Number of copies of document transmitted can be a problem. What if more copies are to be made prior to them being hand-carried, who will copy, what controls will be put in place, is individual authorized to handle the documents to make the copies, what will happen to problem copies (transmission, destruction, or what)?

- Your mailroom personnel are authorized couriers, but are they authorized to have direct access to the sensitive information — even in an administrative sense — or will another individual have to be present to ensure they don't make an unauthorized copy or view the information?

- Restrictions of who has access to the information; be prepared to discuss the limitations that are imposed, and why they are necessary. Again, review the local policy and procedures and summarize that that they are understood and properly interpreted by the attendees to your training session.

13

Moving Security Education into the Work Environment

All organizations have a need for installing the TEAM (training, education, awareness, and motivation) concept as a continuing influence on the job for each employee. We need to be available to our organizational employees all of the time, able to step back from other duties to provide advice and assistance, to answer questions — even the most mundane ones — in order to provide the best possible service, and, finally, to be sure that security is uppermost in the minds of our fellow workers.

The use of promotional materials, such as posters, reference handbooks, mementos, and other published materials are some of the proven methods that can be used to provide continual security reminders to everyone throughout the organization. Depending on the organization, you might even consider interactive video as a possibility. The use of the TEAM concept in meetings and everyday interaction must be seriously considered, carefully evaluated, and then implemented to assure its maximum effectiveness and reception by all organizational employees.

This chapter is somewhat lengthy because of the overabundance of materials related to the subject area. As such, on completion of this chapter, you will be better able to comprehend potential ideas for creating security education products by doing the following:

- Identifying a variety of promotional materials and methods to effectively present TEAM to employees

- Determining materials and TEAM presentation methods that would be effective in their workplace

- Selecting methods that will appeal to employees to get your security education message across

- Considering the design layout, color, illustrative and textual matter in preparing training aids, PowerPoint and other presentation visuals, posters, flyers, and so forth

As you move through this chapter, remember that you are selling a product, a very important product, and its name is security.

SELLING SECURITY

Is there a need to motivate people to support your program, and is selling the angle to use? Security educators, as well as others within the program, are basically salespeople. Security is the product to be sold on a continuing basis. The use of sales marketing techniques, those used by numerous service industries, can be extremely valuable to security managers across the board — no matter whether they are in government, a government contractor, or in private industry.

A Tough Job

Motivating people to care about security is a tough job, but it's one of the most critical responsibilities of any security staff. All security programs depend on people to make them effective, and those people must be motivated to do their part in the program. Yet time and time again, we hear security officers complain:

- "Our boss doesn't care about security."
- "Our management just won't support us."
- "People just don't want to be bothered."
- "The big wheels are always too busy for security."
- "You can't get people to really care."

We hear this kind of complaint from professional defeatists, but we also hear it from dedicated, competent, energetic professionals. The problem is a real one and a tough one. The authors don't have any easy answers. If you're looking for the five easy steps to motivate people to care about security or the secret method that ensures 100% support for your program, look somewhere else. The most we can do is suggest some tools/ideas/ways to approach the subject that may help you work more effectively to solve your specific security motivation problems.

One of the shortcomings in the security profession is that we don't look beyond our field enough to take advantage of ideas (borrow tools) from other disciplines and professions. We seem to see our situations and problems as unique, when, in fact, many of them are much like problems faced by others, in other lines of work. We're going to suggest that you reach out beyond the world of the security profession and borrow a tool kit. Now, this isn't something like the little drawer full of hammers, wrenches, and screwdrivers in your utility room. It's a real, honest-to-gosh, 576-piece mechanic's tool set, just like you see advertised on TV! It's a set of tools that has been carefully developed to motivate specific people to do specific things. It is the product of hundreds of years of research and experimentation, is used by millions of people every day, and is used to plan and control the spending of billions of dollars a year.

The tool kit is the set of principles, strategies, and techniques used in the business of marketing. If one of our key responsibilities is to get people to buy into our security program, then we're going to have to *sell* it to them. If we're gong to do this effectively, we need to step back for a moment and take a good look at what our role in the organization really is.

Security Is a Service Industry

In both government and industry, security of information is the responsibility of management and all those people in the organization who work with the information. Security is *not* the security office's program; it's *everyone's* program! The security staff provides a *service* in carrying out this responsibility by establishing procedures to use, educating employees on the subject, and providing quality control (oversight) and technical assistance. An important part of our job is to get our people, our organizations, and our managers to "buy" our service.

There are two more points for you to think about before we browse in the marketing tool kit. The first is that people learn all the time: not just in planned learning activities, but from everyday experiences. Their attitudes are shaped by their every contact with your security staff and program, not just by your motivation efforts. The other point is that people react to their perceptions, not to reality. Yes, we've covered this idea before, but now, let's view it in terms of selling security throughout your organization.

To influence an organization's attitudes and actions, we have to influence via perceptions. For instance, if people perceive me as a threat, they're going to react defensively. (Sound familiar, security officer?) It doesn't matter that I'm really the nicest guy in the whole world; their reactions are based on their perceptions. To change their attitudes toward me, I have to change those perceptions, and this can be accomplished with a variety of tactics and strategies.

Tactics and Strategy

What sort of ideas will we find in the marketing tool kit? We'll find ideas that can help us on two levels: to plan our strategy for motivation and to devise effective tactics to get the plans to work. There are dozens of examples of how marketing tactics can be useful in promoting security programs. How about advertising? Do marketers use posters? Then why shouldn't we take advantage of all the effort they've spent learning how to make posters effective? When we put notices and reminders in in-house publications, we're advertising. The good principles of print advertising should be useful in adding punch into these items. Can we use sales promotion techniques to help sell our programs? You bet! We're doing it every time we give out that collective variety of items usually referred to as "gimmees." We give out coasters, pens, calendar pads, or pocket protectors — all with security reminders on them. It just makes common sense to learn from all the effort marketing people have spent finding ways to use such strategies effectively.

Even more important, though, are the lessons we can learn about marketing strategy. Before we can use the tricks of the marketing trade though, we need to look at what needs to be done to sell security to our organizational populations and what strategies could pay off for us in doing it.

MARKETING STRATEGY

As examples of applying marketing strategy to selling security programs, let's look at three basic concerns of marketers when they plan a marketing effort. These aren't all-inclusive; there are plenty of other considerations. But these samples will let us see how thinking in marketing terms can give us a fresh and useful perspective on what we're doing. Here are the three requirements for effective marketing that we'll be examining:

- Establishing the credibility of the seller
- Creating the proper positioning and product image
- Promoting customer satisfaction

CREDIBILITY

Credibility means that people must trust you and believe in your competence enough to respect and accept your judgment. Ever heard the expression, "I wouldn't buy a used car from that guy"? There's an element of trust in every sale. We trust the seller to have fairly and accurately represented the product or service and be willing to stand behind it. If you're going to sell your security program to people, they must trust that you are dealing fairly with them and will continue to do so. In many cases, this atmosphere of trust just doesn't exist. Most often, it's been eroded by what happens when something goes wrong. When a security infraction or similar incident occurs, how many of us in security education take an honest and critical look at ourselves, our security staff, and our program, and then shoulder a fair share of the blame? Or do we always look for others to be the targets of criticism and punishment? Trust is also eroded when we try to "snow" someone to cover up a gap in our knowledge. Just get caught at that once, and you can kiss credibility good-bye.

Credibility and trust go together. As an example, suppose you walk by an office (security or otherwise) and hear the department's new boss talking to his staff. You hear, "I don't make mistakes, and you will ensure that I don't make mistakes. This office runs perfect because we know what we're doing." Later, you hear a short give-and-take between the boss and one of his staffers that goes like this:

"Someone asked me a question about XXX and I gave them an answer but not a full one; said I'd get back to them," says the staff member.

"Well," the boss says, "if you don't know it completely, refer them to the regulation, or tell me. I'll tell them what I think they need to know."

"But wouldn't it be better if we explained why we want it done a certain way?"

"That takes time, and my job and that of this office is too important to be wasting time. I'll tell them and refer them to the specifics of our policy and regulatory guidance."

What would be your take on this conversation? In the first instance, the boss has not just inferred, but he has come out and said that nothing will go wrong, and if it does, he is not to blame; his staff will be. How will his attitude translate when you have a problem or concern or misunderstand something that was said or read? The second conversation between the boss and his office staffer again says it all: Do it my way; refer to the policy and regulation. In essence, there is no other way, no other view, except his view and his interpretation of the rules. Also, notice that the boss indicates that his time is much too important to spend it discussing security matters. He gives an answer — more a command statement — and that's the end of it.

Where does this leave you? And what's your view of this new boss? Not a very good one, I suspect, and that view will quickly be translated into behavior that is undesirable, especially in view of the responsibilities of the security program. We require people within the organization who are competent and also can and will work with all other employees to resolve problems, concerns, and differences of opinion in terms of policy and program implementation and the interpretation of same.

Technical competence is another essential element of a seller's credibility. This means more than knowing your product in terms of being able to quote requirements and interpret the technical jargon. It means being able to explain the reasons behind the requirements and the practicalities behind the policies. Have you ever gone to buy an expensive item and run across a salesperson who didn't seem familiar with the product? Oh, she could tell you the model number, the price, and what optional features were included, but she didn't seem able to go beyond that, to really help you understand the product and make sure it was best for your needs. Did you feel comfortable buying from her? People in your organization will feel much more comfortable buying security advice and guidance from someone they feel really *knows and understands* the business.

This is a very important consideration in marketing. Sales organizations spend a good part of their training efforts building product knowledge and helping salespeople understand product benefits. The *appearance* of technical competence is also important. A major electronics retailer introduced a line of home computers in its stores. The product was good, but sales weren't as high as the company had hoped. One of the problems the company uncovered was a hesitancy on the part of potential customers to buy a computer from the same person who sold them stereo speakers, flashlight batteries, and electronic toys. How could that person possibly know enough about computers to help them with their buying needs? So the company partitioned off its computer sales activities into "Computer Centers" to remove this obstacle to sales.

In our case, too, the image of technical competence is important and can easily be promoted. It requires that we become technically competent, of course, and then it requires a bit of time. When someone asks a question about a requirement, take a moment to explain your answer. Let the individual see you aren't just parroting some rule book, but actually understand the issues involved. Don't fall into the common habit of answering every question with a quotation from a manual or security directive. Help people understand what's behind the requirement, and you'll help them also to recognize your competence.

Credibility is also built by displaying a proper *orientation to organizational goals*. This allows your "customers" to feel confident that you understand their situation and share their concerns for having good security while effectively accomplishing other aspects of their mission. There's a sales technique you may have noticed: the salesperson who, when approaching a customer, spends the first few minutes of the conversation trying to determine exactly what the customer needs (or thinks he or she needs). If the salesperson can get a good understanding of the customer's needs, he or she can focus on selling efforts on the products that will best meet those needs. The customer is made to feel comfortable with the salesperson. The customer gets a clear signal that the salesperson is trying to make a sale that will be mutually satisfactory, rather than just pushing a product. Take the time to gain a clear understanding of the non-security missions and concerns of the people you deal with, and let them *know* you understand. It will pay off.

POSITIONING AND PRODUCT IMAGE

People in marketing and advertising spend a lot of effort and money trying to influence their product's position and product image. *Position* is the consumer's perception of where the product stands in relation to similar items that would compete for the consumer's buying dollars. *Product image* is the reaction you have when you see or hear about the product — sort of an instant, automatic picture of what the product is like in one respect or another.

Positioning is often done in terms of cost, and the auto industry provides a good example. Some automobile manufacturers try to position a model on just about every rung of the cost ladder, so they can complete with all the other manufacturers. This leads to such odd descriptions as a "luxury economy" car. Others, like Mercedes-Benz and Rolls-Royce, deliberately position their products at the high end of the cost scale as the ultimate in luxury vehicles. But cost isn't the only way in which products are positioned. Soft drinks provide an example of positioning in terms of a "conservative-to-radical" scale:

- Coca-Cola — conservative and traditional ("The real thing")

- Pepsi-Cola — modern and progressive ("The Pepsi generation")

- Seven-Up — a complete break with tradition ("The un-cola")

- Dr. Pepper — so radically different, you'll join a select elite if you drink it ("Wouldn't you like to be a Pepper, too?")

Product image, however, is less a matter of making comparisons. It's the image or impression that the marketers hope will spring to mind when consumers run across the product. A product image is the answer to the question, "What's the first thing you think of when I mention ____?" A well-implanted product image can then be used as a cornerstone for a marketing effort. Consider these examples: Charmin = soft, Cadillac = expensive, IBM = big, Jordache = stylish, and Maytag = dependable.

Now how about product image and positioning of our security program? First, what's the product image? When people in your organization hear the word *security*, what springs to their mind. I'm afraid that for many people, it would be "hassle," "trouble," "administrative nuisance," "dangerous," "a pain," "stumbling block," "always causing problems," or something less polite. Security has a negative product image for many people, and it's our own fault. We in the security business have allowed this to happen, and in many cases we have caused this negative view. Hardly anyone begins their working career afraid of or resenting security programs. Our program's product image is formed while people are on the job and is based on what they see, hear, and experience.

We promote a negative product image in a number of ways. When we do inspections that are clearly aimed at finding fault — to the point where people expect to hear us cry "Gotcha!" when we find an error — we're forming negative impressions of our programs in the victims' minds. When we concentrate on administrative nit-picking, we're sending signals that there's nothing more substantive to the program. When the security staff bad-mouths policies and requirements, we're encouraging people to see our program as worthless. ("Gee, if even the security people don't think this makes sense, why should I?")

Then there's the favorite security habit — the practice of scrambling to hide in the rule book whenever faced with a question. Let's stop and look at this one for a moment. It's all too common and all too damaging. "Why do I have to do such-and-such?" asks the employee, and the security officers responds, "Because paragraph 17-6b on page 13 of the security manual says so." And that's it. That's supposed to settle the issue and satisfy the questioner. But let's look, not just at what the security officer said, but at what the employee may decide he's heard. Perhaps the questioner heard, "The security manual says so, and that's all I know, because I really don't know my job." Or "The manual says so, and there's probably no other reason, because the security program's just a bunch of meaningless rules that serve no real purpose." Or maybe "The manual says so, and I'm not going to explain it further, because I can't be bothered giving you a better answer." Now, none of these interpretations is true, and, of course, they aren't what the security officer meant. But remember, please, that people react to their *perceptions*, not to what's true or what we mean.

Does this mean you shouldn't refer to the organizational policies, manuals, and various regulations when answering questions? Not at all. But don't let citing them be your whole answer. Common courtesy demands that security educators give someone who asks us a "why" question the respect of trying to give the best possible answer. It's an opportunity for us to educate the employees a bit, to help them recognize that there are good reasons behind security rules, and that the rules serve a purpose and can make an important difference. Point out the requirement in the manual, but also explain the reason behind it. The product image you're promoting when you do this is "Security = worthwhile."

Now for positioning; where does our security program stand in comparison with all the other programs and responsibilities competing for people's time, attention, effort, and resources? As we saw before, positioning can occur on many different scales of measurement. Let's look at two good examples: importance and effectiveness. The scale of importance might run from "mission essential" to "administrative nuisance." Where does security fall on the scale? If we concentrate on paperwork and neglect substance, if we spend inspection time nit-picking forms rather than digging into program quality, and if we fly into a righteous rage if someone doesn't have all the records straight but then we ignore the hard questions of system effectiveness, we position security far down into the "paperwork hassle" category. We almost guarantee that every other program and project will compete successfully against it for emphasis and effort. We need to help people draw clear and compelling connections between the security program and the mission, to be sure they see clearly that the program can make a difference, and lead them to understand that their participation is critical, not just to the security program, but to the organization's reason for being.

Now for effectiveness. The scale might run from "highly effective" down to "futile exercise." And here I think security professionals face a problem that's mushroomed in the past few years. Back in the 1970s, we began to hear expressions of strong concern from the highest levels about leaks and unauthorized disclosures of classified information, and though administrations have changed, this concern has continued. Then, in the 1980s came the flood of espionage cases that have become so familiar — the Walkers, Pollards, Pelton, Chin, Bell, Harper — and on and on. All these were high profile espionage cases involving the theft of classified government information and also information from the private sector, all of which affected America's national security posture. With the Economic Espionage Act of the 1990s, the theft of industrial trade secrets and formulae, including medical, biological, and high-technology information, jumped to the forefront in terms of thefts by spies. These cases have provided a marvelous means of demonstrating to people that espionage is for real and can happen just about anywhere, to just about anyone. The complaints about leaks have let security educators show organizations that someone "up there" does care. But have we been sensitive enough to a possibly dangerous effect?

It seems that we've been hearing a particular kind of problem raised by security people: "How can I get people to care about the protection of information and various forms of data when they figure it's all going to end up in some magazine or newspaper anyway?" Then there's a similar comment: "People don't see why they should go to all the trouble of protecting secrets when somebody like John Walker just hands the stuff over to someone else anyway."

These are tough and nasty issues to tackle, and we have to respect where people with these attitudes are coming from, but to let these criticisms go unanswered and unchallenged just helps position security on the "waste of time" end of the scale. People are hard-pressed to really care about and support a program when they believe it's an exercise in futility. Don't snap back at the people and condemn them for having a bad attitude! Being defensive just signals that you have something to be defensive about. This is a case where reasonable, respectful discussion is essential, and logic is your best tool.

Sometimes, too, you can take the currency of the news and turn it to your advantage. An example of this strategy happened a number of years ago. It involves the theft of classified information contained on several reels of computer tape. Fortunately, though, the theft was caught in time before the tape reels were turned over to an adversarial government. Here's how it went for the security chief. "I was in my office by 7:30, and the telephone was already ringing," he said. Picking up the phone, the first thing the caller said is "what can we do about it?" "About what?" the chief inquired. "You know, look in today's paper," the caller responded. The front page of the paper provided the answer: an attempted theft of stolen information, with the thief caught in the act by the FBI. It had happened across the parking lot and in close proximity to the computer center building for which the security chief had responsibility. As such, it provided an immediate opportunity to perform a number of security education services relative to the threat, espionage concerns, the protection of classified materials, control of materials, access control, and visitor awareness. Positioning and timing of the security product — protecting our nation's secrets — couldn't have been better. The situation allowed security personnel to position themselves as knowledgeable about everyday concerns and actions of employees. The employees viewed the various presentations — one-on-one, small groups, and to the senior staffers — as very beneficial and an excellent use of their time. Employee awareness rose, security became important, and the personal approach throughout the offices worked wonders.

To work with people whose attitudes toward security have been tarnished by an idea that the program is hopeless, consider using an analogy involving money. When employees in the organization complain that protecting information is useless because it will end up leaked to the media anyway, I ask what percentage of information they think will end up being leaked. The percentage is very small, of course. Then I ask them to think about this: If you're walking down the street and lose a dollar bill, what do you do when you find out it's gone? Pull out the rest of your money and toss it away? Of course not. Then why, because some information suffers unauthorized disclosure, should we stop being careful with all the rest? This logic seems to work well, at least to get the employees to think again about the issue.

To counter despair about serious espionage and economic information theft cases, the following argument might be useful: "Sure, the damage to the national security in the Walker (or another recent, well-known case) was serious — *very* serious. But that doesn't mean we should all give up, does it? Let's say you're on a trip, far away from home. You lose your credit cards and most of your cash. What do you do with the money you have left? Wouldn't you be extra careful about keeping it safe? Wouldn't the same sort of logic apply to the information you work with every day?"

The positioning and product image of your security programs depend on people's perceptions of the programs. Influencing those perceptions is something we can all do effectively if we think about it and try.

CUSTOMER SATISFACTION

Ever hear someone in security say, "Security isn't a popularity contest?" Well, they're right, of course. But isn't this often an excuse for having failed to establish a good working relationship with people? In marketing, it's important to keep the customer satisfied. If we are going to market security in our organizations, it had better be important to *us*, too.

First, we should be sure we're clear on who the customers of our service are: they're the people in your organization. Remember that the responsibility for good security falls on everyone in the organization, and our role is to provide them a service in fulfilling this responsibility. They are the ones who have to *buy* the service if it's going to be worthwhile. They pay in terms of time, effort, and other resources they spend on making the program work; accepting our advice, guidance, and help; and responding to our concerns and direction.

The marketers have found out a lot about what makes people buy and what makes for satisfied customers. One is that, while the quality of your product or service is important, it's the *perceived* quality of the product that *really* makes the difference. Particularly for uneducated consumers, any perceived quality of a product is often heavily influenced by satisfaction with the provider. In other words, when I don't have enough knowledge and experience to really judge a product's quality, I tend to make my judgment in large part on the way I'm treated by salespeople, delivery people, installers, and service people.

As an example, take my mother and TV sets. My mother knew a lot about a lot of things, but a TV set wasn't one of them. She knew how to turn it on and adjust the volume, but that was about it. Every time she bought a TV, she bought it from a particular department store and would tell anyone who asked that she wouldn't think of buying a TV anywhere else. Why? The picture was about the same as you'd find on a TV in another store, cabinet styles weren't all that different, costs were about average, and this store's TV seemed to go on the blink about as often as anyone else's. What made the difference wasn't the quality of the product itself (which my mother really wasn't competent to judge), but the quality of the transaction and her satisfaction with the store. The salespeople were always polite and helpful, deliveries were punctual, the delivery people added nice touches like making sure to clean the screen and cabinet before they left, and the repair department responded promptly when called.

Another principle that's important to marketers — and should be to us — is that satisfaction promotes repeat sales. If I'm satisfied with my dealing with a store, I'll be more likely to do business with that store again. If not, I'll avoid the store unless I really *need* what it's selling and can't get it elsewhere. In terms of security programs, "repeat sales" means people come to you more than once for help, advice, or technical assistance. The likelihood of a customer coming back to take advantage of your service can be a critical factor in your success and your program's effectiveness. How willing are people to come to you for guidance rather than blunder ahead on their own? Are people comfortable bringing a problem to you, or will they wait until it becomes a crisis or a full-blown disaster? Do managers invite you into their organizations to help with security education, or does it have to be forced down their throats? Does your boss want you to keep him or her briefed on security developments, or do you have trouble getting on the calendar? Are security incidents promptly reported to you, or does everyone seem desperate to handle them in-house?

BUILDING CUSTOMER SATISFACTION

Before we look at some ways security personnel can build customer satisfaction, let's get one thing straight. To promote customer satisfaction, it is not necessary to compromise your principles, ignore violations, let people off easy, wink at discrepancies, or agree with everybody who walks through the door. You can do a completely honest, competent, and scrupulous job of planning, implementing, and overseeing your organization's security program and still end up with *very* satisfied customers. It's not so much a matter of what you do as how you do it. It's less a matter of making things easy for people than making sure they know they've been treated honestly, fairly, and respectfully and that you've considered their concerns, needs, ideas, and preferences as much as you reasonably could. Here are some ways to do it.

Prompt Delivery

Few things seem to irritate customers more than delays in delivering merchandise. Take the business of computing and mail-order selling of computer hardware and software; it's big business. Almost every complaint you hear about mail-order companies has to do with how long it often takes them to fill an order. People don't like to wait. It makes them feel they're being ignored, and that makes them feel they're not getting the respect they deserve. Prompt attention to a request or question indicates that you think the individuals are important, their questions are important, and their contributions to security are important. If you can't handle someone's problem or question right away, give the person an explanation. Don't just say, "I'm really busy right now." The person might decide that means, "I'm really busy right now, and everything else I have to do is more important than your trivial little problem." Try something like, "I'm not going to be able to get you an answer right away. I have two reports I have to get out by tomorrow, and I'll need a little time to get you a really good answer."

Follow-up

One weekend I developed an abscessed tooth. By early Sunday morning, the darn thing hurt like blazes. Not having a regular dentist, I looked for a nearby medical facility that would be open for business early that morning. I settled on one of those new emergency care centers. I'd always been suspicious of what I considered "fast-food medicine," but at that point I wasn't going to be choosy. I was taken care of promptly, and the doctor sent me on my way with a prescription for penicillin and a stern warning to see a dentist the next day. So far, so good. But what really made me change my mind about these facilities happened the next day, right after I got home from the dentist's office. The phone rang, and it was one of the nurses saying the doctor had asked her to call and see if I'd been able to get to see a dentist that day. So much for my ideas about an impersonal, assembly-line, "we'll-never-see-him-again" attitude! Would I make use of that center again? You'd better believe it!

Following up on a "sale" shows you care about customer satisfaction, and people tend to attach a lot of importance to it. The beauty of it is, following up usually takes very little time and almost no effort. Just calling to see how a new procedure is working out or stopping by someone's office to see if a solution to a problem worked can pay big dividends in customer satisfaction.

Customer Service

When customers buy a product or service, they expect it to work and to get the job done. Smart marketers know that product support (also sometimes called "customer service") can often be the key to creating satisfied customers. The computer business is a fine example. The reputations of hardware and software vendors often depend heavily on the quality of product support they provide. When I buy an expensive software package, I want help readily available if I have problems installing the program on my computer, good answers to my questions about using it, assistance in making it work properly for my purposes, and support in tailoring it to my special needs.

When we sell people a security service, we should be willing to provide them the same sort of customer service. It's dangerous to take the attitude, "Here's what you do; now go do it." We need to be ready to work with people to get new procedures implemented properly and painlessly, answer the questions that new ways of dong things always seem to generate, help them make sure things are working properly, and make necessary changes to overcome unexpected glitches.

When we don't do this, customer satisfaction, our reputations, and the cooperative attitude of the people we're dealing with all suffer badly. Consider this horrible example. While working on a security staff, a new directive from higher management headquarters requires the security team to start a major new function. You talk with your supervisor and coworkers; none can figure out exactly how you could possibly implement the new policy. So you call the office that put out the directive. You explain that you are ready to put a lot of effort into getting this new job done and, in fact, think it is a great step forward, but you are stumped as to how to go about it. You need help. You are told, "We don't want to micromanage your program," and you end up not receiving a single suggestion, let alone any real help. How might this response affect your perception of customer satisfaction? You would be absolutely furious. You're convinced that the people in that office hadn't any idea how (or even whether) the job could be done and had just put out the directive to make themselves look good to their bosses. Their professional reputations hit rock bottom in your eyes, and you resent their leaving you and your security team to "twist in the wind." When we sell our services to the people in our organization, we must stand behind it with good customer service.

Warranty

When we make a major purchase, the warranty that comes with the product is often an important element in our decision to buy. Therefore, problems with warranty repairs can produce dissatisfied customers. Just think of the number of times you've heard people grumble about car dealers and arguments about whether repairs are covered by the warranty.

When we sell our security service, we also need to provide a warranty. If we've provided advice or assistance and something goes wrong, we need to accept a fair share of the blame. The problem should be "our" problem, not "your" problem. Yet the authors themselves have reviewed hundreds of reports dealing with inquiries into security violations and infractions and can recall on one hand the number of times the security staffers admitted that the system was flawed, the requirements were unrealistic, the procedures were ineffective, or support (perhaps, even, security education) hadn't been provided.

At an overseas government installation, where both government military and civilians worked side by side, sitting down and talking with the security people provided one example of an internal problem: There was a clear attitude of "we're right and they're wrong." In this instance, the security people, when investigating a security incident, would always find someone culpable. It was never "our fault" but always "their fault." In essence, the security department made the rules, and everyone else goofed up. The security department was always right; everyone else was always wrong. So ask yourself, when you have a problem or concern, what are the chances that the security department will really help you?

Just after a major espionage case hit the papers, the author was chatting with a neighbor, a midlevel manager in another government department. My neighbor brought up the case, and I commented that it seemed from what I had read (so far in the open press) that the organization's security department had fallen down on the job pretty badly. He was amazed. "I can't believe you said that," he replied. "Around our place, *nothing* is *ever* the security office's fault. Whenever something goes wrong, the security people *always* manage to find someone else to hang!" That's a sad commentary on a way of doing business that's certainly never going to allow a relationship of trust to exist between the security staff and the rest of the organization's population.

Courtesy

The final factor in promoting customer satisfaction that you must think about is plain old common courtesy. Think about going to an income tax preparation service (on April 14, of course). You sit down with a tax preparer who's supposed to help and advise you with your tax filing. She asks for some information, which you don't have because you didn't know it was needed. "I can't believe you didn't know that," she growls. "It's right in the tax law." She then asks for some other information, which you haven't kept track of. With a righteous scowl, she proclaims, "It's your responsibility to know what records are required! You obviously haven't done it." Later on, you question the way she is computing certain deductions. She sighs and says with an exasperated tone, "Look, it's in the tax code, alright?" and turns back to the forms. How anxious do you think you'll be to go back to that service next year, even if the preparer does seem to do a good job on your taxes?

Now think about going to a security office looking for help. You ask a question about how to do something. "Look, you people are supposed to know how to do that," you are told. "We put out a manual with all that information in it. Haven't you bothered to read it?" You plow ahead, and it comes to light that there's a procedure you haven't been following. The security officer bellows, "You mean you people aren't doing that? It's right in the regulation!" Then you ask why a certain procedure is necessary, and you're answered with, "Look, paragraph 4-36, on page 87 of the manual says so. Period." You're sure going to be eager to go back there for help, aren't you? Not if you're sane, you're not!

Working in security isn't easy. A lot of tension, anxiety, and frustration is involved. It's easy to lose patience with "dumb" questions and complaints. But we don't dare have the attitude that our program is so important that we have the right to run rough-shod over people's feelings and self-respect. It's for the program's sake that we must treat people with courtesy and show respect for them and their concerns. The program demands that we keep people willing — and make them eager — to seek our advice and assistance and accept our guidance and direction.

In fact, let's put it more bluntly: The security staff member who willfully or negligently develops an adversary relationship with the people in his or her organization is an incompetent and a menace to the security of the organization and what is supposed to be protected through the security regulations, guidance, and assistance that should be provided to everyone in the organization on a continual basis.

THE BOTTOM LINE

The success of any program for protecting information is heavily dependent on the investment of time, resources, and care by the people who are entrusted with the information. If we — as security professionals — want them to invest in our program, to buy into it, we have to sell. Marketing isn't a mysterious science or arcane craft. It's a system for looking at and thinking about a lot of commonsense actions, many of which most of us do naturally. But thinking about our role in marketing terms can help us make sure we do more of those commonsense actions more often. And that's important!

SECURITY EDUCATION AWARENESS TRAINING (SEAT)

SEAT involves a broad range of ideas, concepts, and techniques. As such, you need to think and work together in terms of development of information and materials. At any time, consider the currency of the information presented. Think about the use of "fact sheets," such as up-to-date newspaper and magazine articles. What about subject matter specialists and experts? Can you update older materials, and if so, why do that instead of starting fresh?

"Case studies" are examples that can apply to your locale or organization, and subject areas that employees can relate to. Ensuring the information they receive is timely, as complete as possible, relevant, informative, and specific should be your goals in formulating a method to get the information across in as positive a manner as possible.

When employees learn something new from a meeting or a discussion, they tend to review the information in their minds. Even if they are provided with a handout, they will carefully read it, pass it on to others, or maintain it at their desks for future reference.

In terms of SEAT, the previous chapters have provided you with theory and the background techniques, our thoughts from many years of experience, and various training concept techniques, which can be successfully used to promote and encourage employees to support the overall security program.

VISUAL AIDS

Most people think of a visual aid as a slide, viewgraph, or a PowerPoint (PPT) slide. While they are right, they are also somewhat wrong, because visual aids have a greater presence and impact than many people realize.

Visual aids are great because they can be used in a variety of settings. At times, you do not have to be present for the visual to interact with the viewer. Other times, the visuals are part of a security presentation for employees. Thus, a visual and any accompanying message can be on a flyer, bookmark, poster, "gimmee" memento item, a 35-mm slide, a computer home page, a viewgraph, or part of a PPT presentation.

Visual Aids for Training

Using slides, viewgraphs, charts, and other show-and-tell supportive items can assist the presentation, highlighting a specific point or further enhancing the subject matter. Visual aids do not have to be something that requires you as the security education person to be present or even currently doing. Visual aids should meet the following goals:

- Should get employee attention (this includes anything that works, such as a bulletin board, butcher paper board, blackboards, or even the lowly slapstick).

- Must be positive.

- Must reinforce a security concept, procedure, or activity practice.

- Must be reasonable.

- May be colorful (pleasing and informative in some manner).

- Cannot offend.

- Should not be too wordy.

- Should be somewhat topical, to include local, national, or international interest, or relate to something that has recently occurred.

- Should not include dated items. History is nice, but on today's super-information highway, people look at the present and toward the future; dated items quickly become ancient history and can be viewed as the instructor's just filling time. Note, though, that some types of historical item subjects can be put to use, although they are an exception to the rule.

- May include "war stories" that directly support or drive home a specific point.

- Should not incorporate the use of videotape for its own sake.

Some Thoughts on Presentation Development

Presentation development is important to consider, from both the viewer's perspective and your own viewpoint. If you are going to use visuals in a presentation, then the following factors and guidelines should be in the forefront of your thought process as the presentation evolves from an idea to actuality.

First of all, think "communication." Consider the communication aspect of the presentation in terms of its design, what you are trying to get across to the audience, and any development that must go within the subject area. One method by which to review this is to consider yourself on the receiving end of the presentation; review it and ask yourself "does it say — *effectively* — what I'm trying to get across to the audience?" If it doesn't, then you should easily be able to discern where the problems lay and remedy them.

Next consider the "what" of the presentation:

- What are your performance objectives (what is the training outcome)?

- What are the employee needs and requirements at this time?

- What is the employee makeup (use a profile for targeting)?

- What is the threat (international, national, regional, local)?

- What are mission-essential items related to the threat?

- What are employee resistance factors or attitudes toward security?

In developing the presentation, you must consider the prime objective and the various subobjectives and how to meet them.

What topic content or issues must be resolved, and how can you best present them? Here is where an outline — with each section and the various steps, substeps, and supporting data — becomes important in the process.

What resources are currently available? Do you have the available audio or video equipment? Are you planning on 'talking off the cuff' or from a prepared speech? Each has its drawbacks and advantages. Talking off the cuff is an informal way of presenting the information. But to do this you must be well sure of the subject matter, its presentation flow, and that you don't miss a step, substep, or get mixed up. The advantages are that you come across much easier with the audience, the message is usually more acceptable, and the informality provides for a better give-and-take relationship with the audience.

What resources don't you have, but can get? Suppose you need an overhead projector, and one is not in the security office. The best place to check would be with the education and training section of the organization, which tends to have about every type of item necessary for training, even those that are not in current use or vogue in terms of presentation equipment. Typically, if this department does not have what you need, someone from the department can tell you where the item can be obtained.

What resources should you have, but don't have and can get later on? Suppose you want some handouts or brochures for employees to use as desktop references. Perhaps you can create these items yourself or you know of someone who has some of these resources left over from a previous presentation. At least jot down the source of the materials. If you're going to have to create these resources yourself, note how long it might take to perform any research and where to get graphics (from the graphics shop, draw them yourself, or perhaps from a graphics library on the computer). How long will it take to put the handout or brochure together, the number of copies required, and whether you will need colored paper are just a few of the thoughts that will run through your mind. Jot them all down, and keep your notes with the presentation. Why? Because (1) you'll forget the ideas for a while and (2) as you continue to develop the presentation or when it is finished, you can see whether or not the handout covers everything it should and stands up to what is talked about during the presentation. There should be no disconnect between the presentation and the handout; they go hand in hand, being closely related in terms of subject matter and the level of specifics covered.

Consider the facts of the training situation and environment, *plus* the various motivation methods you can use. Take these into account when starting to structure the presentation by using this approach.

Remember: Your credibility should be closely aligned with the approaches and the material used. Don't try to put too much into a given presentation. Don't limit the presentation too severely, and consider the effects of the information on your audience (what you say, what they hear, and what they interpret your statements to mean may well be different than what you want).

Presentation Visuals

Think of these as short, informal breakdowns of what you can consider for possible use. There are many types of visuals that can be used in security education, such as PowerPoint, viewgraphs, a chalkboard, posters, 35-mm slides, videotapes, slapsticks, flipcharts, and butcher board charts.

USING VISUALS IN YOUR PRESENTATION

Words

Words tell stories, but the point is to ensure the facts are correct, and in doing so, the limitations on the number of words becomes important. Thus, structure, content, and brevity are critical. Too much text, as all readers know, is a by-product of the computer age. Too much text requires your listeners to stray away from what you are saying relative to the visual text. Their concentration on reading all the text severely limits their hearing input and, further, disallows them the ability to concentrate on the substance of what is being spoken to them.

The 7 × 7 rule — some may want a 6 × 6 rule — essentially means that there should be no more than seven lines of text, and any given line should have no more than seven words in it. Of course, we all know that rules are made to be broken, and this is one of the most broken of all visual text rules.

The size of the font determines the maximum words that can be included on a visual. Size also determines the ability of the audience to clearly *and easily* read the text! If the type is blurry, they squint. If it is too small, they stare and overconcentrate on trying to figure out what is on the visual. If it is too large, you limit the amount of information in your message and leave attendees wondering if you really know how to create visuals.

Are visuals necessary? Do they really add anything to your presentation? Without a visual, all you are doing is talking, and your words may or may not have an impact. Visuals shore up, highlight if you will, what you are saying. A single visual, in a way, is an outline of what you are speaking about at that particular moment in time, or it highlights the specific subject matter under discussion, such as an example being illustrated right after the topic line of the visual.

Visuals also help the audience to further understand, consolidate, and remember what you are saying. In security education, because facts are critical to understanding the message, visuals become much more important. Supplementing your speech with visuals is necessary to get across the facts of the discussion at hand.

Graphic Design and Security Awareness Visuals

No matter what, the primary rule is: *Image is everything*! When preparing your graphic design, consider the following factors.

Rapid Comprehension

While all organizational employees are literate, some are disinclined to read when it is unnecessary. On the other side, some 15% or so will read everything they can.

Relevance

Relevance is established between the visual and the reader within two to eight seconds. For a typical security poster, 10 seconds is usually about the maximum, unless you have something that will hold readers' attention and get them to further think about what is on the poster. For visuals in a training setting, relevance is a given, but the training attendees read with an eye toward (1) getting through everything on the visual, (2) understanding the information without any mental questions, and (3) tying the visual to the words you are speaking and relating those words to the visual.

Impact and acceptance by the viewer is dependent upon several items.

Headlines

Headlines and titles are used to get the reader's attention. It identifies the topic and provides an "invitation" to read more.

Graphics

Photographs, graphics, and artwork should answer the "why" of their inclusion. They shouldn't be included simply to attract attention but to arouse curiosity and inform the reader. Sometimes, in a presentation, a speaker shows a picture but does not discuss it. In this case, a small caption line identifying the relevance of the picture is appropriate — but it should just be a few words long.

Confirmation

Confirmation of the information is established within 30 to 90 seconds for a visual in a training setting. Here again, use a short body text to expand on the picture or other graphic, but don't read it; the audience can read for themselves. There may be the perception that what is shown is "short," but you can expand on the visual and any identifying text with your discussion of its relevance to the overall topic. Also, don't crowd the visual with a lot of text. White space itself can provide emphasis and impact to a viewer. If text has to be several lines long, make the paragraph short, and the width should always exceed the length of a paragraph. Unless the information is very technical in nature, it should be easy reading for everyone.

Numbers and Outlines

In visuals, these features can provide for audience concentration of the subject matter. "Odd" gets more attention than even. In other words, something that should look one way, but actually looks otherwise, draws attention and concentration. An example of this concept is the U.S. flag. If the colors in your presentation image were green, orange, and white instead of red, white, and blue, it would certainly draw attention. In his or her mind the viewer is asking, "Why?" As the presenter, you go on to explain the reasoning behind the change in colors and how it relates to the topic material.

One way of presenting visuals and getting more audience involvement is to use a question-and-answer (Q&A) format. Instead of spelling out specifics, provide several questions — raising the point that they were asked of you — then provide the answers in a discussion format.

A table of contents is really an outline of what is to be covered. If you use this method, limit the listing to one or two visuals. From then on, each succeeding visual should highlight a single outline topic area for discussion.

The use of quotations can effectively highlight what you are talking about. Bartlett's book of quotations (or others) should be one of your desk references. Look to various speeches and articles by subject matter specialists in the field, those that are well known, and extract appropriate quotes for use. Never put too many quotes in a presentation. Limit the use of quotations to no more than three during any given presentation.

Nobody likes a totally dry presentation, so add visuals. However, although clip art, charts, graphs, cartoon sketches, and the like can add impact, they can also detract. You need to know and understand your audience in order to gauge the amount of clip art and cartoons that can be included. As for charts and graphs, these are wholly dependent on the subject matter and their applicability to the subject matter. Don't use a lot of charts and graphs; people either get caught up in them and spend all their time concentrating on these graphics — rather than on you — or they become turned off by them and tune out the entire presentation.

Action

Action happens for the viewer in an unlimited time frame. This piece of wisdom comes from years of experience in giving numerous presentations. The viewers have an immediate reaction to what is being viewed. They agree with it, disagree with it, want to think more about it, or reduce it to something totally insignificant. Thus, what they see, in words or graphics, must be attention getting, of substance, and useful to them.

If the presentation visual is just right, viewers will have an immediate reaction of thinking about it, comprehending the subject matter, and shortly thereafter mentally reviewing part or all of it. Later on, back in their offices, if it is has made any impact or has specific relevance to what is ongoing, they will mentally go over it again.

We've got this far, but let's move backward a moment. You know what you want to talk about in the presentation, that you want graphics, perhaps a handout, but you still haven't developed your subject matter itself — what you are going to say. Now is the time to consider subject content source materials. You have the idea, but the research for the presentation is also important. Look to command-type publications, books, manuals, newspaper articles, your own background experiences, organization subject matter experts, and other organizations for information. I know of no security specialist or educator that doesn't have a wide variety of reference materials, from a current job, from a previous job, from what they have obtained through professional organizations, or from friends in the profession. These are your sources for raw data that you will convert into the facts of the presentation.

Once the presentation is completed and you have reviewed it for accuracy, consider the visuals again. The first time you considered them for what should be on each one, how much data should be included, whether there should be any graphics, and the like. Now, you need to review them again for the following features:

Style

The style of the visual is important to the viewer. You should keep it simple in terms of the fancy fonts that are used. Use only one or two, so that they allow the words to be read accurately. Too many words in different font styles on the same visual means the audience will read, but will do so much slower. This, in turn, means their concentration is on the visual and not on what you are saying while they concentrate on the visual. In this case, select from one of several easy-to-read fonts, such as any of the serif fronts, Times Roman, Chicago Times, Bernhard, Courier, or Perpetua.

Sans serif fonts are nice and can be read faster, but the reading is less accurate than with other font styles. If sans serif fonts are to be used, they are best for headlines and titles. Also to be considered for this area are Helvitica, Century Gothic, and Arial. Try and avoid the use of fancy fonts. Use them sparingly or, better, not at all. These include Algerian, Braggadocia, Stencil, and Marigold.

Now, as to the visual layout, sometimes you will have a single or multiple columns. If you are using straight text, short phrases, and the like, then you really have a one-column layout. The advantage is that single columns are simple and easy to follow — a "no brainer." A concern, though, is the amount of white (or blank) space surrounding them. Also, over time, simple columns sort of become boring; you have nothing interesting, as it were, but a bunch of phrases. Thus, use some level of minor graphics, even if it is a graphic that continues from one slide to the next. In this case, use the organizational logo, or a symbol representing the security office, on a continuing basis.

Charts and Graphs

For charts and graphs, two columns become ideal. The advantages include variation and easy reading. Charts and graphs break the monotony and provide a somewhat formal look to the visual. Concerns include the fact that charts and graphs require more planning, and you may become too conservative in terms of what you actually include.

White Space and Borders

As mentioned earlier, another consideration that can come into play for any visual is the use of white (or blank) space in the visual. Even for handouts or a poster, this is important. When you type a letter, you have margins, usually an inch all around. This gives impact to the message in the letter. White space can be identifying and defining; likewise the use of some form or border can draw attention to the important items on the visual.

White space and borders help direct the eye. The white space tells the viewer there is "nothing here" to read, so look somewhere else. The borders essentially box in the text, again drawing the viewer's eyes to the desired information. You might consider, but only in a limited sense, dividing the page into "bite size" chunks by using several smaller boxes with information within them. Again, each box directs the eye, from left to right, from top to bottom. They also create emphasis, and the viewer will take more care in reading and remembering them.

Rules of Balance

There are several rules of balance that apply to any visual, whether it is part of a presentation, a handout, a poster, or something else. First, large weighs more than small. This means that large letters or words draw attention better than smaller ones. Dark weighs more than light, but only to the extent that it stands out against a light background. Color always weighs more than black and white, thus we tend to put more color into any type of visual. White space has weight and should be used, but again, sparingly; not for the sake of having a lot of white (blank) space on the visual. Also, the unusual always weighs more than the usual (standard or typical). Finally, the most weight for text or a visual is in the upper-left-hand corner. Remember, left to right, top to bottom is the overall rule for laying out text and visuals, and it is the method that people will use to look at the visual and understand it. To put items in another way doesn't necessarily confuse readers, but they spend time figuring out why it was done a certain way and not the expected way. In studying the visual, they are taking up unnecessary time, and you are losing the impact of what you were trying to get across to them in terms of information. Behind every success is a line of failures: Dare to be different, but don't be obnoxious.

POSTERS AND PICTURES

Posters are another form of visual. As such, they must convey a meaning and a message at the same time. Subject matter text, specific phraseology, layout, and any picture or drawing to add impact must be carefully thought out, and the simplicity of the poster is necessary for effectiveness.

Selling Security with Posters: A Marketing Technique Often Forgotten[1]

One lesson we can learn from marketing is the use of visuals, in this case posters. Posters come in all sizes, colors, and locations. You see billboards, stickers, play sheets, window visuals, and other visuals every day. In one form or another, these advertisements are trying to sell you something; actually what they want you to do is just think about it for a moment, because that is all it takes to get the image and very short message into your consciousness and also your sub-conscious. Posters, as we in security visualize them, are a common means of advertising security, a means to sell our product, as it were. There are some good lessons to be learned from marketers on using posters.

---

1. Exerpted from Joe Grau, *Selling Security*, originally published in the *Security Awareness Bulletin*, Issue 2-89, 1989.

A Poster's Main Function Is to Be Noticed

In advertising, posters and billboards are used to draw the attention of potential customers to a product or service — they make the product, service, or seller come to mind and maybe mold the viewer's perceptions of it. That's what posters can do for us in the security field, too. They should be used to bring the security program or some security requirement or procedure to mind for a moment: they're reminders. If this is so, then the main function of a poster is to be noticed — not to dazzle somebody with beauty or impress people with cleverness. An ignored poster is a waste of money. The focus of poster design and use must be to attract attention.

Posters Should Never Be Used to Teach Anybody Anything

Look at advertising posters and billboards. Do they give descriptions of product benefits? Do they have a long text about the advantages of dealing with a certain store? Of course not. Advertisers know that this is better left to other advertising means, like broadcast commercials or the more formal magazine or newspaper print advertising. Posters just remind you of the product and perhaps reinforce a perception you've gotten from those other advertising means. The same should hold true for security posters. We should never rely on them to teach people or provide detailed information. They're just not reliable enough; we can't be sure the message has gotten across. Posters should be used for their legitimate purpose — to remind people about security or a security requirement.

Glitz and Pizzazz Are Great until They Overwhelm Your Message

Advertising books often warn readers to beware of letting the attention-grabber in an ad overwhelm the message. A good example of this is a billboard along a well-traveled road that had a large picture of an attractive young woman in a rather revealing swimsuit. You drive by it about once a week. It got your attention every time. But, offered $100, you probably couldn't remember enough to tell anyone what the billboard was advertising or what any of the text said. The ad attracted your attention — but to the picture, not the product; it was a waste of the advertiser's money. When using a poster, we must be careful that the beauty, humor, or cleverness we use to draw attention to it doesn't obscure the message we're trying to convey. The message has to be an integral part of the poster, sure to be noticed when the poster is noticed.

Humor Is Great — When It's Funny (but Not *Too* Funny)

Humor is often used in advertising to gain attention. When it works, it's a great technique, but nothing falls flatter than the "funny" ad that isn't funny. Radio Shack's Lewis Kornfeld, one of advertising's most famous figures, spent a lot of time keeping humor *out* of his company's ads. He complained that most humor in advertising either (1) didn't work or (2) worked so well it detracted from the ad's message. In posters, too, we should be concerned about both possibilities. Humor can be a great attention-getter. Some of the finest security posters the authors have ever seen were humorous ones in a series created some years ago by Bob Vollten of the Defense Mapping Agency. Because the "message" of our posters should be basic and simple, it shouldn't be hard to keep it from getting lost in the joke. Our main worry, then, should be that any attempt we make at humor is successful. If a poster tries to be funny but the joke flops, the reaction is likely to be: "That's dumb." And the last impression we want to leave in someone's mind is an association between our security program and "dumb."

All Posters Must Be 100% Inoffensive to Everyone

All posters must be totally free of anything that could be viewed as demeaning to anyone based on race, sex, ethnic group, religious beliefs, or occupation. They must be completely devoid of anything that would violate good taste or anyone's moral standards. They have to be "squeaky clean." I'm not making a moral judgment here; you make those for yourselves. What I'm concerned about is a matter of practicality. Lewis Kornfeld wrote, you can't please everyone, but you can certainly avoid displeasing people by being careful about your poster. Anything that offends, such as an implication of racism or sexism, will go a long way towards providing serious damage to your security program, and to you.

Security programs need the cooperation of everyone. We can't afford to leave a bad taste in anyone's mind. Who cares if they're being oversensitive or prudish? The point is that we need their help, and offending them won't get it.

Fortunately, we seem to have become much more sensitive to questions of racism and sexism in posters over the past few years. But one problem that still crops up is posters that are offensive to an occupational group. How do you think security force members feel when they see a "funny" poster portraying a big, dumb, sloppy guard? How about scientists who are looking at the wild-eyed, wild-haired, "zany" scientist in your poster? Or secretaries who see themselves continually portrayed as frazzled and befuddled? These are some of the people whom we have to count on the most heavily to support the security program. It's simply good sense to make sure they don't get the notion that we don't respect them.

Negative Messages Produce Negative Reactions

The message of a poster should almost always be positive. There's a danger that a negative message will become tied to the subject matter (the security program) rather than to what the poster intends to portray negatively (for example, care-lessness or a security infraction in the protection of sensitive information). In one advertising text, the author told the story of a commercial for a restaurant chain we'll call "Fred's Steak House." The ad began with a humorous skit showing diners at another restaurant being subjected to clumsy, careless service. Then came the message: "This will never happen at Fred's, where good service is our goal." The chain did some market research. What did people remember about Fred's from the commercial? Lousy service! When people see posters threatening dire consequences for security failures, are we sure that they will associate the threat with the failure? Just as likely, perhaps, their reaction will be something else: "security = dangerous" or "security staff = menacing."

There Are Many Ways to Get Attention

Look at the posters, billboards, and ads we see all around us. Are they all big, done in fancy colors, or marvels of artistic creativity? No. It's a dangerous mistake to assume that having high visibility has to mean having high cost. The authors, as well as you, have heard security personnel complain that they just couldn't get funds to produce high-quality posters. We're afraid that they were victims of the misconception that high quality in posters means that you have to spend big bucks on them. Some of the most effective posters out there have been produced with a lettering set or with the desktop computer variable fonts, some clip art, and an office copier. An 8½-inch by 11-inch poster can be just as eye catching as a poster-sized one if properly designed. Color can be eye attracting, but so can a good design in black and white. Careful thought and imagination often produce just as effective a poster as a big-budget, flashy pro-duction. As a way of keeping costs down, consider using your computer graph-ics as the artwork and the various fonts for the text. Print out the completed item on heavy-duty cover stock or regular paper and, voila, you have a quickly made effective poster or flyer.

A number of years ago, an effective attention-getting poster was produced with a Kroy-Type machine and a red marking pen. It hung near a copying machine. It was about 10 inches by 14 inches with a 1-inch red border, and the text, crowded in the middle, was only about a half inch high. You would have thought someone had lost his mind; the text was unreadable from any reasonable distance. Curiosity aroused, people walked over and read it. It said, "Are you sure you know the rules for classified reproduction?" The poster was a total success; it attracted the attention of the people it was intended for with its oddness, and curiosity made it impossible for people not to read what it had to say. Not bad for a little, homemade poster.

Novelty Is Noticeable

Something new is more likely to be noticed than something that's become familiar. There's a major retailing chain that regularly uses advertising inserts in the Sunday papers. Every Sunday, there's a new one, with a new gimmick on the cover: "Mother's Day Sale," "Mid-Winter Specials," "Fourth of July Blockbuster Sale," and so on. When readers look inside, they find the contents are almost totally identical, week after week — almost all the products are the same and there are very few changes in price. Why does the chain go to the expense of having new inserts printed each week instead of using the same one over and over? Simply because people's attention is attracted to something new, not to the same old thing.

Novelty can be an important influence in drawing attention to posters and their messages. A poster, even a very catchy, well-designed one, tends to become easily overlooked background noise rather quickly. It's probably better tactics to produce several small, relatively cheap posters that can be changed frequently than to put your dollars into a single, expensive one that may have to hang for an extended time.

The Only Right Place to Put a Poster Is Where It Will Be Noticed

If the purpose of a poster is to be noticed, the proper place to put it is where it is most likely to be seen — not just looked at, but *seen*. In one article, a billboard company owner described the best place to locate a billboard on a highway was on a long stretch of straight road with rather dull scenery. That way, motorists will tend to notice the billboard and pay more attention to it because they have nothing better to do with their eyes. (Watching the road didn't seem to be a consideration!) The principle is a good one.

The best place for a poster is where people will look while they have nothing better to do with their eyes. For example, if you're putting up a poster in your copying machine area, put it on the wall behind the machine where people tend to look when they're waiting for their copies. In a hallway, put it at the end of the hall (not on the side walls) so people will have it in front of them as they walk down the hall. Do you have waiting areas in places like the personnel office, visitor control center, break rooms, or an employee clinic, where people sit and wait with nothing much to occupy them? These are great places for posters.

Proximity Lessens Effectiveness

In some organizations, there are designated poster areas, where all posters are supposed to be placed. If that's the way it is in your organization, try your best to get the policy changed. Burying a poster in a swarm of others just dilutes its power. Just look at a street-corner phone pole sometime, where a slew of posters have been tacked. Notice how hard it is for any of them to draw your attention.

These are just a few ideas we can glean from observing how advertising professionals use media that are similar to our security posters. How about other ideas? Well, there are plenty of them for you to find out for yourself. Keep in mind that every day we must market the security program to all employees, and the tricks of the marketing trade are there to use. Watch for techniques and methods that work on *you*, and then make them work *for* you and your security program.

Continuing Theme Posters

Theme posters that rely on a given background, a continuing "character or sketch," or something similar have positive results. Viewers look forward to the next poster in the series, realizing, of course, that while the individual poster subjects change, the overall theme of security awareness and motivation continue from one to the next.

For example, one character sketch, depicting a "Security Bear," continues on in different poses and situations over many posters for the organization, and has continued to provide security advice and assistance over a number of years. The character sketch has become a positive security symbol for the company, and employees look to see how he will be applied to a security situation or message in the next poster.

Sometimes the concept of a character can be used by another organization. For instance, one organization used the picture of a clown to provide security information. A lot of time went into filling out the data on the poster, but another organization can use the clown concept in its education program — not necessarily the same clown, or even the same costume, but the *concept* of the clown with a totally different face and in a totally different situation.

Further, those who have the time and always present a multicolor poster may extend the concept by creating a more detailed visually appealing poster. What is different is the subject matter covered; each poster used will have the clown graphic, allowing for a continuing visual theme character. As to any character variation, a slightly different clown design could be used, with the variation being further developed by the organization. What is different from one poster to another is the subject matter and the text on the poster.

The Politics of Posters

There will be times in your security education program when an item or specific idea that you wish to use for an educational poster may be thought provoking, of current interest, or have a viewpoint that is not necessarily that of senior management. Because of local or even national politics, the subject matter is of interest, but *someone, somewhere* does not like the idea or, having seen the end result, feels it is in poor taste. Some level of politics has come into play.

This is not to say that politics rears its ugly head every time a poster is relevant, useful, thought provoking, or may be misinterpreted, but the fact remains that if someone above you doesn't like the poster — no matter what the reason, or for no true reason at all — it probably won't ever see the light of day outside of your office. Interpretations of the visual or the poster text are hard to determine, but if in any way the poster visual or text offends, it should be eliminated and not used. But there can be an exception to this rule, as will be discussed further on in this chapter.

A poster was originally developed over a decade ago and was partially distributed. It consisted of a photograph showing an inside view of an airplane. What it actually showed was a cargo bay full of coffins, with an American flag tastefully draped over each. The poster text had just a very few words: Poor Security . . . Has Its Price. It was *very* powerful, thought provoking, and clearly had a security message of interest to everyone. Someone decided that it shouldn't be distributed, and copies were recalled while many others were destroyed. It wasn't the message as much as the picture that was the determining factor in recalling the poster. Even many security education professionals who viewed it saw the positive features of the poster. Fortunately, a few copies of the poster still survive in various archives.

While posters should not be offensive in any way, this one is an exception to the rule. It is realistic, current — even today — and sends a specific message to the viewer. Such posters as this one do not come along often, but when they do, they should be used because of the message that is being sent to the viewer.

If you look back at some posters of World Wars I and II, you will find amazingly powerful visuals that send a clear message and have stood the test of time. Reprints of these posters are usually available on the Web, in major library poster collections, at American Society for Industrial Security (International) (ASIS) headquarters in Alexandria, Virginia, and in private collections. There is seldom more than two generations separating any great security poster design, but, as the generations continue, variations of early powerful poster themes reoccur and are hailed as items of value because of their overall positive influence in helping shape the minds of a new generation to be more positive about security. The subtle but unspoken reason behind such posters is that they provoke a desire for the viewer to do something positive about security, because the viewer can easily realize the fallout and long-term impact of not doing something positive.

COLOR THEORY

Here are some basic guidelines for using color to its fullest advantage and allowing you to be practical at the same time. Color can enhance the visuals in your presentation. This is accomplished through attention, location, simplicity, contrast, meaning, expectation, coding, and readability of the subject matter. We discuss each briefly.

Attention

Color speaks loudly, calling attention to important information. The best colors include bright reds, oranges, and yellows as attention-getters.

Location

Color use helps readers to locate information easily when that information may be of a different color than the rest of the visual. It also helps readers to recall where information is located (in hard copy, location assists in recall and can easily help you to find something when the same colors are used at different points, in essence, speeding up your ability to retrieve desired information).

Simplicity

Don't overdo a good thing (too much of anything — even good — can be bad); color is no exception. Reserve color for important areas, and use the color consistently.

Never use more than four or five colors at a time for charts and graphs; never use more than three in the text. Inconsistent use or the overuse of color confuses rather than clarifies.

Contrast

Use contrasting colors; the viewer cannot always distinguish similar shades of the same color. Avoid those colors (hot pink/fluorescent) that can clash or cause eye fatigue. Remember, too, that good color combinations have strong levels of contrast. Pairing colors of similar brightness levels creates vibration effect and can make reading difficult. This is especially important for any type of slide shows, such as PPT and viewgraphs. Good contrast color combinations include yellow on blue, white on green, and black on yellow.

Meaning

Color conveys meaning (green = go, nature, environment, money; yellow = caution, bright and happy messages; red = danger/stop; blue = stately, regal, and "solid" type themes). Color meanings can vary within groups, individuals, cultures, so choose your colors carefully; consider your audience. The use of an inappropriate color for an audience diverts their attention from the point that you are trying to make.

Expectation

There are about 30 basic color names, but there are thousands of colors (shades, hues, variations, etc.). The variations include colors such as apple red, royal blue, and lime green, to name a few. It is better to show a color than to try and describe it to an audience. Color and image are important and people expect to see them used in a certain way. The audience immediately notices color if it is not what people are expecting to see; if that is your intent, fine; if not, the audience may become distracted by your unexpected use of color and you may lose the opportunity to make a certain point.

Coding

Color is helpful for placing information into categories. This becomes important in charts and graphs where multiple colors are used. It is important to use color choices consistently to avoid confusion. Thus, information on lists, charts, sheets, graphs, and the like requires consistent color coding. Please realize the importance of being selective in your selection and use of color choices.

Readability

The use of color enhances readability of information. Try to match the color backgrounds to the light level of the environment in which the materials are presented (see Table 13.1).

HANDOUTS AND GIMMEES

Handouts are just that: something handed out, given away, or left on a table for your employees to pick up and take back to the office. They can be just about anything, but the continuing theme is one of security awareness. They include such items as pocket reminders, desktop reference and referral guides, two- and three-fold mini-information sheets, employee awareness alerts, notepads with different messages on them, bookmarks and variations, calendars, letter openers, cups, pencils, rulers, bags, keychains, and ice scrapers. These items are produced and made available to help the security program. Each has a practical application, but each is also a security reminder. Every time an

Table 13.1 Using Color to Enhance Readability

If room light is:	Use background colors:	Text colors:
Dark or subdued	Navy blue, forest green, scarlet, black	White, pale yellow, pink
Light	Light yellow, magenta, light green, white	Dark blue, black, saturated green, dark green

employee uses the item, even infrequently, a subtle reminder comes into his or her mind to consider security in that particular task (see Figure. 13.1). Of course, one will say, handouts cost money to produce; some do cost money, others cost your time and effort. But realize the cost when the employee doesn't think about security as he or she goes about everyday duties.

These are all methods of communicating security messages and promoting a heightened security awareness among employees with a minimum of security personnel. You receive an optimum impact from an ongoing educational effort

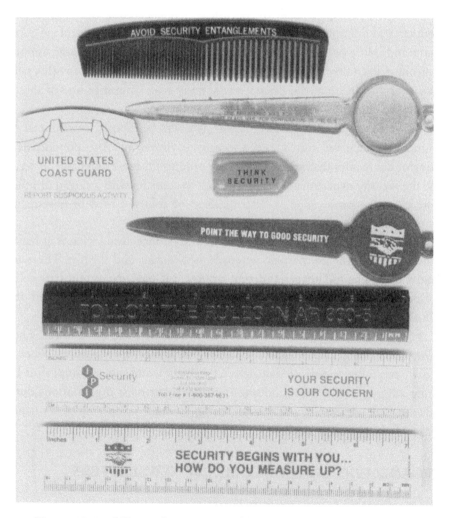

Figure 13.1. *"Gimmee" items are useful and provide a security message every time they are used.*

when you tailor the content and medium to meet the many needs and interests of your audience and then fit the program specifics into their regular work habits and routine.

"Gimmees" is that catch-all term used to denote a wide variety of handouts and other miscellaneous items. You attend a trade show or convention or go to the opening of a new store in town, and what do you see but items that are handed out to the various potential customers. It may be a hat, a ruler with the business name and logo on it, a cloth shopping bag that can be used over and over again (also with the company or organizational name and logo on it), various flyers, perhaps a small 6- to 10-page reference book detailing various products and examples of how you can use them in your home, and even key chains and bottle openers. How did the name "gimmee" come about? Simple. Someone walked down the aisle and saw someone else at a booth or with a sales clerk receiving an item, the person instinctively said, "Gimmee one of those" — thus the name.

As we continue through this chapter, you will be exposed to examples of gimmees that are well suited to the security environment. Also provided is a listing of companies that make a variety of products that are amenable to security; the security department is only required to come up with a slogan or other short blurb, perhaps a logo, a determination of colors, a total of how many items it wants to order, and the colors to be used.

You can create some gimmees yourself, in the office, using what is at hand. The easiest to make are coasters, notepads, bookmarks, and the like. These are created using graphic images and text, printed out onto the appropriate color and thickness of paper, copied in number, and then cut (if necessary) and distributed throughout the organization.

Handouts and gimmees are value-added security program features. They allow you as the security educator to provide some measure of security concern to each employee as part of that person's work life, and you accomplish it by taking advantage of a communications channel that most organizations don't consider: that of security information being available in an employee's hand, pocket, writing pad, or desk.

ORGANIZATIONAL AND COMPANY NEWSLETTERS

Organizational and company newsletters are very valuable. Employees read these newsletters because they can provide some insight into current and possibly future events of interest. News of new products, new people, new ideas, and new programs are always found here. Why not include some security information along with it?

The newsletter is an accepted medium that is easily accessible to everyone, one that most people will read, and your participation in passing on security ideas, topics, and hints is really free — your time to come up with the subject matter and writing a little is all that is necessary. The outcome for an hour's work is a product that can be in the hands of every employee, and you have been able to pass on a security message at the cost of minimal time and effort.

Whenever possible, make newsletters colorful in terms of the variety of information; they can become somewhat interactive when you put in word puzzles, quizzes, and so on. Vary the selection of topics for each issue; don't concentrate on just one topic area. Show the positive as much as possible; show the negative only as the basis for informing readers about a technique that will resolve the negative situation. Getting regular information to your staff is a key component that must be included within every aspect of your security education program. Having employees read it is much more important.

Topics covered in newsletters should be varied, never just a list of reminders, policy or regulatory requirements, or summaries of what has gone on before. News, humor, puzzles, questions and answers on a given topic, questions (answers located elsewhere in the newsletter), and even interviews are appropriate. Many topic ideas come from questions that are raised in one-on-one discussions, from a local newspaper or national magazine, from questions posed by supervisors, and from various security projects that raise potential security issues and concerns.

Consider including updates about major security changes or improvements that will make the employee's life easier, changes in requirements and procedures that save time and work, and always try to include some form of security activity that has a positive benefit.

Make regular contributions to the company newsletter. Don't just put something in when you have a problem; include something in every issue, if possible, but at least every other issue. Work to get feedback from employees on the program, and acknowledge their contributions and efforts.

As you see your efforts rewarded, consider the possibility of publishing a security newsletter. While still contributing some material to the company newsletter, develop your own. The advantage here is that there are no space limitations, which means more flexibility for developing ideas into specific articles. For example, describe a security problem, analyze it, and then show the solution and benefits that are reaped from it. Some areas you may wish to cover include security inspections (pros and cons) with the end results published, guest commentary columns by people outside the security office who have positive views that can affect the viability of the organization, security quizzes, details on upcoming security presentations, and the like.

Use a continuing format, and consider a distinctive logo. If you don't have a logo, suggestions or a contest may be the way to go. Employees with an interest in desktop publishing and playing with computer graphics will typically come up with ideas for a logo — and they will even help with the labor involved. For ideas, look to other newsletters outside your organization, or find ideas in professional security trade journals and magazines. Use the ideas and redefine them as they apply to your own organization. Be unique and develop illustrations to add to articles.

The great thing about publishing your own newsletter is that you can carefully select the information that will be included. It must be timely and appropriate for the employees, and it must speak to their best interests — in addition to the overall interests of the organization. Well conceived and written, you can develop an audience if what you write is informative and interesting. Emphasize material that creates and enhances organizational support for your security programs.

Printing the newsletters is as close as your nearest reproduction machine. Larger organizations may have a printing facility. Use thick, heavy-weight paper (60 lb.) for the front cover, and consider the same for the back also. Use the back page or cover as a place to put a computer-designed or employee-developed security poster. Employees will likely remove the back cover and post it in their office area. In numerous instances, the authors have found that the right poster with a great design concept, the right security message, and its ease of availability ("It's in every security newsletter!") will get people to hang onto them. Making a security poster in black and white allows employees to use their creativity to color the posters before putting them up around the office. Try it; you'll find that some employees collect the posters or make a few more copies and provide different color schemes to them. Others will see how they can make the security message stronger or relate the poster visuals to another topic area when the message is changed. All in all, what is accomplished is that employees begin thinking more about security, their role, and how they can improve security — a win-win situation for all concerned!

Many organizations with newsletters — security or otherwise — love to have a contest for their employees. Use the newsletter to promote a contest, such as naming the newsletter, designing a security logo, naming the logo character if there is one, developing a continuing security slogan, finding ways to improve security policy and procedures without reducing the level of security, presenting ideas or designing security posters, and so on. Another possibility is to insert a cartoon that drives home a point in relation to an accompanying article. For example, a short article discussing the protection of data classified or company-sensitive material from unauthorized ears could benefit from a related cartoon.

CONTESTS

Contests, whether formal or not, help to build employee awareness about security. Contests build reader interest and response, in addition to measuring employee participation and concerns for topical security matters. Take a unique or intriguing approach to developing the purpose of the contest. If the contest, for example, were to revolve around a security poster for the computer division, contestants could be asked to develop a cryptogram or they could learn to apply security procedures to the protection of information on the computer. Only your mind and the minds of employees involved in the contest will determine the level of creativity that will result from a simple idea.

Contests, like newsletters and gimmees, are another method of moving security's importance to the forefront of your employee's mind. Instilling the importance for security and keeping it there requires continual planning and thought about new and better ways to reach members of your organization. Take advantage of their minds, and let them do some of the thought via contests.

Important to all of this is the reward system that goes along with a contest. Positive rewards for positive input have a continuing positive influence on employees. It may sound trite, but it works and will continue to work so long as you have something to offer that has a value to others. Remember the value may be miniscule, but it still counts to the employee. Sometimes just having a reward that other employees find hard to obtain because they didn't put forth a little creative effort is all it takes to get others to become more involved with the program.

Having a unique security mug available, a new security-related T-shirt, a hat, dinner with the boss, a saving bond, or an award certificate for training received (with a positive note added to the employee's personnel file) may be all it takes to get people to better support the program. Again, all these items are just different types of security awareness reminders that help to promote the

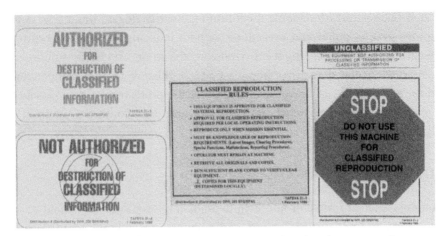

Figure 13.2. *Stickers or magnetic signs can be placed in many places for effectiveness.*

program and allow employees to continually think about security as they go about their everyday job duties. Figure 13.2 illustrates some of the various items that can be considered for employees. Security stickers are another form of reminder; they may also come in the form of magnets.

OTHER TIPS FOR EFFECTIVE POSTERS AND HANDOUTS

Use humor in security handouts. When humor is incorporated, consider also spreading cartoons out throughout the pamphlet or handout. Cartoons are more memorable than typical graphics. When you have the right cartoon character, use it as or in your logo, and make it a part of as many security awareness posters and products as you can.

Remember that posters not only convey a security message, but that they also represent and present an image of your security office. Ensure the posters are in good taste, and be aware and beware of posters or any visual that may have an unintended interpretation.

It isn't always necessary to have a picture; simple text phrases are great also, as shown in Figure 13.3. Such items can be created on the office computer, and by using different-colored paper, a variety of two-color posters or flyers are quickly created. If desired, your printing office can blow up the items into wall-sized posters that can be quickly printed. The examples here show two possible poster type signs. Once can be near the office door where it is seen as employ-

```
LOCK YOUR SAFE BEFORE YOU LEAVE
```

```
DO NOT DISCUSS
SENSITIVE
INFORMATION
OUTSIDE THE
OFFICE
```

Figure 13.3. *A simple message that is both informative and educational.*

ees leave; the second could be near the same location or appropriately placed where personnel leave a controlled area, larger office area, or building.

Effective Security Poster Examples

Figures 13.4 and 13.5 show effective posters that have been created over the last quarter century. You will notice that even the older posters are still effective in getting the security message across to the viewer. These have been extracted from the ASIS poster collection residing in the O. P. Norton Resource Center at ASIS headquarters. Should you ever have the opportunity to visit, please don't forget to request a look at the posters in the collection. Upon viewing them, you will probably want to get more involved in creating and producing effective security posters for your organization.

"GIMMEE" SHOPPING: SOME IDEA PLACES FOR "STUFF"

The following is but a partial list of places where you can go to obtain mementos or gimmees that relate to security education. Actually, you probably already

Figure 13.4.   *Posters should target a specific security subject.*

have a variety of these catalogs, as many are shipped in the mail to homes and offices. Get on the Internet and browse using such terms as *knick-knacks*, *advertising handouts*, *promotional items*, or *promotional materials*. There are some Web sites that deal in limited types of security related products, but not many.

You will notice that the catalogs and Web site products are not necessarily security related in terms of specific items. It's up to you to determine what words

Figure 13.5. *Tie poster subjects to ongoing events which can impact your people or organization.*

or phrases would go on a selected item and then coordinate with the appropriate dealer to get what you want.

When you do develop or obtain such items for use in your security education awareness and training program, it would be greatly appreciated if a sample or two could be forwarded for inclusion at ASIS. Also appreciated for their reference collection would be such items as brochures, training manuals, or desk-side reference aids, which would be useful to other security personnel who visit ASIS in search of items and materials that can provide them with ideas for improving their own security education program efforts. As a last resort for questions or comments on security education training aids, posters, and the like, contact Mr. Roper, one of the authors, at roperc@rcn.com.

Notice of Disclaimer: The authors neither support nor recommend any specific company listed have. Addresses are provided for your information as possible contact points relative to items that can be used in a security education program. There are other companies — large and small — that also have a variety of items available. Perhaps one is located in your city.

- Motivation Productions, Inc.
  1475 N. Broadway, Suite 420
  Walnut Creek, CA 94596

- Sales Guides, Inc.
  10510 N. Port Washington Road
  Mequon, WI 53092-9986

- D&G Sign and Label
  P.O. Box NA-157
  Northford, CT 06472

- Crestline Co., Inc
  22 W. 21st Street
  New York, NY 10010

- Dynamic Graphics, Inc.
  6000 N. Forest Park Drive
  P.O. Box 1901
  Peoria, IL 61656-1901

- Positive Impressions, Inc.
  225 Westchester Avenue
  Port Chester, NY 10573

- Brighton Associates
  P.O. Box 3316
  Long Branch, NJ 07740

- Best Impressions
  348 N. 30th Road
  P.O. Box 800
  La Salle, IL 61301

- Paper Direct
  205 Chubb Avenue
  Lyndhurst, NJ 07071

- Success Builders
  Baldwin Cooke
  2401 Waukegan Road
  Deerfield, IL 60015-9952

14

How Not to Train:
A Commonsense Alternative

In this chapter we're going to look at how you can avoid training — and how you *should* avoid training whenever you can. That may seem like heresy to a lot of people who are really big on training, but we're going to see how it's just common sense. First let's remember what was traditionally called "training." It's when we help people stuff information into their heads so they'll remember it when they need it. It can be information about what to do, who should do it, when it needs to be done, where it has to or should be done, and how to do it. People need to know all of this if they're to do what needs to be done, right? Well, we'll see.

Doing some training is probably an absolute necessity in your security program. There are certainly people — on and off your security force — who will need to be trained to perform their security roles. The problem is that we do too much training. We train people when the problem with their performance isn't a skill or knowledge deficiency at all. We don't do a good front-end analysis, and training ends up being the knee-jerk solution. And we do training when it's *a* solution, but not the *best* solution, to a performance problem.

There are two major problems with training people. The first is that training is expensive. It costs the trainer's time, but much more expensive is the time that the people who are doing the learning are away from their jobs. But what if we could work it out so that people could do all the training they need in a fourth of the time? How about a tenth? That's big savings in people hours for your organization. How could we reduce training time so drastically? By training employees to remember only a small part of what they need to "know." The second problem with training is that it doesn't last. Unless people are doing a task regularly, they tend to forget how to do it. Think about that nifty digital watch you're wearing. When you bought it, you carefully studied those instructions in the teeny, tiny print and followed them to set your watch. After you'd done it, you remembered how. You'd trained yourself to set the watch. Now along comes daylight saving time. You go to set the watch again. But which of the six buttons do you push for what? You root around in the drawer for the instructions. You've been a victim of the notorious forgetting curve. When you learn something, you immediately begin to forget it. Maybe not much. Maybe just a few details. If you use the information often enough, you refresh your memory; but if it's something you do infrequently, the forgetting curve jumps up to bite you.

We're going to suggest a way to help yourself avoid both of these problems. It's a technique borrowed from performance technology called job aiding (it's also called job performance aiding and several other equally impressive names). The basic idea of job aiding is this: Don't try to stuff information in people's heads if you can find a better way to make it available to them. In other words, don't train what you can job aid. Job aids have two advantages that can be very important to our security program. People forget; job aids don't. And giving people a job aid costs a whole lot less time (theirs and yours) than trying to train them to recall something reliably. There are several types of job aids. There are times when job aids work well and times when they're not right for the situation. And putting together a good one takes some thought and effort. Let's look at all these issues and see if we can't spark your imagination about where job aiding may work for you.

Just what exactly is a job aid? A job aid is a set of step-by-step procedural instructions that a performer is given so that he or she can use them as a guide while performing a task. Job aids are guides that take you by the hand, lead you through the steps of a task, and maybe give you some information you need while doing it. They are *not* learning aids or teaching tools. The whole point of the job aid is that the person won't have to learn what's in the job aid and you won't have to teach them! They are to be used while actually doing the job. There are several different kinds of job aids and dozens of catchy variations on each kind. But they all share these common characteristics: step-by-step guidance to be used while performing the task.

To keep things from getting too complicated, we'll stick to three types of job aid that seem to have the most application to security programs: the cookbook, the flowchart, and the checklist. The best example of a cookbook is a recipe. You have a task to do: bake a cake. The recipe tells you, step by step, what to do (fold in two eggs), when to do it (after the flour is well mixed), where to do it (in the bowl), and maybe a little bit of how to do it (carefully).

Because you're doing the cooking, it assumes you know the "who." The cookbook takes you step by step through the task. If you follow the recipe, you don't have to remember what ingredients to add, what steps to take, or what sequence the steps should take. The needed information is all there in front of you — on that neat little card or page that won't forget and leave anything out or get anything wrong. The flowchart type of job aid is similar in that it gives you step-by-step instructions for a task, but it also helps you figure out the "ifs." It branches to different steps depending on your situation. An example would be a chart that shows how to figure out how to ship a package. It might be going along in the task and asks, "Does the package have to be delivered the next day?" If the answer is yes, it might send you to instructions for using your express carrier; if not, it goes on with the instructions for regular shipping. Then at another point it tells you to weigh the package and asks, "Is the weight more than 20 pounds?" "Yes" sends you one way, "no" a different way. The checklist type of job aid does just what the cookbook and flowchart types do, with one addition. The checklist has you record each step as you take it. Maybe you will simply have to make a check mark or jot your initials in a column, or maybe you will have to enter some data. An example of the first kind is the checklist airline pilots use for their preflight checks. An example of a not-so-good checklist job aid is the 1040 form you learn to hate every April.

Pretty nifty, huh? But I'm sure you figure there's a catch. Actually, there are several. To get them out of the way, let's look at when you *shouldn't* try to use a job aid. There are four basic disqualifiers for using job aids:

1. When the task is so simple that people will easily remember how to do it (turning on your computer).

2. When the task is something people do all the time, and there's no chance of their forgetting how to do it (tying your shoes).

3. When the task has to be performed so quickly that the person can't stop to use a job aid. A good example here is a police officer making a decision about drawing and firing a weapon. He or she certainly couldn't take the time to read some card; he or she has to remember all the steps in the decision process and take them immediately.

4. When the task has to be performed under conditions where using a job aid isn't practical (in the dark, while driving at high speed, etc.).

What sort of conditions suggest you really *should* consider job aiding?

1. When the consequences of making an error are serious. (Like forgetting steps in a preflight check.)

2. When the task is a complicated one with lots of steps and lots of things to remember.

3. When the task is performed so infrequently that people might forget how to do it right in the meantime.

4. When performance needs to be documented. A good example here is the "Miranda Warning" card that smart police officers pull out and use to give rights advisements. Using the card documents their actions for later prosecution. Another is the income tax form, which shows the IRS exactly how you went about figuring your taxes.

It boils down to the fact that people have a task to do, and they need information to do it right. If they need to have the information in their heads (knowledge), train them. If it is enough to have the information readily available to them when they need it, think about job aiding. At this point, you may be thinking, "Hey! We use a lot of these things already!" (At least, we hope that's what you're thinking.) You're probably right. Common sense leads us to put together job aids even when we don't know what to call them. We'd like to suggest that you take a good, hard look at the training you're doing (or planning) and make sure you're using job aids whenever they're the best choice. We'd also like to help you make sure your job aids are up to snuff and really doing the "aiding" they're supposed to. So let's move on to how you put together a good, solid, effective job aid.

Here are a few tasks that might lend themselves to job aiding, at least in part:

Who	What
1. Shipping clerks	Determine proper shipment method for sensitive items
2. Alarm monitor	Respond to coolant system alarm in Building 22
3. Receptionist	Process visitors to restricted laboratory area
4. Security specialist	Conduct security processing of terminated employee
5. Technical librarian	Process request for sensitive technical data

First, figure out which type of job aid you're going to build. It may be that, as you work on the job aid, you'll decide to change the type. Don't worry about it. You probably won't have wasted any effort. But it's nice to have at least a preliminary idea of what the final product will look like. Our guess would be that the first, third, and fifth examples in the table will end up with flowchart job aids. The second example will take a cookbook, and the fourth will use a checklist.

Now take a good, hard look at the task or set of tasks you're going to be covering in the job aid. If you've done a good front-end analysis, you already know a lot about the process. But now you have to break things down into chewable chunks, discreet steps you'll be listing in the job aid. You want to reduce the task to a series of if/then, stimulus/response steps: "If this is the situation, then you do this." You won't always put things in those terms in the job aid, but that's what the steps should look like. Sometimes, the "ifs" will be completing the previous step, but you won't have to say so. For example, "Tighten the clamp. (If you've done that,) Remove the wire binding. (If you've done that,) Check the pressure."

Write the steps down in order. Add extra information if you think it's needed. Be careful, though, not to load the job aid up with too much unnecessary text. Remember, this is not a learning tool. Its purpose is to walk a person through a task. About the only good reason to add extra information to a job aid is to give the performer a little reassurance.

Let's look at a little chunk out of a job aid. Here's the situation. A member of your security force mans a central alarm station. There are three annunciator panels, each with 25 alarm displays and a variety of lights and buttons for each. Each display is identified with a number. There are about 30 different types of action your employee is expected to take, depending on which alarm goes off. You make up little job aids for each alarm and put them in a looseleaf binder, kept beside the panels. Each one-page job aid has a tab with the corresponding alarm number on it. Here's a part of one of the pages:

Alarm # 441

Coolant System Alarm, Building 22

If the alarm light turns RED:

   Jot the alarm number (441) and time in the alarm log.

   Press the RESET button right under the light.

If the light turns GREEN, write "Reset to green" on the same line in the alarm log. (The alarm probably was caused by a momentary power drop.)

If the light stays RED, call the duty engineer at 555-1212 and report the situation.

Follow his or her instructions.

Write "Duty engineer notified" in the alarm log.

As you can see, the job aid is simple and clear, with all the information your employee needs to handle the situation.

TESTING AND INSTALLATION

Once you have your job aid ready to go, you will want to test it. The best way is to give it to one of the people who will be performing the task and have them walk you through exactly what they'd do while following the job aid's instructions. Look out for any steps you might have missed and for any ambiguous instructions. Listen carefully to questions the users might have, like "But what about . . . ?" and "But what if . . . ?" Those are usually good signals that something is missing from the job aid.

Once you've tested your job aid, make any needed changes. There's one more thing you have to do. It's called installing the job aid, and it's really a little bit of training. You have to make sure your performers know three things: when to use the job aid, how to use it, and that they should use it instead of trying to remember how to perform the task. The first two items are usually pretty simple to explain. In our example, you'd tell them that when an alarm goes off, they look at the number, pick up the book, turn to the numbered page, and follow the instructions. Period. The last item sometimes takes a bit of doing.

In our society, many people have a prejudice in favor of knowledge versus performance. They think it's how much you know about a job that counts, forgetting that it's how well you do the job that really matters. So they hesitate to seem like they "don't know what they're doing" or "have to look things up all the time." This is something you'll run into as you try to get your performers to understand that they're expected to use the job aid to guide them through the task, every time they do it. They need to be convinced that this is the proper way to perform the task, and it's the smart way. One argument that often works well is telling them that if they use the job aid correctly, do exactly what it says, and something goes wrong, they can't be faulted for it. If they refuse to use the job aid, the blame will be all theirs. Another technique is to liken the job aid to a dictionary, a phone book, or a book of recipes. Nobody thinks less of anyone for using those.

AN ADDED BENEFIT

I think you can probably see for yourself how job aids can cut down dramatically on the time and effort needed for training in many situations and how they can contribute to consistent, quality performance. But there's one added benefit you probably won't find mentioned in the job aiding textbooks. Using job aids can contribute to motivation.

Remember expectancy — the performer's perception that he or she can do the job successfully? Providing a job aid almost guarantees successful completion of a task. At least the person doesn't have to worry about leaving out a step or two. Expectancy rises; so does motivation.

FINALLY

We hope this chapter has whetted your appetite for job aids and given you a few ideas to think about as you consider using them (or more of them) in your security education efforts. Here are a few final thoughts to consider. Job aids don't eliminate training, but they can dramatically cut down the amount of training you have to do. Job aids promote consistent, uniform, quality performance: a job aid never forgets. When procedures change, it's a heck of a lot easier to hand out new job aids than it is to retrain a workforce. Job aids promote confidence and, consequently, motivation. Job aids are *not* a magic solution to all performance problems, but they're a marvelously cost-effective way to attack some of them.

This isn't the place for a detailed technical discussion of job aid design and construction. If you want to give job aiding a serious try, there are plenty of books and articles to steer you right. Your library, management engineering organization, or employee development staff should be able to help you find them.

15

Evaluating Security Education Programs

The importance of evaluating your educational program cannot be overemphasized. Oddly enough, this critical task is often neglected or given little thought. As educators, we must be able to demonstrate that what we are doing has *value* for the organization and its employees. We must be able to show that security education is essential to the mission of the organization, whatever it may be. This is a tall order, and as with the delivery of the education, awareness, or training itself, it requires careful thought and a realistic strategy.

Regrettably, some practitioners tasked with providing security education embrace the view that security education (even other security activities) is being carried out simply to comply with some regulation or policy imposed by a higher authority. This unfortunate attitude filters down to the workforce and creates an atmosphere that is both almost beyond repair and, in some situations, dangerous. A compliance-based security education program that meets only minimum standards hardly needs evaluation. It is a failure by definition. A mission-driven program, however, depends and thrives on systematic evaluation, not only to become more effective, but to compete successfully for adequate resources to remain viable. Program evaluation documents and proves to both management and the workforce that security education adds value to the organization and that it, as part of the overall security program, is a mission-critical function.

What does it mean to evaluate an educational or awareness program? How do you judge whether your program is a "success" by having the desired effect? What are the indicators of effectiveness that we should be looking for to justify the time and effort we put into security education?

Back in the 1980s at the height of the Cold War, we experienced an escalation in the number of damaging espionage cases in the Department of Defense and its contractor community. A high-ranking Pentagon official gravely concluded that there must be something wrong with the way we were doing security education. A government report issued at about the same time stated that we can look at the number of reports of unsolicited foreign contacts with cleared government personnel to demonstrate the success of security awareness programs in sensitizing the cleared workforce about the activities of foreign intelligence agents.[1] Both authorities were grasping at some easy measure to assess the effectiveness of security education at that time, possibly because there were no other visible or reliable measures of program effectiveness. Each of these arguments had some merit, but it is often difficult to make such causal linkages between educational experience and systemic patterns or statistical trends.

In general, program evaluation should mean that your educational program can be judged in terms of its desired effect in creating new and demonstrated competencies or in molding the behaviors of an employee population that were intended by those who designed the program and possibly funded it. However, we find that the measures or "metrics" often used for program assessment provide only a superficial assessment at best. Management may be satisfied with evidence only that a program is actively communicating with an employee population. Others may be particularly concerned with the content of that communication — that, for example, a briefing includes facts and advice on all of six items mandated for coverage in a regulation or that required briefings are being delivered on schedule to an employee population.

Other managers may want to know how many members of a designated population have actually received a specific briefing or completed an online interactive training module. Those of us who have worked in government have from time to time been required to participate in mandatory training on such topics as sexual harassment in the workplace or professional ethics. Often directors or commanders are then required to certify to their headquarters that all personnel have in fact completed the prescribed training. These head counts are well and good as far as they go, but this begs the questions: How well have they been received and understood by the intended audiences, and will the training have a positive effect on how individuals interact with coworkers or the general public?

One method of evaluation was discussed in Chapter 8, in which we urged the security educator to test every aspect of the educational or awareness

---

1. Office of the Secretary of Defense, *Keeping the Nation's Secrets: A Report to the Secretary of Defense by the Commission to Review DoD Security Policies and Practices*, 1985, p. 69.

program against clearly articulated performance objectives that specify measurable outcomes. The logic of this strategy is that if something seems not to address an objective, it gets cut — saving money and making room for other educational efforts that do meet the criterion. And if the measurable outcome is determined in advance of the educational experience, it is possible to engage in before and after testing.

LEVELS OF PROGRAM EVALUATION

One way to make sense of the array of evaluation techniques and strategies that security educators commonly employ is to distinguish among activities at three levels: management, audience, and effectiveness levels. Each level has differing purposes and methods for addressing those purposes. Consequently, you can select evaluation methods to undertake the assessment of your program or an element of that program according to what kind of evaluation you wish to accomplish. As indicated by Table 15.1, evaluation efforts at each level have a somewhat different purpose and different metrics used to determine success. What these methods or techniques have in common is that they all reflect an attempt to measure effectiveness or quality objectively, but their selection depends on how one defines evaluation.

Probably the best strategy for the security educator who is rightly concerned about program evaluation is to attempt evaluation at all three levels whenever feasible and on a recurring basis. At the management level, not to maintain simple records would be both negligent and risky (if you value your job). However superficial these measures are, they at least document the coverage and scope of your activities. Information at the end of Chapter 9 contains a table in which the program manager can enter completion data for each communication event. This type of scheduling form would serve as a management level evaluation tool.

Three examples of audience level evaluation instruments for different elements of a security awareness program follow at the end of this chapter. All have been used at various times by federal agencies to evaluate a single element within a security education program. The first is a readership survey that was published in an issue of a security newsletter that provided a monthly news summary (before the days of the Web access to news items). The second instrument was frequently used to check audience opinions about new awareness videos presented as part of a program for formal instruction for security managers. (The

Table 15.1　Levels of Evaluation*

Level	Purpose	Examples of Metrics/Methods
Management level evaluation	To document that information and the appropriate message is reaching the designated audience or to verify that you are meeting mandated requirements	Attendance records Content evaluation Number of Web site visits recorded
Audience level evaluation	To determine that the content — ideas, facts, arguments — are understood and retained by audience members and that it has made a positive impression on them	Employee surveys Product evaluations Course critiques Verbal feedback
Effectiveness level evaluation	To determine whether the educational effort has had a positive effect on the performance and behavior of audience members with particular focus on organizational goals	Performance indicators Reporting frequency Security violations Employee inquiries Decrease in theft, accidents, loss of assets, trust betrayal

* This table shows types of information metrics that are typically collected for differing levels of evaluation.

heading on the form was changed each time to reflect the title of the video being viewed by the audience.)

The third example of audience level evaluation is a briefing evaluation form used by the Department of Energy Office of Counterintelligence. Like the others, this short form has the advantage of producing a considerable amount of data about audience reaction to a particular educational experience without appearing to be long or burdensome. The essential seven questions are presented in what is called a Likert format in which the audience member is simply asked to respond to a positive statement with fixed choices ranging from strongly agree to strongly disagree. A program evaluation that rests on any of these three examples, however, would require similar and regular evaluations of various types of educational events and communications that are part of the same program.

Also found at the end of this chapter is another example of an audience level instrument for evaluation, a model security survey. Rather than testing audience reaction to one briefing or event, one can use a survey like this to assess how much a target population knows or has learned from your communication strategy as a security educator. With a very large target population it would be feasible to execute a before-and-after experiment by selecting a difference sample of audience members drawn randomly from the same population early on in your educational program and then a year or 18 months later. If you can show a significant improvement in response scores, your program is a winner. If not, you need to go back to the drawing board. With the right amount of promotion plus assurances of anonymity, you should get a reasonably high participation rate. Create a simple self-explanatory heading such as "Test Yourself! How Much Do You Know about Security?" Keep both the questions, answers, and the total number of questions short. Be sure to publish the preferred answers with explanations later. The survey itself is obviously an educational tool that should stimulate discussion.

Metrics utilized by the security educator at the next level of evaluation, the effectiveness level, must, however, be interpreted with care. These indicators are generally behavioral in nature. Does, for example, an increase in reported security violations after an educational experience mean that violations are on the upswing or that now, unlike before, people know what a violation is and where to report it? If unsolicited inquiries to your office increase, does this mean that employees are more confused than ever or that something you have done has got them interested in security?

One example of the use of a systemic indicator to show the impact of a very focused educational effort occurred in the early 1980s, while the author was employed as the editor of a Department of Defense quarterly bulletin that was designed to help security educators to promote awareness in their cleared employee populations. A serious concern among policymakers at that time was the low level of coworker reporting in the defense industry about employees who were exhibiting signs that they might not be able to adequately safeguard classified information or who, out of ignorance or disregard for policy, were committing security violations.

A number of articles were published in the bulletin that stressed coworker responsibility for reporting, in confidence, personal vulnerabilities to a security

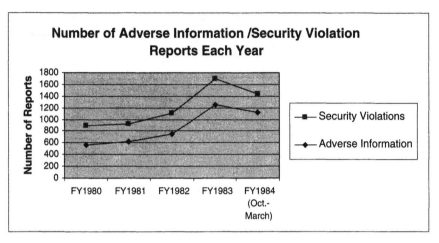

Figure 15.1. *An example illustrating the results of adverse information/security violation reports over a period of years.*

manager. After a couple of years of promoting this idea, which by the way is difficult to "sell" in our culture, we decided to check the records. Fortunately, at the time, reporting frequencies were centrally tabulated for the Defense Industrial Security Program. The diagram in Figure 15.1 was prepared for the edification of higher management to illustrate the behavioral impact of the awareness effort to encourage reporting.

COMPREHENSIVE PROGRAM EVALUATION

Occasionally top-to-bottom reviews of agency or industry-wide security educational programs are commissioned when executives or policymakers become concerned about the direction and overall efficacy of the current program of security education for larger employee populations. Such assessments are best carried out by an impartial and external team of researchers or professional program evaluators. For example, in the mid-1990s, the National Counterintelligence Policy Board agreed on a need to review the effectiveness of the U.S. intelligence community's Foreign Intelligence Threat Awareness (FITA) programs. The review, conducted by the DoD Personnel Security Research Center, was based on the concern that with the end of the Cold War, security educators were not conveying messages that reflected new international realities about the international threat.

Although all aspects of the FITA review and its final report cannot be discussed here, it would be useful to identify some of the methods of program evaluation employed at that time.[2] The research team undertook the following program of data collection in 31 executive branch agencies:

- Interviews with senior-level agency representatives to get their overall perspective and opinions.

- Interviews with 71 security educators (briefing providers) about how they conduct briefings, the topics covered, and their sources of information.

- Actual observations of 61 awareness briefings to record topics covered.

- A questionnaire survey of 1401 audience members to obtain their assessment of whether eight key learning objectives were effectively met and the quality of presentation.

- Five post-briefing focus groups of audience members to discuss in detail their response to a briefing. This method provided richness and depth to the survey results.

- Researchers also systematically evaluated other materials used for security educations such as briefing slides, videos, brochures, bulletins, and newsletters.

Among several important findings, the research team concluded that the "presentation content is up-to-date and reflects the post–Cold War climate. But greater emphasis is needed on the issues of insider threat and personnel security indicators."[3] The researchers conducting this program review have included several of their data collection instruments as an appendix to the final report. At Appendix A is the Focus Group Protocol used in the FITA review. This document not only describes how to conduct a focus group, but is a model protocol that could be used for conducting a program evaluation within a smaller organization to supplement results of a general survey or where a survey may not be feasible.

---

2. Defense Personnel Security Research Center, *Foreign Intelligence Threat Awareness Programs: A Review*, February 1998, Monterey CA.

3. Ibid., p. 46.

BUILT-IN EVALUATION

Another approach to the evaluation of educational programs has been offered by Professor Robert Brinkerhoff of Western Michigan University. In his presentation on the evaluation of training programs and their application to security awareness in particular,[4] Professor Brinkerhoff proposes that program evaluation should be a continuous process in which the security educator engages in continuing measurement and evaluation. Evaluation, he stated, should be embedded into training. He advises, "begin doing evaluation when you begin to think about training and embed the evaluation into the training. Good training has invisible evaluation; it's built into the training."[5] Brinkerhoff outlined a generic evaluation model that he described as a training evaluation cycle in which evaluation is defined as the information-gathering function that informs each of six critical training decisions. Each stage in the cycle has a set of critical questions to be answered. He also makes the point that "what you do before [awareness] training and what you do after training is what makes training pay off." That is, the total value of training for the organization is achieved when preceded and followed by a support system, and that we need to get better in the *before* and the *after* zones.

Brinkerhoff's approach to evaluation has a couple of clear implications for the security educator. In attempting to instill a basic understanding of security principles, threat awareness, or knowledge of how to react to indicators of elevated risk, we must ensure that

1. Educational or communication events must tie in and reinforce each other as a coherent program with a common set of messages.

2. Whatever else is done in the security arena, from inspections to personnel security interventions, must be in harmony with the ideas, commitments, and goals promoted through education.

Table 15.2 identifies the key questions at each stage of Brinkerhoff's training evaluation cycle and the methods that could be used to address each set of questions at each stage in the cycle.

---

4. Robert O. Brinkerhoff, "Security Awareness Program Evaluation," *Security Awareness in the 90s*, Monterey CA: Defense Personnel Security Research Center, 1990.
5. Ibid., p. 109.

Table 15.2 The Six-Stage Evaluation Model: "Evaluate Your Way to Worthwhile Training"

Stage	Some Key Questions	Some Useful Methods
I. Goal setting: are training needs and opportunities worth pursuit?	• What's the problem or opportunity? • Is it worth fixing? • Who could be changed? • What kinds of learning and behavior changes are needed? • Would these changes happen? • If these changes happened, would the problem or opportunity be fixed?	Surveys; performance audits; records analysis; "front-end analyses"; interviews; panel and group reviews; nominal group technique; research studies; brainstorming; site visits; case studies; expert opinions
II. Design evaluation: is the design good enough to implement?	• What alternatives exist? • Which alternative is best? • How good is training plan "X"? • Is Design A better than Design B? • What revisions need to be made? • Is it likely to work? • Is the plan ready to implement?	Literature reviews; trainee reviews; expert reviews; checklists; pilot tests; visits to other programs; experiments; research data; feasibility studies; comparative analyses
III. Program implementation: is it working?	• Is it installed as per the design? • What is really happening? • Is it on schedule? • Is it on budget? • What problems are cropping up? • Are enabling (interim) objectives being achieved? • What in fact took place?	Observations; checklists; logs and diaries; participant feedback; "happy sheets"; record reviews; participant observers; key informants; interviews; artifact and refuse analysis; "wear and tear" analysis; user records

Table 15.2 The Six-Stage Evaluation Model: "Evaluate Your Way to Worthwhile Training" (continued)

Stage	Some Key Questions	Some Useful Methods
IV. Immediate outcomes: were skill, knowledge, attitude objectives achieved?	• Did they learn it? • How much did they learn? • Who learned it? • What did they learn (unanticipated outcomes included)? • How well was it learned	Knowledge and performance tests; attitude measures; pre- and posttesting; self-reports; trainer reports; observation checklists; simulations; work-sample and product analyses; quizzes
V. Usage and retention: are on-job usage and retention objectives achieved?	• Who is using it? • How well are they using it? • How is it being used? • What parts of it are being used? • What is not being used? • Who is not using it?	Self, peer, and/or supervisor reports; records analyses; surveys; visits; observation; "success case" studies; follow-up surveys; work-sample analyses; logs and diaries; performance appraisals
VI. Impact: did it make a worthwhile difference?	• What difference did using it make? • Has the need been met or reduced? • What else has resulted? • How much difference did it make? • How much are differences valued or worth? • How do results compare to costs?	Surveys; performance audits; records analyses; interviews; panel and group reviews; nominal group technique; profit-loss studies; productivity measures; cost/benefit analyses; corporate performance measures

SUMMARY

Security professionals have the reputation for putting out fires — that is, responding to urgent and unexpected crises and problems in the workplace. It may be serious security incidents, workplace violence, compromises of critical information, or a sudden management assignment that must be completed by the following day. Whatever the "fires" may be, the security specialist, manager, or officer engaged either in day-to-day operations or in recurring educational activities is called on to place organizational goals and needs ahead of all other considerations. We in fact are and should be goal oriented in our work and educational efforts.

With some effort, these goals or organizational priorities can be translated into educational or performance objectives. Let us say, for example, after a number of injuries sustained by employees while on the job, management has decreed that the top organizational objective is to ensure that everyone has a safe and secure workplace. Given this scenario, how would the security educator respond? One reasonable reaction might be to immediately re-gear the continuing educational program to focus on the problem of the day, possibly adopting Brinkerhoff's method of embedding evaluation or by determining the measurable educational objectives so that the impact of the program modification can be evaluated. Along with this would go the selection of techniques appropriate to the level of evaluation for which you are aiming.

There is a caveat to all of this that the security educator must always keep in mind. Not all security problems or high-priority organizational issues can be solved by education or training. Sometimes "more training" is too easy an answer, and when it doesn't work, the educator gets the blame. Too often in government, and this may be true of industry as well, inadequate training, awareness, or education are identified as the culprits when a mission is not being met. The real causes of a bad situation are as likely to be poor executive management, inadequate or unevenly implemented policies, or an unwillingness to commit sufficient resources (personnel) to get a job done.

There may be times when part of your professional responsibility is to raise the issue with management that training may not be the problem or even the solution to a systemic problem. To do this, however, in addition to being tactful, you need to have your ducks in a row, your data firmly in place, and your facts on the table. This is when the importance of program evaluation becomes clear. We evaluate what we are doing in objective ways so that not only we ourselves but others know that we add value to the organization, so that we know what to do to make our educational program more effective in meeting mission-related objectives.

Readership Survey

It's time to tell us what you think!

Now and then we need to check with our readers to make sure that we are on target with this publication. We want to make sure that the *Security Awareness News* is getting to people who need and appreciate it. At this time in our history, when we must make every dollar count, your response to this simple questionnaire will help us (or your component) decide whether to keep your office on the mailing list.

Answer the following short questions, cut out the page, fold it in half, tape the end (please, no stables), and drop it in the mailbox. As a token of our appreciation for support, we will send you a new security awareness poster.

1. **About how many people share this one copy of the *News*?** _____

2. **To what type of office or field unit has this copy of the *News* been sent?**
   a. Defense investigative service _____
   b. Army, Navy, or Air Force unit _____
   c. Other department of defense component or office _____
   d. Other federal agency or department office _____
   e. Other, please indicate _____

3. **How useful do you find the *News* in your professional role?**
   a. Extremely useful _____
   b. Moderately useful _____
   c. Only slightly useful _____
   d. Not useful at all _____

4. **To what extent do you or any of the other readers of this copy use information in the *News* as content for security awareness activities, such as briefings, for cleared employees?**
   a. Extensively _____
   b. Occasionally _____

   c. Rarely   _____

   d. Not at all   _____

5. The *News* comes out monthly. Is this the right frequency? What is your preference?

   a. Twice monthly   _____

   b. Monthly   _____

   c. Every two months   _____

   d. Quarterly   _____

6. How would you rate the production quality (layout, general appearance, printing, paper) of the *News*?

   a. Very high   _____

   b. Good   _____

   c. Just acceptable   _____

   d. Less than acceptable   _____

7. In general, how do you and your coworkers evaluate the timeliness of the news items reproduced in this publication?

   a. Very up to date and of current interest   _____

   b. A bit dated, but still useful   _____

   c. Somewhat out of date by the time we receive each issue   _____

   d. Too outdated to be of any value   _____

8. Lastly, are we covering the right kind of news in each issue? Please indicate your degree of interest in the following:

News about:	High	Moderate	Slight	None
a. Espionage	____	____	____	____
b. Foreign intelligence threat	____	____	____	____
c. Information security	____	____	____	____
d. Communications security	____	____	____	____
e. Technology transfer	____	____	____	____
f. Illegal export	____	____	____	____
g. Computer or IT security	____	____	____	____
h. Terrorism	____	____	____	____
i. Personnel security	____	____	____	____
j. Government security programs	____	____	____	____
k. Security policy issues	____	____	____	____

Audience Questionnaire for Video Evaluation

Video: _____ **(insert title here)**

Please complete this short questionnaire so that the producers of the video you have just seen can evaluate its effectiveness and determine what else would be helpful in an accompanying presentation guide. There is no need to provide your name.

We would like your evaluation of this product's specific qualities. Please circle a numerical rating on the scales below for each element, ranging from 1 (poor) to 10 (excellent).

a. Overall assessment: What is your immediate impression of this video's effectiveness as a motivational product?

1   2   3   4   5   6   7   8   9   10

b. Production quality: Does this have the look of a high-quality professional product?

1   2   3   4   5   6   7   8   9   10

c. Interest: Does it hold your attention over its total run time?

1   2   3   4   5   6   7   8   9   10

d. Strength and clarity of the message: Is the central message unmistakable and compelling?

1   2   3   4   5   6   7   8   9   10

e. Tone and impression: Is it generally positive and constructive?

1   2   3   4   5   6   7   8   9   10

f. Use of time: With regard to length and pacing, are they on target?

1   2   3   4   5   6   7   8   9   10

g. Orientation: Is this product suitable for all audiences?

1   2   3   4   5   6   7   8   9   10

h. Credibility: Does this video convey a high degree of realism and consistency with the truth?

1   2   3   4   5   6   7   8   9   10

Does anything you saw in this video need further explanation to make it better understood? Additional information might be covered by a presenter before or after the video is shown.

If changes could be made, how might this video be improved to make it a more effective awareness product? Feel free to comment on any of the above assessments.

Lastly, in order to help us understand how people with different backgrounds and levels of experience might have different opinions about this product, we need to find out something about the people in our test audiences.

Please check the appropriate selection for each question:

a. Gender   Male   ☐   Female   ☐

b. Age category   Twentysomething   ☐
                         Thirtysomething   ☐
                         Fortysomething   ☐
                         Fiftysomething   ☐
                         Sixtysomething   ☐

c. Professional Group: Government civilian security professional   ☐
                        Government civilian counterintelligence   ☐
                          professional
                        Military security professional   ☐
                        Military counterintelligence professional   ☐
                        Other government civilian employee   ☐
                        Other military personnel   ☐
                        Security professional in defense industry   ☐
                        Other industry employee   ☐

d. About how many years of experience can you claim in your present profession?

_____

Thank you very much for your cooperation.

United States Department of Energy
Science, Security, and Energy: Powering the 21ˢᵗ Century

Office of Counterintelligence
Briefing Evaluation

Topic/Briefing Type: (circle one)

Core	Hosting Foreign Visitors
Foreign Travel	Polygraph
Reporting Requirements	New Hires/ Uncleared Employees

Date of Briefing: _____

Name of Briefer: _____

Please use the following scale to indicate the extent to which you agree with the statements below:

1	2	3	4	5	6
Strongly disagree	Somewhat disagree	Neither agree nor disagree	Somewhat agree	Strongly agree	Not applicable

1. Information provided in this briefing was clear and easy to understand.	1	2	3	4	5	6
2. Handout material was useful and informative.	1	2	3	4	5	6
3. The instructor's approach to presentation was effective.	1	2	3	4	5	6
4. This briefing will help me in my performance of related duties.	1	2	3	4	5	6
5. This briefing gave me a better understanding of counterintelligence issues.	1	2	3	4	5	6
6. I better understand my roles and responsibilities related to counterintelligence awareness.	1	2	3	4	5	6
7. I better understand the purpose of the counterintelligence program and the office of counterintelligence.	1	2	3	4	5	6

Suggestions for improvement:

Other comments:

16

Security Education in the Electronic Age

For almost three decades now, security educators have worried and fussed over the vulnerabilities to organizational assets created by this wonderful, new-fangled electronic age. Computers are everywhere, it seems, having moved out of those air-conditioned, vaultlike rooms in the basement to perch on everyone's desks and even keep our organization's travelers company in their hotel rooms and cramped airplane seats. We've done a lot of work eliminating vulnerabilities and combating threats, but we haven't spent nearly enough time exploiting the opportunities — particularly the opportunities a computerized environment presents for security education.

This chapter is going to provide a hodgepodge of ideas for you to think about as you decide how to exploit those opportunities. A few of them might be just the ticket for your security education program; others may be completely worthless. It all depends on how computers fit into the life of your organization. As we go through the list, we'll assume that the folks reading this book are a typical mix of security professionals. Some of you are probably genuine experts on computers; others barely know how to turn the gadgets on. Many of you are perfectly comfortable whizzing around the electronic world; others try to avoid those horridly complicated machines as much as they can. Some of you work in organizations where just about everyone uses computers constantly and zips around the Internet at will; others work in organizations where only a few people, in a few parts of the activity, use computers at all. We're also going to avoid all that information systems "technical talk" as much as we can. Those of you who are fluent in computerese will please forgive us for taking longer to say something in plain English than it would if we used computerese.

As we think about this topic, we'll focus on three areas that seem to us to have particular potential for security education: the World Wide Web, CDs (compact disks), and e-mail. There are other possibilities, which we'll leave to your creativity. Three items is enough for starters. Also, you may be disappointed to discover that we don't provide Web addresses (URLs) for some of the online resources we mention. Sorry, but our experience is that Web sites and URLs change faster than twirled kaleidoscopes, and a print publication with lists of URLs tends to be out of date before the ink dries. A good Web search engine like Google, AltaVista, or Yahoo! should let you find these sites quickly and easily.

ASSESSING THE POSSIBILITIES

For most of you, an essential first step in evaluating the potential of the ideas in this chapter for your program is to build a strong alliance with your organization's information systems professionals. There are many factors to be weighed before you can determine if something we're suggesting will be worth trying in your company or agency. We believe the best way to make sure all of them are properly considered is to sit down with the information systems people and develop a good, sound understanding of just who in your organization actually uses computers and how they use them. Here are some examples of the kinds of things you need to know. (We say "some examples" because we're sure we've forgotten something.)

First you need to consider a few questions. How many people in the organization *regularly* use computers on the job? Are they concentrated in one or two elements of the organization or spread pretty evenly? A lot of times the question is posed as: "How many people have access to computers?" That misses the point. Just because someone "has access" to a computer doesn't mean that he or she can get access *conveniently* or is comfortable with the computer. When you get an answer to the first part of this two-part question, make sure you think about the reverse: How many people *don't* use the things regularly? Make sure you think about employees like drivers, maintenance people, the janitorial staff, and so on.

How many people have CD readers on their computers or access to CDs via a network? If it's through a network, how much trouble is it for a person to get access to a specific CD just when he or she wants it?

How many people have the ability to do telecomputing on their work computers? (*Telecomputing* means computers "talking" to one another and sharing information by means of telephone systems or similar means.) Do you have just a simple network? Does your organization have an intranet? (An *intranet* is an internal corporate or agency setup that looks like the Internet, walks like the Internet, quacks like the Internet, but isn't really the Internet, because it exists within your own organization. People outside the organization can't get access to it and people within the organization may or may not be able to use it to access Web sites outside the organization.) Do people have access to the Internet?

There are other important questions to pose as well: How many people have and use e-mail? Does your organization have a corporate or agency Web site? How does someone go about adding a subsite or Web page to it? What sort of display or reader software do people have convenient access to? Here we mean Web browsers, graphics viewers, readers for special types of files (PDF document files are a good example), and so forth. How about printers?

Once you get answers to these questions, you can start looking at the various ideas we're going to offer and see which of them look like they have potential for your security education program. Before we start going through the list, there's one word of caution we feel duty bound to offer, even though we hope it's unnecessary. Make very sure you consider security as you work on this. There have been a few very unfortunate situations of security organizations themselves compromising sensitive information because they just didn't quite understand the security aspects of their electronic environment. Don't let it happen to you.

WEB SITES

The World Wide Web has become one of the most astounding phenomena of modern culture. More and more people are becoming accustomed to using this part of the Internet to do everything from reading the latest news, to buying airline tickets, to finding recipes, to doing academic research, to locating pictures of cats. A security Web site is something you really ought to consider adding to your security education program. Not only can you provide good information yourself, but you can also include links (technically, *hypertext links*) to other Web sites of value. Be careful to consider security and legal constraints, but give a Web site some serious consideration.

How you can and should go about setting up a Web site will depend heavily on your organization's information systems structure. If your organization has a Web site for the overall company, agency, or facility, you may be able to add your site as a page or subsite of that. Or you may set up your site on its own Web server or on an intranet server. This decision has to be left to you and your supporting information systems staff. We'll concentrate on what you might include on the site.

SECURITY CONTENT

The first and most important question is, what do you want to put on your site? A Web site is a communications tool, so just what information do you want to communicate to your organizational population that might fit nicely on a Web site? How about these possibilities, for starters?

Security Office Contact List

Offer a list of phone numbers in your security office that people can call with specific problems. Give the names of your staff members and their phone numbers, but also show which areas of security each one covers. And make sure the subject areas are listed in terms that nonsecurity people can understand, maybe something like this:

Locks and keys	Joe Gray	555-1764
Security badges	Tisha Lincoln	555-2190
Sensitive document control	Paul Wyczyk	555-3956
Travelers' briefings	Marian Stern	555-0595

Make the last item something like "Everything else," so those who aren't sure which category their problem falls into will have someplace to call. Doing this can create a time-saver for your security staff by reducing the number of times they have to transfer callers to another number.

Online Documents

Include security regulations, directives, Standard Operating Procedures (SOPs), and policy documents in HTML or PDF format. This not only makes the documents readily available, it helps make sure your staff members are using the most up-to-date versions. It can also be a money-saver by cutting down on the number of paper copies you'll need to produce and distribute. And these same electronic versions can easily be included on a security CD, which we'll discuss in a moment.

Hot News from Security

Timely information about time-sensitive items like gate or access point closings, policy or directive updates, new procedures being implemented, and security education events will enhance your site. A word of warning here: Don't only rely on your Web site to distribute this information. Keep on using the same means of getting the word out that you always have. But having the items here is just one more way to try to make sure everyone gets the message. It also gives people a means of getting the straight scoop about items they may have heard about second- or third-hand.

Security Reminders

Right in the middle of the main page of your site, include a reminder about something the staff needs to be reminded about. Don't put this at the top of the page; experienced Web users tend to ignore stuff up there. And don't put it way down at the bottom; people may not scroll down far enough to see it. This can be a general reminder or something specific, like the time and place of a security education event or the need to show up for rebadging. Make it short (one sentence) and clear.

Security Education Materials

Include documents, charts, and transcripts to help employees recall what they learned from presentations. Don't rely on your Web site to *do* security education. It's simply not reliable enough. But you can use it to *support* your other efforts. For example, if you passed out a chart during a presentation, you may also want to post it on your Web site. People may lose the paper copy, but they can access it on your site. Or maybe post an outline of a presentation, to jog people's memories about important points.

There's one popular feature found on many Web sites that we'd recommend *against* putting on yours: a message board. This is a place where visitors can ask questions and make comments, and the board moderator (you) and other users can provide answers or reply to the comments. There are two reasons for avoiding this. The first is that it's too easy for visitors to inadvertently include sensitive information in their questions or comments. Bingo! The sensitive information has just been published to anyone who visits the board. The second reason is that message boards are a magnet for congenital whiners and gripers to post their whines and gripes. That's not going to be constructive and can be quite destructive. Message boards can serve good purposes, but we don't think they belong on security Web sites.

A QUICK WORD ABOUT DESIGN

The key to designing a good security Web site is the tried and true old maxim: Keep it simple, stupid! These days the Web is loaded with sites that are unbelievably jazzy and true works of graphic art, but they are so inefficient to access that they become a major turn-off. The more spiffy artwork you add to a site, the less efficient the site is to access for people with slow Internet connections or when the server is operating under a heavy load. The more fancy webcrafting techniques you use — like Java, JavaScript, Flash, or exotic subsets of HTML — the more chance there is that your site might not be accessible to people operating under heavy security constraints or using old or nonstandard Web browsing software. You want your site to be attractive, but more important, you want it to be efficient and accessible for your whole intended audience.

GETTING HITS

Once you've decided to put up a Web site and come up with some good security-related content and a good design, you've got one problem left. How do you get people to visit the site? (In the Web world, this is called *getting hits.*) There are few things sadder than a good Web site that nobody ever visits. It's like planning a fine party and then nobody shows up. One solution is to provide good, useful content *not* related to security — content that will make people think your site is a convenient source for information they can use — along with your security material. Even if they don't access the security-related information very often, they'll still get a reminder about security every time they visit. Here are some ideas to consider, all of which are *free*:

- *The local weather.* The National Weather Service has an excellent Web site that provides local weather conditions and forecasts for every zip code in the country. You can set up a link that takes people to a page with weather info for your specific location.

- *School closings.* This information can be extremely useful for the parents in your employee population. Almost every school district in the country has a Web site, and most of them provide notices about student holidays, weather-related school closings, and late openings. You can pick the district or districts where your employees live and provide a link or links to those sites.

- *Maps.* Several services on the Web provide maps of local areas, plus maps and driving directions for travelers. You can set up a link that provides a map of your local area, and from there people can access other maps they need. If you work in a large facility, consider providing a map or diagram showing locations of points of interest: perhaps the cafeterias, personnel office, payroll office, employee clinic, and, of course, the security office.

- *A dictionary.* Several major dictionaries have had their contents placed on Web sites. Check out a few, and add a link to the one you like best. You might also consider linking to one or two subject-specific dictionaries that cover terms used in the technical fields your staff may deal with or, if your company deals with the military, a dictionary of military terms.

- *The correct time.* The U.S. Naval Observatory has a site that provides the "official" correct time. People like to use this information to check their watches.

- *World time zones.* "Let's see. I have to call the plant in Oregon/ Pittsburgh/Stockholm. Now, what time is it there?" Quite a few Web sites display the time in various time zones. Some of them are well done and easy to use. Some are thoroughly confusing. Poke around the Web and find a good one, then link to it.

- *Organization-specific sites.* Whatever type of organization you support, there are probably some Web sites that your people would find particularly useful. Perhaps the Web sites are those of major customers, professional organizations, or major suppliers. And don't forget to include your organization's main Web site, if it has one.

These are just a few examples. If you're at all Web savvy, you can probably think of others. Or maybe you'll want to ask some of the people on your security staff or in the larger organization for suggestions. Be careful to avoid links to major time wasters like news and entertainment sites, but try your best to include enough useful sites to make *your* site a popular place to visit.

CD-ROMS

As you probably already know, a CD-ROM (or just CD) is a compact disc on which you put computer files that can be read with a reader in or attached to a computer. Their biggest feature is that you can store an absolutely incredible amount of data on them, which can include documents, graphics, photos, animations, and just about anything else that can be digitized. The holder can view the material on the computer screen or print out documents and graphics for use away from the computer.

CDs have excellent potential for supporting your security education efforts. How about giving people their own personal library of security regulations and directives on a CD? How about placing your security office directory on a CD for users to print out and keep handy? Outlines of security briefings or perhaps the full texts on CD might be useful. Job aids can be distributed by CD for users to print out if they need them. You can make forms handily available on CD. Lists of addresses and phone numbers of security support organizations can be included. Maybe you have a security handbook that you provide to your employees. That can go on the CD. Use your imagination! The really neat thing is that you can probably put all of the above on a single CD and still not fill it up!

CDs are easy to produce in quantity and are almost always *much* cheaper to produce than the equivalent amount of paper documents. CD writers are fairly cheap and can be attached to just about any computer. Often CDs can be produced more quickly than waiting for bulk printing to be done, and they're handier for people who regularly use computers than shelves and desk drawers full of paper. If people need or want a paper copy of something on a CD, they can print it out.

There's another advantage to CDs over paper documents, but you have to set things up to take advantage of it. When we did security inspections and staff visits, one thing we always wanted to do was make sure people had the latest, up-to-date copies of security regulations and directives. That usually meant having them pull a number of paper documents off their bookshelves or wade through their stuffed desk drawers trying to find them. If you provide copies of these publications via CD, make sure the date of creation of the CD is placed on the label. Now your security staff can just glance at the label of the CD and know whether everything's current. They can also make a habit of having a couple of the CDs in their briefcases to give employees when they find outdated material in use.

CDs won't eliminate all needs for paper publication. A CD is only worth-while if the user has a CD reader *readily* available for use when the content is needed. But CDs can be a cost-effective way of helping people have information available when they need it. That's good management and may even help earn you a gold star (or at least a silver one) on your next performance evaluation.

E-MAIL

E-mail has become one of the most popular means of communication. Like just about any other means of communication, it has potential to support your security education efforts. What sort of services might e-mail offer? Use it to do any of the following:

- Notify employees of changes in procedures and requirements

- Let people know about upcoming security education activities

- Advise people of changes in access routes (temporary gate closings, etc.)

- Provide occasional reminders about security responsibilities

- Announce changes in contact information (new members of the security staff, changed phone numbers or office locations, etc.)

- Give people the "straight scoop" on security issues that might be floating around the rumor circuit inaccurately

- Provide a word of thanks or praise to people for good security performance — by an individual or a group

We're sure you'll probably be able to find other good uses for e-mail, but *please* use it wisely and cautiously. Used properly, it can be a fine security education tool. Used improperly it can be ineffective, irritating, and dangerous. Let's look at some problems and how to avoid them.

If you use e-mail yourself, you're probably well aware of the problem of electronic junk mail, often called *spam*. One of the authors opened his e-mail box the other day to find eighteen e-mails about how to buy cheap Rolex watches, four e-mail ads for Viagra, two e-mails from people about a scheme for getting $3.5 million dollars from a bank in some country he'd never heard of, and one offering the most wonderful credit card in the world. And, oh yeah, there were two e-mails from friends and one from his insurance company about a claim. Be extremely cautious about letting your security office get a reputation for spamming. Make sure your e-mails provide useful, relevant information to the recipients. And make sure employees come to realize that, when they see they've gotten an e-mail from the security office, it's going to be worth reading. If employees start thinking otherwise, clicking that Delete button without bothering to read the mail will become a habit. One security office developed a program of sending a daily "security reminder" e-mail to all employees. Nice try, but we're willing to bet that after a week or so most of those e-mails were deleted unread. What was particularly unfortunate was that some of them contained useful, timely, and relevant information. But busy people probably aren't going to be willing to spend their time separating the wheat from the chaff.

E-mail can also promote an unrealistic sense of speed and reliability. A lot of people seem to think that e-mail is a nearly instantaneous means of communication. (One of the authors once worked for a boss who had the irritating habit of stomping into his office and asking why he hadn't answered an e-mail the boss had sent an hour ago!) Well, maybe so, but maybe not. Keep in mind is that an e-mail is only received when it's read. Some people check their e-mail several times a day; some have those nifty setups where you get an onscreen notice when you get new e-mail. Other people check their e-mail once a day or even less often than that. Remember, too, that e-mail can be "delayed in the mail." We've had many instances when e-mail has been received in our mailboxes literally seconds after it's been sent. We've also had cases where e-mail has gotten hung up on a mail server somewhere and hasn't been delivered for several days. Also, being sent and received does not equal being read. We refuse to admit how many times we've accidentally deleted a piece of e-mail when we hadn't checked our mailboxes for a while and the item was tucked in with a long list of spam.

A final problem concerns security. Many people consider e-mail a private form of communication: It goes only to the intended recipient and it can't even be overheard — as telephone conversations can — by others in the office. It's a continuing problem to get people to remember that *private* doesn't necessarily mean *secure*. This isn't the place for a lecture on computer security, but we do have one piece of advice. Unless you operate in a *very* secure computing environment, we'd suggest you do *not* encourage people to ask questions of the security office by e-mail. It's just too easy for them to inadvertently slip a bit of sensitive information into their mail. This is a judgment call you'll have to make based on your knowledge of your information systems security posture, but please give it some thought.

Enough of the negatives. E-mail can be a useful tool for security education, and here's a tip for making it pay off well. You may be familiar with mailing lists. A *mailing list* is a group of e-mail addresses that you keep on your system. You write an e-mail and send it to everyone on the list, without having to tediously enter all the addresses. These lists can be a super tool for making sure your e-mails go to the people who need the information, but *only* those people. Some examples of possible mailing lists include the following:

- All employees
- Division security representatives
- Store managers and assistant managers
- All personnel in the procurement branch
- Scientific and engineering personnel
- Company, battalion, and brigade executive officers
- Mail clerks
- Employees whose last names begin with *S*
- All security staff members
- All gates and building access control points
- All employees at the Chambersburg plant
- All supervisors at Henrico County facilities

You can see that using mailing lists gives you all sorts of possibilities for tailoring distribution of your e-mails to the specific needs of people in the organization. If you don't know how to set up mailing lists, check with your information systems team. If you use e-mail, creating mailing lists should be possible for you.

DO YOU HAVE THE RESOURCES?

Now let's talk about just who's going to do all this stuff. We've left this issue for last because, unfortunately, a lot of people consider it first. In one workshop on using computers in security education, a couple of the attendees were curious about the subject and wanted to know more just for their own professional development, but had already decided they probably couldn't make use of a Web site in their programs. They just didn't have people in their organization who were able to do the necessary work. When they left the workshop, they weren't so sure.

The first thing you should do is check around among your security staff and see if there are any hidden possibilities. For example, one small organization recognized that it should have a Web site of its own. Management kept hesitating, though. The organization just didn't have the resources at the time to send someone off to learn Web crafting. Then the head of the organization happened to find out that one member of his professional staff had created a fairly large and rather popular Web site about one of his off-duty interests — the Civil War — which had even been written up favorably in a history magazine. When asked, the employee was happy to pitch in, and the organization quickly had a presence on the Web. The site was nothing fancy, but it did the job and brought a lot of favorable reactions from customers. Web crafting is a popular hobby, and you just may find you have a talented Web site creator in your midst. The same goes for computer graphics to include in computerized and paper publications. Don't overlook the lights that may be hidden under bushels on your own staff.

Find out what help is available in your supporting information systems organization — not just what it says on people's job descriptions, but also skills and abilities they use off the job that might be put to good use in your program. If your organization has a Web site, who created it and who maintains it? Could that person do the same for a security Web site? Is contract help available through the information systems staff? Are there computer graphic artists who could support you? Does the information systems staff have people who are expert in creating computerized documents? Do they have CD-ROM production capability?

You may not have in-house capabilities to support computerized security education efforts, but how about contracting for services? You may be able to find a few dollars to obtain outside help. Be careful. There are zillions of people out there looking to make a little cash producing Web sites, computer graphics, and so on. Some of them are truly creative and expert. Some of them are walking disasters. The best way to tell the difference is to look at their products. For example, a person providing Web site creation service should be able to give you a list of addresses of Web sites he or she has built. Give these sites a once-over, and look at the person's own Web site. Are the sites well designed?

Can you navigate around them easily? Do they present a nice appearance? Are they efficient in delivering information as well as navigation? Figure that the sites they refer you to are what they consider their best work.

But what if none of this solves your problem? You don't have anyone on your staff who can help, the information systems people are already overloaded, and there's no money for contracting. There's one last possibility. Talk to the computing faculties at your local high schools and colleges. Many high school and college students are extremely savvy about computing and telecomputing. Thousands of fine Web sites have been created by people who aren't old enough to legally buy a beer. And some of the computer graphics you see at school art shows are marvelous. See if some of the students might be willing to give you a hand. You'll want to reward them appropriately for their help, of course. You may be able to do this even if you don't have any money available. Many of these young folks are looking forward to careers in the field, and they may be happy to work on your security education program in return for the chance to include the effort on their resumés. A letter of appreciation from one of your organization's senior executives might be all the reward they'd want. Or how about a nice lunch in the executive dining room with one of your top managers? In one case, building a security Web site for a small company was even made an in-class project with the approval of the school's administration. When the project was completed, the company had a wealth of material to use in putting together its "final product" site. The security director visited the class to thank the students for their work and to drop off several large bags of candy bars and a letter from the CEO to the school's principal thanking the class and the teacher. Don't overlook this as a possibility.

A BOTTOM LINE

Depending on the information systems environment in your organization, using computer capabilities in your security education efforts can be anywhere from sort of useful to a *major* asset. Learn as much about how your organizational population uses computers as you can, poke around to find out what resources are available to you, then do some hard thinking about whether and how these electronic advances can contribute to security education quality. Be particularly alert for possibilities for tailoring efforts specifically to discrete parts of the population. Remember, too, that using the electronic environment to support security education isn't *the* answer — it's simply an often useful tool.

APPENDIXES

Introduction: Security Products and Presentations

The following appendixes provide a wealth of materials that may be used in developing security presentations and included in organizational newsletters. Many of the items can be further broken down into handouts, pamphlets, and the like and may be used as a handout in a given security presentation or provided as one of many security awareness products that are of great information value to your employees.

Use these materials as you will. They are from open sources, and those from government organizations have been authorized for public release, so feel free to fit them into your security education program. The reader may go to the Defense Security Service Agency Web site and look up many of these materials that can be downloaded directly for your use.

Additionally, as an initial appendix the authors have also included a short discussion of focus groups. This may seem a strange topic area, but like with large businesses, you create a variety of security-related products for employees of the organization. One method to obtain feedback and get a better feel for your security education items is via the time-tested and accepted focus group. Please consider the focus group method as a way of learning what works and what doesn't always work.

APPENDIX A

Focus Group Protocol

From time to time in larger organizations, a focus group might be an option to evaluate a forthcoming security program. This section discusses the purpose, group size, selection criteria, meeting time, and roles for focal groups. Although the administrative tasks remain relatively the same for all focus groups, the type of presentation and, thus, the objectives of the focus group change with the subject matter under discussion. In the discussion that follows, we will be using a threat-based presentation protocol. Whatever your specific presentation topic area, the objectives and specifics can easily be modified or rewritten to meet your specific needs and requirements.

PURPOSE

The purpose of a focus group is to obtain audience reactions to the content and presentation style of a given presentation. Through the focus group, you are attempting to glean insights into what makes for an effective presentation. You are looking for specific examples and anecdotes of what captures and holds the attention of the viewing audience, and these are what you hope to receive in terms of feedback from the focal group attendees.

TYPE OF PRESENTATION SELECTED

Focus groups should be conducted following the more generic presentations or refresher briefings/reviews with larger audiences. If possible, avoid having to conduct a focus group following a very specific briefing with a limited number of participants (e.g., travel or specialized small-group briefings).

GROUP SIZE

Each focus group should be comprised of seven, plus or minus two, participants. Allowing for absentees, at least seven participants should be selected prior to the presentation. (Note: Some organizations use focus groups of up to 15 to 20 people. When this is the case, consider using the objectives response sheet as a handout for participants to complete. A variation of the handout is to use 1 to 5, 1 to 10, poor to excellent, and so on as the basic response to a question and then leave a few lines for written comments. When using this option, keep the number of questions on the list reasonable and short; never more than 10 to 15. Also allow time for some verbal discussion. Keep the group happy when it is larger than seven to nine people by having coffee or soft drinks available for the participants.

SELECTION CRITERIA

To the extent possible, the Point of Contact (POC) or presentation provider should be given an explicit set of criteria for selecting group members in advance of the presentation. This will allow the group members to plan their schedules so they can participate in the focus group. The selection criteria should be followed as closely as possible and should include the following:

- Include a cross-section of employees who will be attending the presentation. These employees should represent the various units, bureaus, divisions, and services within your organization.

- Include individuals with different types of skills (e.g., administrative types, management types, scientists/researchers, line managers).

- Avoid selecting individuals who work for one another (e.g., a supervisor and his or her subordinates).

- In selecting group members, rank is important. If possible, try not to mix higher-ranking individuals with much-lower-ranking individuals. That is, avoid mixing high and midlevel managers with nonsupervisory employees of the same group.

- In cases where the attendees are not known in advance, an alternative strategy should be developed in cooperation with the POC or presenter. If no alternative exists, volunteers may be sought from the audience.

MEETING TIME

The focus group should start as soon as possible after the presentation is concluded, allowing for only a quick break. The focus group session should last approximately 1 to 1.5 hours and be conducted in a meeting place that is quiet, comfortable, and private. If possible, the room should be arranged so that the participants sit facing one another around a conference table; if not, rearrange the room so the chairs are in a circle, creating an atmosphere conducive to discussion.

ROLES

There should be two facilitators. One has the role of leader who will do most of the talking. The other facilitator will observe and record the proceedings. This person may support the leader by offering occasional observations or suggestions. But the first facilitator should be clearly viewed as the leader of the group.

FOCUS GROUP OPENING

Introductions

The leader should open the focus group by making introductions and thanking participants for taking the time to help in the endeavor. Ask the participants to briefly introduce themselves by giving their first name, job title, and service, department, or office. At times, even within larger organizations, it is possible that participants will all know each other. Do the introductions anyway. You may not know all of the participants, what office they come from, and what they do.

Explain the Purpose of the Session

The leader should explain why the facilitators are conducting the session and why the participants have been asked to take part.

1. Why is the session being conducted? Your organization has been asked to review this program presentation, receive feedback — both good and bad — and identify ways to improve the current and future security awareness presentations.

2. Why are the participants there? A cornerstone of the study is the evaluation of security awareness presentations by recipients. The goal of doing these presentations is to inform and assist people like themselves. Because they are the intended audience for these presentations, you want their views on the value of the experience. They are the key; if they are not getting something from the experience, the whole focus group exercise is a waste of time. Further, the presentation itself may be a waste of time, and as security educators, you want to fix the problem and create a valued product for the organization's employees.

You may mention, where appropriate, that this is just one of a number of focus groups with people like themselves, which will be spread across this organization and possibly others. Also explain that they have been selected to represent different areas or specialties within the organization.

Definition and Ground Rules for a Focus Group

Explain what a focus group is and what is expected of the group members by saying the following or something similar:

- "A few ground rules are associated with focus groups. First, the term 'focus group' is just another way of saying we're going to have a group discussion. We will ask you to focus on various topics and would appreciate hearing your honest opinions. We want to hear all your ideas, thoughts, and comments.

- "The most important ground rule is that there are no right or wrong answers. Please feel free to say what's on your mind. If you don't agree with someone else who's talking, please speak up when the other speaker has completed his or her thought. We want to hear from all of you.

- "Concrete examples are especially helpful in our discussions, but please do *not* use any actual names.

- "Everything you say in this room is confidential. You will never be identified with anything you say. Some of your responses may be quoted in any report that may be developed, but we will never use your names or other identifying information. We also request that you *not* repeat anything that is said today outside of this group."

How the Focus Group Works

So that group members are not surprised, mention the following: "___ is taking notes during this session to help us remember the point you make. He/she will not be associating names or titles with these comments. Because time is limited, I may have to cut you off occasionally to move on to a new topic."

How the Group Discussion Will Work

The leader will explain that the members of the group will discuss the presentation they just observed in the context of eight objectives. Each objective will be explained and discussed in turn. The members of the group will be asked whether or not they agree that the objective was achieved. (Note to facilitators: Do not press members who cannot decide.)

The group will discuss why each objective was or was not achieved. If members thought that the objective was met (agreed), they will explain what the presenter did to be successful. If members thought that the objective was not met (disagreed), they will explain what the presenter did that precluded success. Members will also be asked to indicate what the presenter could (or should) have done to be successful. The leader will encourage group members to provide concrete examples and anecdotes in their explanations.

The facilitator will use a flipchart to guide and record the discussion. The objective to be addressed will be printed at the top of a sheet on the flipchart. The facilitator will explain the objective using specific questions from the "List of Objectives" section that follows. The proceedings will be recorded in the appropriate areas of the flipchart. The facilitator will proceed through flipchart sheets, one for each of the eight objectives.

Close by offering an opportunity for group members to add any further comments or suggestions about the presentation that cause it to be successful (or not, as the case may be). Thank participants for their cooperation in this important task. Explain that results of the focus group will be put together with other information collected. The results will be used only for the redefining and betterment of the organization's security education and awareness program.

List of Objectives

1. *Threat existence.* Did the presentation convince you that foreign intelligence activities exist, are a serious concern, and are not just an imaginary threat?

2. *Threat signals.* Did the presentation help you recognize indicators of possible foreign intelligence interest or activity? Which examples of suspicious or improper activity were most helpful?

3. *Targeting.* Did the presentation help you understand the types of situations in which you might be targeted? Did it show you how your own behavior may unintentionally attract foreign intelligence interest, especially in foreign countries?

4. *Reporting.* Were you convinced to report incidents of security concern? Was your obligation to do so made clear, as well as the procedures for reporting such activities?

5. *Deterrence.* Do you believe that the presentation will help deter individuals from committing espionage or other deliberate security breaches?

6. *Relevance.* Was the briefing relevant to your job?

7. *Provider.* What was your overall evaluation of the provider? Was the provider credible? Well prepared?

8. *Overall presentation.* What was your reaction to the presentation as a whole? Did the presentation have clear objectives? Was it interesting? Were the aids used in the presentation very good or effective?

APPENDIX B

Security Presentations

Presentations — you might call them briefings — are typically standard to a great degree, being modified or customized to meet the specific requirements of individual organizational policies and guidelines.

This appendix provides a short variety of some basic security presentation outlines that can be used to enhance your security presence, provide specific information to your employees, and keep all employees updated as to their responsibilities. They are presented with some general discussion as remarks to the attendees.

Customize the outlines to meet your specific and continuing security needs. Remember the TEAM process, and consider also appropriate research of your files and open source information in order to obtain the latest information that will be of value to each and every employee.

As you review the various outlines, you will notice that they are detailed in terms of the amount and types of material covered. The number of items included will allow you to select those portions that may apply to your particular situation, and then you can extract and customize the outline portions as necessary for local use. Using the Initial Briefing presentation as an example, you will see there is actually the potential for more than a dozen specific and unique presentations.

The presentations include the following:

- Initial Briefing: An Introduction and Overview of Security Responsibilities
- Security Refresher
- The Threat and Your Security Responsibilities

INITIAL BRIEFING: AN INTRODUCTION AND OVERVIEW OF SECURITY RESPONSIBILITIES

Introduction and Opening Remarks

Each of you has now officially received your security clearance and you have authorized access to classified information in the course of your official duties. This initial security indoctrination will explain your responsibilities for handling and protecting classified (sensitive) information within our organization.

Objectives

At the conclusion of this presentation, you will be able to do the following:

1. Use correct security procedures.

2. Send and receive classified (or sensitive) information.

3. Properly handle classified (or sensitive) materials.

4. Be aware of the requirements for storing classified (or sensitive) materials.

5. Understand how to reproduce classified (or sensitive) materials.

6. Identify steps that must be taken to protect materials.

7. Understand your responsibilities in the work environment.

8. List the actions that require reporting relevant information that may have been lost, stolen, or compromised.

9. Describe the appropriate actions to be taken when a security violation, infraction, or potential infraction occurs.

Motivation

As guardians of national defense (or company sensitive) information, we continually need to practice good security practices and procedures in order to preclude unauthorized disclosures and the compromise of classified (or sensitive) information. Practices dangerous to security, whether caused by negligence, lack of knowledge, or carelessness, may result in serious violations as well as the loss of information should that information fall into the hands of people whose interests are inimical to that of the United States or our organization.

A. The hostile intelligence threat.
   1. Targeting of U.S. defense information.
   2. Recruitment techniques used against U.S. citizens.
   3. Damage done to U.S. security by recent espionage cases (from current news media and various Web sites).
   4. Involvement in espionage.
   5. Illegal activities as defined by U.S. constitutions, statutes, and various state laws.

B. Effective security practices as preventive actions.
   1. The nature of classified or sensitive information.
   2. Custodial responsibility for the protection of such information.
   3. The ability of good security to prevent the loss of information.

C. Access to classified information.
   1. Appropriate level of security clearance.
   2. The "need to know" principle.

D. Releasing classified information to others.
   1. Proper identification of the information.
   2. Appropriate level of security clearance verification.
   3. Determination of the recipient and requirement to have the information.
   4. Accountability of the information.

E. Sending and receiving materials.
   1. Receipting and accountability records.
   2. Sending materials through the mail.
   3. Receiving materials through the mail.
   4. Telephone security and secure voice telephone systems.

F. Use of classified (or sensitive) materials on the job.
   1. Physical protection in the work area.
   2. Proper handling of documents; use of warning sheets.
   3. Preventing access to uncleared personnel.
   4. "Sanitization" of working papers and after-hours security.

G. Reproduction of classified (or sensitive) materials.
   1. Authorization for reproduction.
   2. Warning notices on documents.
   3. Document control markings and procedures.
   4. Document destruction procedures.

H. Accountability for materials designated for destruction.

I. Storage of classified materials.

J. Safe and security container combinations.
   1. Safeguarding combinations as classified or sensitive information.
   2. Requirements for changing combinations.

K. Storage of classified (or sensitive) materials while in transit.

L. Information technology/computer security.
   1. Classified (or sensitive) information processing on approved systems.
   2. Access control to systems processing classified (or sensitive) material.
   3. Protection of classified (or sensitive) storage media.

M. Security violations.
   1. Most frequently seen violations.
   2. Action to be taken when violations are identified.
   3. Procedures followed by your security office.
   4. Corrective action and consequences for the individual.

N. Reporting requirements to security officer or other relevant authorities.
   1. Projected foreign travel to or through a designated country or antici-
      pated attendance at a conference or meeting where designated country
      nationals may be present.
   2. Any contact, intentional or unintentional, with a foreign individual.
   3. Information about coworkers reflecting on the security protection of
      sensitive information.
   4. Security violations.

In summary, recap the following topics:

1. Hostile threat

2. Security practices as preventive action

3. Two basic requirements for access

4. Releasing classified information

5. Sending and receiving

6. Use of classified materials on the job

7. Reproduction of classified materials

8. Destruction of classified materials

9. Storage of classified materials

10. IT security

11. Security violations

12. Reporting requirements

Tie-in Obligations

1. The obligation to provide adequate protection for classified (or sensitive) information and materials as prescribed in our policy and procedures manual

2. The obligation to report relevant security information

3. The nondisclosure of classified (or sensitive) information: execution of a nondisclosure agreement

SECURITY REFRESHER

Introduction and Opening Remarks

You received an initial security briefing when you first came to work at this facility or when you were granted access to classified (sensitive company) information or other materials at this location. At that time you were informed about the handling and protection of classified materials and about your responsibility to report security-relevant information to the security officer or other designated authority. Today we will briefly review reporting requirements and look at any special problems at this facility that require the attention of cleared personnel.

Objectives

At the conclusion of this security presentation, you will be able to do the following:

1. Identify five situations that require reporting of relevant information to a security officer.

2. Describe appropriate action to be taken when a security violation or a compromise of classified information occurs.

3. Identify the most frequently occurring security violations.

Motivation

We all need to be aware of basic information about the safeguarding of classified information and why the granting of a security clearance needs to be refreshed and reinforced periodically. In addition, we must challenge people who want access and demand that cleared employees be kept up to date with new policies and concerns about the foreign intelligence threat. We must address any failure to provide periodic reinforcement of the procedures within the security regulations for the safeguarding of sensitive information and materials within our organization. The foreign intelligence threat has many aspects:

A. New information on the threat.
   1. Foreign priorities and known targets in this geographical area.
   2. Any appropriate update on foreign or other targeting and recruitment methods.
   3. Current information on the multidiscipline threat (e.g., technical intelligence, illegal export, exploitation of open sources).
B. Discussion of the most recent case or cases where situational factors come closest to those at this facility (select a recent case and review it in some detail with emphasis on lessons learned).
C. Personal vulnerability factors (which may lead to the recruitment or self-involvement of a U.S. citizen in espionage).
   1. Situational factors: effectiveness of the facility security posture.
   2. Damage to organization and/or national security: what was lost and what are the long-term implications?

A cleared employee has continuing responsibilities:

A. Reporting requirements.
   1. Report contacts with Soviet bloc or designated country citizen or entity anywhere, even if it appears to be unintentional.
   2. Review list of designated or high-risk countries if necessary.
   3. Discuss real examples from recent past or hypothetical situations that might happen to an employee ("What if . . . , what should you do?").
B. Report information indicating that an employee may be representing or assisting another country.

C. Report information that reflects adversely on the ability of any cleared employee to continue to safeguard classified information.
   1. Report in confidence; let the security officer decide whether it's serious or not.
   2. Examples: involvement in illegal activities, intoxication on the job, financial irresponsibility, bizarre, suspicious, or irrational behavior, drug use, or substance abuse.

D. Report any questionable or illegal or unauthorized access to classified or sensitive information.
   1. Discuss a real or hypothetical situation ("What if . . . , what should you do?").
   2. Comment on implications of unauthorized disclosure of information if there is no foreign agent involved.

E. Report any attempt or actual deliberate compromise of classified defense information.

F. Notify appropriate authority or security officer before contacting or visiting any establishment of a communist or designated country, including those located in the United States or in a friendly country.

G. Notify security officer in advance of anticipated travel to or through a communist or designated country or before attendance at any professional conference or meeting where designated country citizens are expected to be present.

H. Discuss typical situations where reporting was required.
   1. Requirement of a defensive security briefing before travel.
   2. Reporting of unusual events to the security officer.

I. Report information concerning any international or domestic terrorist organization. Sabotage or subversive activity that may pose a direct threat to U.S government, its activity, people, businesses, organizations, and so on.

J. The current security posture of this facility.
   1. Recent or unusual problems that pose a definite threat to personnel, facilities, and so on.
   2. Most frequently occurring types of violations.
   3. Particular examples of violations that could have been avoided.
   4. Corrective actions taken.

K. Vulnerability to domestic and international terrorism.
1. The domestic and international terrorist threat at this time.
2. Local concerns and physical security measures at this facility.
3. Review precautionary guidelines for personnel who travel to high risk areas.

In summary, conclude on a positive note:

1. Reemphasize major points of the briefing, new developments in the hostile threat, and most important reporting obligations for the cleared employee.

2. Comment on the favorable aspects of the security program at the present time.

THE THREAT AND YOUR SECURITY RESPONSIBILITIES

Introduction and Opening Remarks

To put it simply, the *threat* is why we are here; in a sense, it is our purpose in being. If it weren't for the foreign intelligence threat, there would be little justification for putting so much money and effort into such things as personnel security investigations, regulations for controlling classified information, and security countermeasures.

Objectives

Following this presentation, security professionals will be able to do the following:

1. Identify the principal sources of the foreign intelligence threat operating in the United States.

2. Describe the four stages of recruitment modus operandi of agents of hostile intelligence services.

3. Accurately evaluate the relative importance of personal motivations and vulnerability factors leading to involvement in espionage.

4. Identify several indicators of possible espionage involvement revealed by investigative activities and what action needs to be taken when information of this type comes to light.

Motivation

All the mechanics for determining the suitability for access to classified information are determined based upon investigations into an individual's background. These include the National Agency Check (NAC), Background Investigation (BI), and the Special Background Investigation (SBI). Each of these have different levels of investigation, with the NAC being the least intrusive and the SBI the most intrusive. Once the investigation is completed, the results of the investigation are adjudicated to determine if the individual qualified for access to classified information and, if so, the level of access that may be granted. The investigations are also a part of the countermeasure response to known and potential treats. An individual without a positive investigation outcome obtains a level of trust in protecting the information that he or she will have access to, and also they receive appropriate training sessions and briefings in terms of how to handle and protect the information against threats. It, then, becomes important that all of us as security professionals have a sound, general understanding (an overview) about the pervasiveness and magnitude of the intelligence threats. Not only can we then recognize the threat when it is staring us in the face, but also when we confront our routine daily tasks, we can do so with the conviction that what we do is really important. Each of us can then look into such matters as drug use or excessive indebtedness, knowing there is a legitimate reason for it.

A. What is being threatened or targeted?
1. Information helpful to potential adversary.
2. Targeted information.
3. Adversaries after more than just "classified" (or sensitive) information.
4. High-tech information is highly desirable.
B. Targeting priorities of foreign intelligence. The source of the threat: Where is it coming from?
1. The threat from hostile countries.
2. The threat posed by "friendly" countries.
3. The new Russian intelligence services, among many others who are still plying their trade.
4. Competitor organizations.
C. Methods: The all-source collection effort.
1. Open source collection methods.

    2. Covert methods: IMINT and SIGINT.

    3. HUMINT: Exploitation of human sources.

D. Use of case studies in awareness training.

    1. The "actors" in espionage.

    2. Foreign agents: The case of Larry Wu-Tai Chin.

E. Exploitation of U.S. citizens by hostile intelligence organizations or services.

    1. The heart of the problem: Citizens having access.

    2. The contemporary face of espionage.

    3. Trends in the past 10 years.

    4. Recruitment of vulnerable U.S. citizens.

       a. The case of William Holden Bell.

    5. Self-initiated involvement in espionage.

       a. Preponderance of self-recruitment cases.

       b. The Boyce and Lee Case.

F. Espionage: Motivations and contributing factors.

    1. The problem of prediction.

    2. Primary motivations.

    3. Examples of money as the primary motivation: The Walker spy ring; the Cavanagh case.

    4. Other motivations and contributing factors.

G. The role of investigative agents in counterintelligence.

    1. Information indicating the violation of laws.

    2. Reporting requirements.

    3. The case of Samual L. Morison.

In summary, recap the following topics:

1. What is being threatened?

2. Source of the threat.

3. Operation of hostile services.

4. Exploitation of U.S. citizens by Hostile Intelligence Service (HOIS).

5. Motivations and contributing factors of espionage.

6. Investigative agents' role in counterintelligence.

Appendix C

Security Articles: The Protection of Information

PROTECTING CLASSIFIED INFORMATION

Overview

A security clearance is a privilege, not a right. When you accept the privilege of access to classified information, you are also accepting the responsibilities that accompany this privilege.

This guide informs you of your responsibilities and provides information to help you fulfill them. Briefly, you are expected to do the following:

- Comply with security regulations and procedures to protect classified information. The nondisclosure agreement you signed when accepting your clearance is a legally binding agreement between you and the U.S. government in which you agreed to comply with procedures for safeguarding classified information and acknowledged that there are legal sanctions for violating this agreement. Some of your responsibilities for protecting classified information are discussed in the following topics: need-to-know, classification guidelines and distribution controls, handling classified information, marking classified information, mailing and carrying classified materials, appropriate use of computer systems, and using the Secure Telephone Unit III (STU-III).

- Comply with standards of conduct required of persons holding positions of trust. This includes recognizing and avoiding behavior that might cause you to become ineligible for continued access to classified information.

- Report to your security office changes in your personal life that are of security interest, including planned marriage or cohabitation, certain outside activities, foreign contacts, and other changes as described in "Self-Reporting on Your Personal Activities."

- Report to your security office or a counterintelligence office any information that comes to your attention regarding known or suspected foreign intelligence activity directed against yourself, a fellow coworker, your organization, or any other national interest.

- Report to your security office any information that raises doubts about the reliability or trustworthiness of any coworker or other person with access to classified or other protected information. This responsibility is discussed in "Reporting Improper, Unreliable, or Suspicious Behavior."

- Understand the foreign threats that make these security measures necessary. These threats are discussed in "Foreign Threats to Protected Information."

Failure to comply with these responsibilities may result in adverse administration action including revocation of your security clearance. Deliberate violation for profit may be prosecuted. The nondisclosure agreement you signed when accepting your security clearance assigned to the U.S. government the legal right to any payments, royalties, or other benefits you might receive as a result of unauthorized disclosure of classified information.

When we study the history of foreign intelligence activities against the United States, one thing becomes very clear. When our adversaries or competitors are successful in obtaining classified or other sensitive information, it is usually due to negligence, willful disregard for security, or betrayal of trust by our own personnel.

The Bottom Line

Pogo, a popular cartoon character from the 1960s, coined an oft-quoted phrase: "We have met the enemy, and he is us." That sums it up. We — not our foreign adversaries or competitors — are the principal source of the problem, but we can also become the solution. You and I and all others who hold a security clearance are the first line of defense against espionage and loss of sensitive information. Together, if we fulfill our responsibilities, we have the power to protect our national security and economic interests.

Receiving your security clearance is a bit like a school graduation or a religious ceremony such as marriage. It is a rite of passage that marks a permanent change in your life. You accept new responsibilities and will be expected to meet them. Your responsibility to protect the classified information that you learn about is a *lifelong* obligation. It continues even after you no longer have an active security clearance. Your signed nondisclosure agreement is the only form held on file long after you retire (50 years!).

Need-to-Know

Your security clearance does not give you approved access to all classified information. It gives you access only to:

Information at the same or lower level of classification as the level of the clearance granted *and* that you have a "need-to-know" in order to perform your work.

Need-to-know is one of the most fundamental security principles. The practice of need-to-know limits the damage that can be done by a trusted insider who goes bad. Failures in implementing the need-to-know principle have contributed greatly to the damage caused by a number of recent espionage cases.

Need-to-know imposes a dual responsibility on you and all other authorized holders of classified information:

- When doing your job, you are expected to limit your requests for information to that which you have a genuine need-to-know. Under some circumstances, you may be expected to explain and justify your need-to-know when asking others for information.

- Conversely, you are expected to ensure that anyone to whom you give classified information has a legitimate need to know that information. You are obliged to ask the other person for sufficient information to enable you to make an informed decision about the person's need-to-know, and the other person is obliged to justify his or her need-to-know.

- You are expected to refrain from discussing classified information in hallways, cafeterias, elevators, rest rooms, or smoking areas where the discussion may be overheard by persons who do not have a need-to-know the subject of conversation.

You are also obliged to report to your security office any coworker who repeatedly violates the need-to-know principle.

Need-to-know is difficult to implement as it conflicts with our natural desire to be friendly and helpful. It also requires a level of personal responsibility that many of us find difficult to accept. The importance of limiting sensitive information to those who have a need-to-know is underscored, however, every time a trusted insider is found to have betrayed that trust.

Here are some specific circumstances when you need to be particularly careful:

- An individual from another organization may contact you and ask for information about your classified project. Even though you have reason to believe this person has the appropriate clearance, you are also obliged to confirm the individual's need-to-know before providing information. If you have any doubt, consult your supervisor or security officer.

- Difficult situations sometimes arise when talking with friends who used to be assigned to the same classified program where you are now working. The fact that a colleague formerly had a need-to-know about this program does not mean he or she may have access to the information. There is no "need" to keep up to date on sensitive developments after being transferred to a different assignment.

- The need-to-know principle also applies to placing classified information on computer networks. Before doing so, make sure it is appropriate for this information to be seen by all persons with access to the system. Although every individual gaining access to a particular computer network is cleared for the clearance level of that system, the person may not have a need-to-know all of the information posted on the system.

HANDLING CLASSIFIED INFORMATION

As an approved custodian or user of classified information, you are personally responsible for the protection and control of this information. You must safeguard this information at all times to prevent loss or compromise and unauthorized disclosure, dissemination, or duplication. Unauthorized disclosure of classified material is punishable under the Federal Criminal Statutes or organizational policies.

Your security officer or supervisor will brief you on the specific rules for handling classified information that apply to your organization. Here are some standard procedures that apply to everyone.

Classified information that is not safeguarded in an approved security container shall be constantly under the control of a person having the proper security clearance and need-to-know. An end-of-day security check should ensure that all classified material is properly secured before closing for the night.

If you find classified material left unattended (for example, in a restroom or on a desk), it is your responsibility to ensure that the material is properly protected. Stay with the classified material and notify the security office. If this is not possible, take the documents or other material to the security office, a supervisor, or another person authorized access to that information, or, if necessary, lock the material in your own safe overnight.

Classified material shall not be taken home, and you must not work on classified material at home. Classified information shall not be disposed of in the wastebasket. It must be placed in a designated container for an approved method of destruction such as shredding or burning.

E-mail and the Internet create many opportunities for inadvertent disclosure of classified information. Before sending an e-mail, posting to a bulletin board, publishing anything on the Internet, or adding to an existing Web page, you must be *absolutely* certain none of the information is classified or sensitive unclassified information. Be familiar with your organization's policy for use of the Internet. Many organizations require prior review of *any* information put on the Internet.

Classified working papers such as notes and rough drafts should be dated when created, marked with the overall classification and with the annotation "Working Papers," and disposed of with other classified waste when no longer needed.

Computer diskettes, magnetic tape, CDs, carbon paper, and used typewriter ribbons may pose a problem when doing a security check, as visual examination does not readily reveal whether the items contain classified information. To reduce the possibility of error, some offices treat all such items as classified even though they may not necessarily contain classified information.

Foreign government material shall be stored and access controlled generally in the same manner as U.S. classified material of an equivalent classification, with one exception. See "Foreign Government Classified Information."

Top Secret information is subject to continuing accountability. Top Secret control officials are designated to receive, transmit, and maintain access and accountability records for Top Secret information. When information is transmitted from one Top Secret control official to another, the receipt is recorded and a receipt is returned to the sending official. Each item of Top Secret material is numbered in series, and each copy is also numbered.

Some classified Department of Defense information is subject to special controls called alternative or compensatory control measures (ACCM). ACCM are security measures used to safeguard classified intelligence or operations and support information when normal measures are insufficient to achieve strict need-to-know controls and where special access program (SAP) controls are not required. ACCM measures include the maintenance of lists of personnel to whom the specific classified information has been or may be provided, together with the use of an unclassified nickname and ACCM designation used in conjunction with the security classification to identify the portion, page, and document containing such specific classified information.

WHAT ARE WE PROTECTING?

One of the first steps a good defense lawyer will do in defending a client in a trial involving espionage is convince the judge and the jury that her or his client did not know the information or equipment stolen was classified or proprietary. The defense lawyer may place an employee of the company — corporate official or security officer — on the witness stand and ask her or him what reasonable measures were taken within the company to clearly identify classified or proprietary information and ensure its protection. If the witness cannot satisfactorily articulate the reasonable measures and safeguards used to protect the classified or proprietary information, the case could be dismissed.

Within the United States, we have various federal laws to help ensure the protection of "classified" U.S. government information. These laws have been used numerous times to prosecute U.S. and foreign citizens for committing espionage against the U.S. government. Until recently, we did not have a federal law to protect the unclassified proprietary information or trade secrets of private U.S. companies. The Economic Espionage Act of 1996 was specifically enacted to provide some protection to U.S. companies to cover this oversight.

One responsibility every company official has is to clearly identify to employees what classified or proprietary information requires protection. In other words, a company has a responsibility to take reasonable measures to protect classified U.S. government information or its company trade secrets.

The term *trade secret* means all assets such as financial, business, scientific, technical, engineering, or economic information. This includes patterns, plans, compilations, program devices, prototypes, formulas, designs, procedures, methods, techniques, codes, processes, or programs — whether tangible or intangible and whether or how stored, compiled, or memorialized physically, electronically, graphically, photographically, or in writing if the owner has taken reasonable measures to keep such information secret; and the information derives independent economic value (actual or potential) from not being generally known to, and not being readily ascertainable through proper means by, the public.

Recognizing that not all assets and activities warrant the same level of protection, a company needs to identify which assets need safeguarding and to assess their relative value or importance. Asset value need not be assessed in dollars. However, the cost of the security countermeasures used to protect assets must be reasonable in relation to their overall value. Assets can be valued relative to their potential loss impact. Within the Department of Defense, the impact of the loss of an asset might involve human lives or national interests.

An asset to the U.S. government is any person, facility, material, information, or activity that has a positive value to the U.S. government or a company. The asset may have value to an adversary, as well as the U.S. government or company, although the nature and magnitude of those values may differ.

The following five categories may help identify the general types of assets relevant to a U.S. company:

People

- Government personnel
- Contractors
- Military personnel

Activities/Operations

- Intelligence collection/analysis
- Sensitive movement of operations/personnel/property
- Conduct of sensitive training
- Communications/networking
- Research, Development, Testing & Evaluation (RDT&E) and sensitive technology
- Production of sensitive technology
- Protection of nuclear/chemical/biological materials
- Protection of weapons, explosives, and equipment

Information

- Classified
- Sensitive compartmented information
- Top secret
- Secret
- Confidential
- Unclassified
- System designs
- Intellectual property
- Patents
- System capabilities/vulnerabilities
- Sensitive methods
- Sensitive financial data

Facilities

- Industry sites
- Headquarters
- Field offices/administrative buildings
- Training facilities
- Contractor facilities
- Storage facilities
- Production facilities
- R&D laboratories
- Power plants
- Parking facilities
- Aircraft hangars
- Residences

Equipment/Materials

- Transportation equipment/vehicles

- Maintenance equipment

- Operational equipment

- Communications equipment

- Security equipment

- Weapons

- Automated information systems equipment

Information about critical assets can be gathered from a variety of sources. The "asset owners" or program managers (often company officials) are generally the most knowledgeable about the assets in need of protection. Sometimes it may be an engineer or scientist. These individuals generally have the best idea as to which assets are the most sensitive and valuable.

Understanding the nature and value of the assets being protected allows security professionals to make more rational decisions about related vulnerabilities and about the allocation of security countermeasures. It also helps ensure that critical assets will be protected first and that resources will be allocated where they will be the most effective.

NATIONAL SECURITY THREAT LIST

The FBI's foreign counterintelligence mission is set out in a strategy known as the National Security Threat List (NSTL). The NSTL combines two elements:

1. *The Issues Threat List.* A list of eight categories of activity that are a national security concern regardless of what foreign power or entity engages in them.

2. *The Country Threat List.* A classified list of foreign powers that pose a strategic intelligence threat to U.S. security interests. The activities of these countries are so hostile or of such concern that counterintelligence or counterterrorism investigations are warranted to precisely describe the nature and scope of the activities as well as to counter specific identified activities.

Only the Issues Threat List is discussed here, as the country list is classified. The FBI will investigate the activities of any country that relate to any of the following eight issues:

Terrorism

This issue concerns foreign power–sponsored or foreign power–coordinated activities that do the following:

- Involve violent acts, dangerous to human life, that are a violation of the criminal laws of the United States or of any state or that would be a criminal violation if committed within the jurisdiction of the United States or any state;

- Appear to be intended to intimidate or coerce a civilian population, to influence the policy of a government by intimidation or coercion, or to affect the conduct of a government by assassination or kidnapping; and

- Occur totally outside the United States or transcend national boundaries in terms of the means by which they are accomplished, the persons they appear intended to coerce or intimidate, or the locale in which their perpetrators operate or seek asylum.

Espionage

This issue concerns foreign power–sponsored or foreign power–coordinated intelligence activity directed at the U.S. government or U.S. corporations, establishments, or persons, which involves the identification, targeting, and collection of U.S. national defense information.

Proliferation

This issue concerns foreign power–sponsored or foreign power–coordinated intelligence activity directed at the U.S. government or U.S. corporations, establishments or persons, which involves the following:

- The proliferation of weapons of mass destruction to include chemical, biological, or nuclear weapons, and delivery systems of those weapons of mass destruction or

- The proliferation of advanced conventional weapons.

Economic Espionage

This issue concerns foreign power–sponsored or foreign power–coordinated intelligence activity directed at the U.S. government or U.S. corporations, establishments, or persons, which involves the following:

* The unlawful or clandestine targeting or acquisition of sensitive financial, trade, or economic policy information, proprietary economic information, or *critical technologies* or

* The unlawful or clandestine targeting or influencing of sensitive economic policy decisions.

Targeting the National Information Infrastructure

This issue concerns foreign power–sponsored or foreign power–coordinated intelligence activity directed at the U.S. government or U.S. corporations, establishments, or persons, which involves the targeting of facilities, personnel, information, or computer, cable, satellite, or telecommunications systems that are associated with the National Information Infrastructure. Proscribed intelligence activities include the following:

* Denial or disruption of computer, cable, satellite, or telecommunications services;

* Unauthorized monitoring of computer, cable, satellite, or telecommunications systems;

* Unauthorized disclosure of proprietary or classified information stored within or communicated through computer, cable, satellite, or telecommunications systems;

* Unauthorized modification or destruction of computer programming codes, computer network databases, stored information, or computer capabilities; or

* Manipulation of computer, cable, satellite, or telecommunications services resulting in fraud, financial loss, or other federal criminal violations.

Targeting the U.S. Government

This issue concerns foreign power–sponsored or foreign power–coordinated intelligence activity directed at the U.S. government or U.S. corporations, establishments, or persons, which involves the targeting of government programs, information, or facilities or the targeting or personnel of the following:

- U.S. intelligence community;

- U.S. foreign affairs, or economic affairs community; or

- U.S. defense establishment and related activities of national preparedness.

Perception Management

This issue concerns foreign power–sponsored or foreign power–coordinated intelligence activity directed at the U.S. government or U.S. corporations, establishments, or persons, which involves manipulating information, communicating false information, or propagating deceptive information and communications designed to distort the perception of the public (domestically or internationally) or of U.S. government officials regarding U.S. policies, ranging from foreign policy to economic strategies.

Foreign Intelligence Activities

This issue concerns foreign power–sponsored or foreign power–coordinated intelligence activity conducted in the United States or directed against the U.S. government or U.S. corporations, establishments, or persons that is not described by or included in the other issue threats.

MILITARILY CRITICAL TECHNOLOGIES LIST

The Militarily Critical Technologies List (MCTL) is a detailed compendium of information on technologies that the Department of Defense assesses as critical to maintaining superior U.S. military capabilities. The MCTL contains definitions of thresholds that make technology militarily critical. The acquisition of any of these technologies by a potential adversary would lead to the significant enhancement of the military-industrial capabilities of that adversary to the detriment of U.S. security interests. It includes, for example, technologies associated with the proliferation of nuclear, chemical, and biological weapons and missile delivery systems.

The MCTL provides us all with a greater degree of sophistication and sensitivity about what technology must be protected and what may be freely exchanged with our foreign counterparts. The majority of the MCTL technologies are dual-use technologies, which means they can be used for both military and civilian applications. A foreign intelligence collector may use alleged civilian use as a plausible cover for seeking information that has military applications.

The MCTL is the technical foundation for decisions on the following:

- Proposals for export control and for implementation of licensing and export control policies

- Prepublication review of scientific papers prepared by government, industry, and academia

- Tasking for intelligence collection, which includes research and development planning and international technology cooperation and transfer

The overall document is several hundred pages in length. A hard copy is generally published annually. However, the MCTL is updated almost daily, so the hard copy should be used only as a general guide. The Department of State and Department of Commerce should be consulted for up-to-date information relating to specific cases.

The major technology categories in the MCTL include the following:

- Aeronautics systems

- Armaments and energetic materials

- Chemical and biological systems

- Directed and kinetic energy systems

- Electronics

- Ground systems

- Guidance, navigation, and vehicle control

- Information systems

- Information warfare

- Manufacturing and fabrication

- Marine systems

- Materials

- Nuclear systems

- Power systems

- Sensors and lasers

- Signature control

- Space systems

- Weapons effects and countermeasures

For each of these technology categories, there are tables showing country-by-country estimates of the general status of technological capabilities. One can see from these graphics which countries might be in a position to challenge our technological superiority and which might be so devoid of specific critical technologies that they might engage in aggressive and costly intelligence operations to gain them. (Note to briefer: You may access the MCTL on the Internet at www.dtic.mil/mctl.)

Appendix D

Security Articles: Espionage and the Theft of Information

Take advantage of your security responsibilities in providing a variety of security items of interest to your employees. This appendix includes various items that can be used for creating pamphlets, general and specific handouts at security presentations, and items that can be customized to fit within an organizational or security-specific newsletter. For some of the longer items, consider breaking them down into smaller sections for a newsletter, or use the entire item for a pamphlet. During your security presentations, you can also take sections of various items and revise them, if desired, for individual handouts.

GETTING INFORMATION OUT OF HONEST PEOPLE LIKE ME

Methods of Operation

Topics in this module discuss methods that foreign intelligence services, foreign corporations, and other intelligence collectors use to obtain protected information of both a military and civilian nature.

Some of these methods are entirely legal. We don't distinguish between legal and illegal methods, because the same foreign intelligence services, corporations, and other intelligence collectors frequently employ both legal and illegal methods in a coordinated effort. Both types of methods can have the same damaging result — loss of a technological edge in either military weapons or the global marketplace.

Moreover, the distinction between legal and illegal is itself sometimes questionable. For example, there is no law against stealing discarded documents from your organization's dumpster or from a trash container outside your home. Until 1996, the United States did not even have a law against industrial espionage.

Elicitation

In the spy trade, *elicitation* is the term applied to subtle extraction of information during an apparently normal and innocent conversation. Most intelligence operatives are well trained to take advantage of professional or social opportunities to interact with people who have access to classified or other protected information.

Conducted by a skillful intelligence collector, elicitation appears to be normal social or professional conversation and can occur anywhere — in a restaurant, at a conference, or during a visit to one's home. But it is conversation with a purpose, to collect information about your work or to collect assessment information about you or your colleagues.

Elicitation may involve a cover story or pretext to explain why certain questions are being asked. Some elicitation efforts can be aggressive, imaginative, or involve extensive planning. For example, a professor from a south Asian country was teaching a night class in business administration at a Maryland university. In one assignment, her students were assigned a term paper on the company where they worked. One student reported to the FBI that the professor returned her paper three times. On each occasion, the professor asked for more details on the company. The student became concerned when the directed expansion of the assignment began to involve sensitive, possibly proprietary information.

For the foreign intelligence operative in the United States, one attraction of elicitation as an intelligence-collection technique is that it is a very low risk activity. It is hard for the target to recognize as an intelligence collection technique and easy for the operative to deny any intentional wrongdoing. It is just a pleasant conversation among colleagues or friends.

Another attraction is that it often works. Through elicitation, intelligence collectors may confirm or expand their knowledge of a sensitive program or may gain clearer insight into a person's potential susceptibility to recruitment.

As an intelligence technique, elicitation exploits several fundamental aspects of human nature:

- Most of us want to be polite and helpful, so we answer questions even from relative strangers.

- We want to appear well-informed about our professional specialty, so we may be tempted to say more than we should.

- We want to be appreciated and to feel that we are doing something important and useful. As a result, we often talk more expansively in response to praise about the value or importance of our work.

- As open and honest people, we are often reluctant to withhold information, lie, or be suspicious of others' motives.

Testing willingness to talk about matters of intelligence interest is one step on the road to recruitment. If you provide useful information once, you may be considered a "developmental contact." If you do so regularly, you may be classified as a "trusted source."

You should feel free to expand your professional and personal horizons by meeting with foreign colleagues, as long as you keep in mind that not everyone you meet has the best intentions. Follow these rules when talking with foreign colleagues:

- Never talk about your personal problems or about the personal problems or weaknesses of an American colleague. Such information may be exactly what the other side is looking for.

- If the conversation is moving into a sensitive area, change the subject or simply ignore any improper question. You are not obliged to tell anyone any information the person is not authorized to know.

- To discourage someone who seems to be too pushy about discussing sensitive information or arranging a private meeting with you, state that you would have to clear this with your security office. That is the *last* thing an intelligence operative wants to hear. It usually causes him or her to back off immediately, as no intelligence operative wants the FBI or CIA to become aware of his or her contact with you.

UNSOLICITED REQUESTS FOR INFORMATION

Direct, unsolicited requests for U.S. defense or industry program information or other proprietary science and technology (S&T) information is the most frequently reported foreign collection activity against defense industry. The requests may be faxed, mailed, e-mailed, or communicated by phone. This procedure is so popular because it is low cost, low risk, and often works.

Unsolicited requests are often directed to individual employees by name, rather than to corporate marketing departments. There are two reasons for this. First, individuals are more likely to be unaware of or not care about company or organizational policy in responding to such requests. Second, the purpose may not be to actually collect information. The purpose may be a preliminary screening to identify those who are willing to be helpful by responding to such a request. The few who respond may then be targeted and assessed further by other means.

Various ploys are used to increase the likelihood of an initial response, such as the following:

- The request is sent to individuals with the same national, ethnic, religious, or other background as the requestor.

- The requestor claims to be a student requesting help with a thesis.

- The requestor asks for a copy of a trade journal article authored by the recipient of the request. If the recipient responds, the requestor follows up with detailed questions about the subject of the article.

Many companies label an unsolicited request as suspicious when the information requested is on the Militarily Critical Technology List or is covered under the International Traffic in Arms Regulations (ITAR) and would require a license for export.

OBTAINING INFORMATION UNDER FALSE PRETENSES

When foreign intelligence services or business competitors can't obtain information openly, they may devise some more or less elaborate scenario to get it under false pretenses. Among the gambits used are the marketing survey, the phony headhunter, and phony competitive bidding.

Marketing Survey Ploy

Foreign consultants or a consortium of foreign companies ostensibly looking for business relationships in the United States often fax or mail or e-mail various kinds of market surveys to U.S. companies. Sometimes, the survey sponsors state they are working on behalf of their country's armed forces. In any case, the final recipient often remains unknown.

These surveys sometimes exceed generally accepted procedures for soliciting marketing information. For example, they may solicit proprietary information concerning corporate affiliations, market projections, pricing policies, program or technology directors' names, purchasing practices, and dollar amounts of U.S. government contracts. Customers and suppliers of a company may also be surveyed.

This is a standard ploy for collecting competitive intelligence. In one case, the foreign consultant was identified as working on behalf of a foreign company that was the primary competitor of the U.S. defense contractor and was preparing a competitive bid on a multinational program. The surveys were sent to individual engineers, not the marketing department. Other surveys were sent to the company's suppliers asking about the company's prices and supply line.

One foreign defense organization sent out a survey requesting detailed information to include number of employees, areas of activities, products, foreign collaboration, joint ventures, and infrastructure. The marketing survey clearly exceeded generally accepted terms of marketing information. The stated goal was to develop an international aerospace directory. A more likely goal was to develop a targeting guide for collection of information on specific aerospace technologies.

The following indicators suggest that an ostensible market survey may be an effort to collect intelligence for a competing firm or another government:

- Marketing surveys are faxed or mailed to an individual instead of the company marketing office.

- You are unable to find independent sources of information about the sender.

- The Internet address is in a foreign country. Note that a foreign Web site usually has a two-letter country designator after the .com or .org. For e-mail, however, there is no visible indicator of the country from which it was sent. An e-mail from an aol.com address, for example, could be sent from almost anywhere in the world.

- Technology inquired about is classified, International Traffic in Arms Regulation (ITAR) controlled, is on the Militarily Critical Technologies List, or has both commercial and military applications.

- The requestor identifies his or her status as a student or consultant or says the work is being done for a foreign government.

- The requestor insinuates that the third party he or she works for is "classified."

- The requestor says not to worry about security concerns or assures the recipient that export licenses are not required or are not a problem.

- The requestor says to disregard the request if it causes a security problem or if it is for information the recipient cannot provide due to security classification, export controls, and so on.

- The requestor admits he or she could not get the information elsewhere because it was classified or controlled.

The following measures are appropriate when you receive any survey request that may not be legitimate:

- Follow your company or organization's policy in responding to requests for information. It there is no company or organization policy, check with your security officer before responding to any unusual request.

- Unsolicited contacts with defense contractors should be viewed as suspicious and reported to the local supporting counterintelligence activity. The purpose of reporting unsolicited contacts is to develop a database of information about possible foreign technology or intelligence collection requirements. This information can then be used to support future analysis or investigations. It can also be consolidated and returned to other U.S. companies to help them protect their classified or proprietary information.

False Headhunter Ploy

If you have knowledge and experience in a specialized field, you may be contacted, usually by telephone, by a headhunter who identifies himself or herself as representing a company that seeks applicants for a job position. This is a legitimate, common practice, but not all headhunters are legitimate.

During the interview, a phony headhunter may use skilled elicitation techniques to obtain information from you. In your zeal to impress the headhunter and obtain a better job, you may, without even realizing it, provide sensitive information sought by a foreign organization employing the headhunter. If you are not interested in the job, the headhunter may elicit information on other experts in the field. The headhunter or the foreign organization can then target these individuals in other ways.

A variation of the headhunter ploy is the repatriation of émigré and foreign ethnic scientists. One country, in particular, claims to have repatriated thousands of ethnic scientific and technical personnel back to their home country from the United States. Skilled scientific and technical personnel are asked to return to aid the economic development of their native country.

These are frequently naturalized U.S. citizens, some of whom have a security clearances. This is an effective means of transferring technology. Contacting and screening scientific and technical personnel for repatriation also offers excellent opportunities for assessing and recruiting persons as agents who remain in this country. Frequently, foreign intelligence operatives appeal to a person's patriotism and ethnic loyalty.

Some countries' intelligence services resort to threatening family members that continue to reside in their home country.

Request for Competitive Bids Ploy

A request for competitive bids is a standard business practice, but it can also be used as a means of collecting information when there is no intention to let a contract.

Officials of a U.S. defense contractor reported an incident in which their company was invited to prepare a proposal for an electronic control system and bid on a defense contract for a West European government. The company prepared what it believed was the best, most detailed proposal of all other bidders for the foreign government contract, and also the lowest bidder. Despite this, after all the bids were in, the foreign government decided to build the control system itself.

The U.S. company believes in retrospect that the foreign government never had any intention of awarding the contract to a U.S. company, but was only interested in obtaining technical information. Later, while attending an international trade show, the U.S. contractor saw a foreign-built control system from the same country that rejected its bid, and the foreign country's control system looked identical to the U.S. company's own system.

By deceiving the company, the foreign government acquired preliminary concepts and designs from proven systems and saved money and time in the R&D process. While the U.S. firm may have anticipated some risk in providing technical proprietary information to the foreign government, it also expected an honest competitive process.

It is not unusual for foreign organizations to demand that U.S. companies divulge large amounts of information about their processes and products, at times much more than is justified by the project being negotiated. U.S. contractors can reduce the risk of losing such information by conducting research on their prospective foreign partners and by factoring the potential for being the victim of industrial espionage into their cost-benefit analysis. If a particular country or foreign government has a documented history of economic or industrial espionage, companies may decide that it is not in their best interest to conduct business with that country or company. At a minimum, companies may elect to provide the absolute minimum amount of information necessary to compete for the contract.

Front Companies

A number of governments use front companies to gather intelligence and provide cover for intelligence operations. They are often used to purchase high-technology products legally and then export them illegally to an unauthorized recipient.

Front companies are also used by countries and corporations that do not wish to show their hand when conducting competitive intelligence activities such as market surveys, collection of information at conferences and seminars, or purchasing reports from the Defense Technical Information Center. Countries that do not have diplomatic relations with the United States commonly use front companies as cover for placing their intelligence officers in this country.

COLLECTION FROM OPEN SOURCES

Information doesn't need to be Secret in order to be valuable. During the Cold War, Soviet intelligence found the journal *Aviation Week* so valuable that copies were rushed to a waiting aircraft as soon as it appeared on the newsstands. The plane was staffed with translators so that key articles could be translated in the air, en route, and be ready for dissemination as soon as the plane landed in Moscow. One indicator of how much things have changed since the end of the Cold War is that *Aviation Week* now publishes a Russian-language edition.

A vast amount of competitive intelligence is legally and openly available from commercial databases, trade and scientific journals, corporate publications, U.S. government sources, Web sites, and computer bulletin boards. Collection of information through open sources often has a dual purpose: to obtain the open information, but also to refine the clandestine targeting of individuals who have access to protected information. These individuals may then be contacted and assessed by other means.

Because they believe that they are closely monitored by U.S. counterintelligence, some intelligence collectors resort to clandestine methods to collect even open-source materials. They have been known to use false names when accessing open-source databases and at times ask that a legal and open relationship be kept confidential. They may take steps to hide their true interest, affiliation, or location when accessing information through the Internet. For example, they may use public access Internet connections at public libraries or educational institutions for browsing Web sites, or they may route e-mail through one or more other countries to hide its true point of origin.

Exhibits, Trade Fairs, Conventions, and Seminars

Foreign intelligence collectors find these gatherings provide rich opportunities, especially when they bring together a concentrated group of specialists on a key topic of intelligence interest. The Paris and Farnborough (England) International Air Shows are especially noteworthy as attractions for a large number of government, corporate, and freelance intelligence personnel. In addition to obtaining all the available literature, intelligence collectors use these opportunities to elicit information and for networking to meet or at least identify knowledgeable personnel who can then be targeted for further contact and assessment.

There have been many cases when Americans met at international conferences have been contacted at a later date and asked to provide information on a given technology or proprietary data. These approaches often play on a common cultural heritage as a reason to cooperate.

Some countries routinely debrief their citizens after travel to foreign conferences, asking for any information acquired during their trip. Some foreign scientists describe these debriefings as heavy handed and offensive. In other countries, they are simply an accepted part of traveling abroad.

Indicators of security concern include the following:

- Topics at seminars and conventions deal with unclassified versions of classified or controlled technologies or applications.

- The country or organization sponsoring the seminar or conference has tried unsuccessfully to visit your facility.

- A foreign organization issues invitations to brief or lecture in the foreign country with all expenses paid.

- Photography and filming appears suspicious.

- Some attendees wear false name tags.

Good risk management requires careful consideration of who and what are being exposed to whom at these meetings, attention to the physical security of sensitive information or equipment, and an appropriate balance between effective security countermeasures and marketing or other goals.

Surfing the Internet

Foreign governments and companies are increasingly using the Internet as a tool for collecting basic data on their intelligence collection targets. The World Wide Web was not designed with security in mind, and unencrypted information is at high risk of compromise to any interested adversary or competitor.

It is very easy to search the Web and put together related pieces of information from different sites. For example, the search engine www.searchmil.com specializes in indexing sites with a .mil domain name. It claims to have indexed more than 1 million pages of military sites, with the number of pages still growing. The Department of Defense (DoD) has been among the first government departments to take the lead in spelling out rules for what should and should not go on a Web site and how information should be reviewed before it is posted on a Web site.

Information on a corporation's organization, leadership, products, or programs, and the kinds of people it is seeking to hire may often be found on the company's Web page. Quarterly financial reports submitted to the Securities Exchange Commission, newspaper and magazine stories about a company, and, in many cases, discussions of new technology being developed by a company can be accessed on the Internet by using various search engines. Employees can often be identified and assessed by searching Usenet and Newsgroup postings.

Internet Discussion Groups

The anonymity of the Internet makes it a perfect medium for collection of information using e-mail, search engines, and discussion groups. One technique is the exploitation of listserv, an e-mail-based discussion group organized along topics of interest and open to anyone. Subscribers who join a list may send an e-mail message to the listserv. The listserv then sends the message to all other members of the group. This provides subscribers with the e-mail addresses of all other members interested in the same topic.

This procedure facilitates discussion of research on various technical challenges, and these discussions are permanently archived and searchable. Such exchanges can pose a serious threat to economic and technical security for two reasons. First, it is not uncommon for discussion of concepts, research, development, testing, and evaluation of new technologies to take place in an open or unclassified environment. The availability of these discussions on the Internet is a security concern when they deal with sensitive unclassified, dual-use, export-controlled, or proprietary technologies. Second, a foreign national collecting information on U.S. programs can participate in the listserv using an e-mail address that makes it appear that the person is in the United States.

Competitive Intelligence Professionals

Many corporations and some countries hire specialists in the collection of competitive intelligence to sort through the huge volume of openly available data. On its Internet site, the Society of Competitive Intelligence Professionals claims nearly 5000 members in 44 countries. Most competitive intelligence professionals try to stay within the limits of the law, although those limits may be stretched almost beyond recognition. Their research modus operandi generally involves extensive use of the Internet; phone interviews with employees, industry experts, customers, competitors, suppliers, and government officials; gathering information at trade shows and conventions; and, as needed, utilizing human intelligence networks.

U.S. Government Sources

The Defense Technical Information Center is a major source of unclassified research on defense issues. Its database of available information may be searched on the Internet. The U.S. Patent Office provides free copies of U.S. patents to interested parties of all nationalities.

Requests for information submitted under the Freedom of Information Act (FOIA) are another major source of information. When a major corporation in a friendly Asian country decided in 1986 to enter the space industry, for example, it made extensive use of FOIA requests as a means of obtaining information from NASA. By some estimates, the corporation filed more than 1500 FOIA requests in 1987 alone.

THEFT AND "DUMPSTER DIVING"

This discussion of theft focuses on theft by outsiders, not by insiders, although such theft may be aided by information provided by an insider. Principal targets for theft are laptop computers (stolen for the information on them as well as for the value of the computer); sensitive papers taken from wastebaskets, trash containers, or dumpsters (often called "dumpster diving"); and sensitive equipment (stolen or diverted briefly so that it may be copied).

Laptop Computers

Laptop computers are a prime target for theft from your office, your home, or at airports, hotels, railroad terminals, and on trains while you are traveling. They are an extremely attractive target for all types of thieves, as they are small, can be carried away without attracting attention, and are easily sold for a good price. They are also a favorite target for intelligence collectors, as they concentrate so much valuable information in one accessible place.

Safeware, the largest insurer of personal computers in the United States, paid claims for the theft of 319,000 laptop computers during 1999. Of course, most laptops are not insured, so this is only a small fraction of the total number of laptop computers that were stolen during that year.

The risk of having your laptop stolen is especially high while you are traveling. Two incidents at separate European airports demonstrate the modus operandi of thieves operating in pairs to target laptop computers:

- Airport security at Brussels International Airport reported that two thieves exploited a contrived delay around the security X-ray machines. The first thief preceded the traveler through the security checkpoint and then loitered around the area where security examines carry-on luggage. When the traveler placed his laptop computer onto the conveyer belt of the X-ray machine, the second thief stepped in front of the traveler and set off the metal detector. With the traveler now delayed, the first thief removed the traveler's laptop from the conveyer belt just after it passed through the X-ray machine and the thief then quickly disappeared.

- While walking around the Frankfurt International Airport in Germany, a traveler carrying a laptop computer in his roll bag did not notice a thief position himself to walk in front of him. The thief stopped abruptly as the traveler bypassed a crowd of people, causing the traveler also to stop. A second thief, who was following close behind, quickly removed the traveler's laptop computer from his roll bag and disappeared into the crowd.

All travelers, both domestic and international, should be alert to any sudden diversions when traveling, especially when transiting transportation terminals. If victimized, travelers should report the thefts immediately to the authorities and be able to provide the make, model information, and serial number of their laptop computer or any other item of value.

Dumpster Diving

There is an old saying that "one man's trash is another man's treasure." That is certainly true in the intelligence world. Taking papers from dumpsters outside offices is called "dumpster diving" and is a common tactic used by commercial information brokers as well as foreign intelligence services. "Trash cover" is a standard methodology used by investigators and intelligence agents throughout the world. It involves collecting and going through the trash left out for collection in front of residences and businesses. Trash may also be stolen from wastebaskets by cleaning crews.

In 1991 a guard observing the home of a senior executive of a defense contractor in Houston, Texas, noticed two men in an unmarked van take trash bags that had been put out for routine trash collection. The guard obtained the van's license number and later identified one of the men as the consul general from a friendly Western European country that collects economic intelligence in the United States. When confronted, the consul general claimed that he and an assistant were simply trying to collect bags of grass cuttings for filler — to fill a hole dug at the consulate compound for a swimming pool that could not be completed because of a zoning dispute.

Stealing trash is not illegal. The Supreme Court ruled in 1988 that once an item is left for trash pickup, there is no expectation of privacy or continued ownership.

Strict procedures govern the disposal of classified information. For disposal of sensitive unclassified waste, however, each government office or private company sets its own regulations. These procedures depend on the sensitivity of the information and the likelihood that a foreign group or domestic interest may want to obtain that information. If unclassified documents need to be destroyed prior to disposal, a commercially available cross-cut shredder should be used. A cross-cut shredder cuts the paper both vertically and horizontally. Destruction should not be entrusted to paper recycling vendors.

Sensitive Equipment

Sensitive equipment may be stolen so that it can be copied through reverse engineering. For some purposes, it may be sufficient to gain access to the equipment for only a brief period.

For example, a cleared company participated in an air show that took place overseas. The company shipped over an operational $250,000 multimode radar system that can be used on fighter aircraft. At the conclusion of the air show, the radar system was packaged for return shipping by company personnel, and the radar assembly was actually bolted to the shipping container. The shipping container was routed through a third country with the customs seals intact.

Upon being opened by company personnel, it was discovered that the radar was no longer bolted to the shipping container. As a result, the radar system was damaged beyond repair. It was determined that the radar was properly bolted down at the time it was prepared for shipment. It also was determined that the country that sponsored the air show was keenly interested in the radar's technology. It is not known whether the intruder's failure to re-bolt the radar was an oversight or was done deliberately to destroy evidence of whatever was done to examine the radar.

The lesson learned here was that the company did not really need to take the entire radar assembly to the air show. A mockup without the internal mechanisms could have been set up along with photographs of the internal components.

ILLEGAL TECHNOLOGY TRANSFER

The U.S. government — often in collaboration with its allies — controls the export of certain technologies and commodities to countries that for various reasons are judged to be inappropriate recipients. The violation of these export controls is commonly referred to as illegal technology transfer and is a serious security concern.

The Arms Export Control Act regulates the export of defense articles and services. Such exports may be licensed only if their export will strengthen U.S. national security, promote foreign policy goals, or foster world peace. The Arms Export Control Act is administered by the Department of State, the Center for Defense Trade Controls, through the International Traffic in Arms Regulations (ITAR) and the U.S. Munitions List. The Munitions List is a list of defense articles that require a license prior to export.

The Export Administration Act regulates the export of dual-use items — that is, items that have both military and civilian uses. Dual-use items that would make a significant contribution to the military potential of another country are on the Department of Commerce's Commodity Control List, and a license is required for their export. The Commodity Control List includes items from the Defense Department's Militarily Critical Technologies List and technology that could support the proliferation of chemical, biological, or nuclear weapons or missile technology.

A number of countries conduct major programs to avoid U.S. export controls. The potential magnitude of such programs is illustrated by the program conducted by the former Soviet Union. After the demise of the Soviet Union, the Russian government made public annual reports from the chief of the KGB (Soviet Intelligence) to the secretary general of the Communist Party, Mikhail Gorbachev, for the years 1985, 1986, 1988, and 1989. These reports state that the KGB acquired 12,000 to 13,000 samples of equipment or products each year from the West. Principal customers for these samples were the Ministry of Defense, the Military-Industrial Commission, and the State Committee for Science and Technology. Not all of these samples were obtained from the United States, and not all of them were obtained illegally, but a majority probably were.

In many cases of illegal technology transfer, the intended end user is a country whose policies are unfriendly to the United States, but this is not always the case. Some friendly countries obtain U.S. technology illegally to seek economic advantage. One study of illegal technology transfer operations during the 12-year period from 1981 to 1993 identified 56 different end-user countries. The same study found the following:

• The types of goods being exported illegally were 38% dual-use equipment (e.g., high-performance computers, laser mirrors, oscilloscopes); 31% weapons components (e.g., radar tubes, aircraft parts); 15% entire weapons (e.g., TOW missiles, fighter aircraft); 13% nonlethal military equipment (e.g., night-vision goggles); and 3% commercial commodities (e.g., commercial jet engines).

- Various schemes were used to get around the requirement for an export license. In over half the cases, the goods were simply purchased and shipped by another U.S. company (often a front company) without a license in hopes they would get past Customs without incident. Fraudulent end-user certificates were used in many cases. In other cases, military items were declared as civilian, high-tech items were declared as low-tech items, shipping documents were falsified, export licenses were forged, or a partial license was used rather than a full license.

- By far the most common means of shipping the goods out of the United States was to export them first to a friendly country, then transship them to a proscribed end user. Half the transshipments during the time period covered by this study were via Europe, most commonly via Germany, Switzerland, or the United Kingdom. The next most common procedure was for goods to be ordered by a U.S. individual or company, which then mislabeled them and repackaged and reshipped them illegally to the end user. Less frequently, goods were concealed in personal luggage, delivered directly to a foreign diplomatic mission in the United States, or smuggled in a chartered transport.

The initial buyer in illegal technology transfer operations is often a front company in the United States set up to acquire technology legally and then export it illegally to an unauthorized recipient.

Security Countermeasures

The best security countermeasure is for a business to know its customers. When a "new company" enters the picture requesting sensitive or classified information or technology, prudent risk management would suggest doing some checking of the company's history.

To help U.S. businesses recognize indicators of possible intent to circumvent export regulations, the Department of Commerce's Bureau of Export Administration developed the following checklist:

- The customer or its address is similar to one of the parties found on the Commerce Department's list of denied persons.

- The customer or purchasing agent is reluctant to offer information about the end use of the item.

- The product's capabilities do not fit the buyer's line of business, such as an order for sophisticated computers for a small bakery.

- The item ordered is incompatible with the technical level of the country to which it is being shipped, such as semiconductor manufacturing equipment being shipped to a country that has no electronics industry.

- The customer is willing to pay cash for a very expensive item when the terms of the sale would normally call for financing.

- The customer has little or no business background.

- The customer is unfamiliar with the product's performance characteristics but still wants the product.

- The customer declines routine installation, training, or maintenance services.

- Delivery dates are vague, or deliveries are planned for out-of-the-way destinations.

- A freight forwarding firm is listed as the product's final destination.

- The shipping route is abnormal for the product and destination.

- Packaging is inconsistent with the stated method of shipment or destination.

- When questioned, the buyer is evasive and especially unclear about whether the product being sought is for domestic use, export, or re-export.

The Bureau of Export Administration hotline for reporting suspected export violations is (800) 424-2980. Information on export controls is available on the Internet in an up-to-date database at www.gpo.gov/bxa. This Web site contains the entire Export Administration Regulations (EAR), including the Commerce Control List, the Commerce Country Chart, and the Denied Persons List.

WHO'S DOING WHAT TO WHOM?

Overview

America's role as the dominant political, economic, and military force in the world makes it the Number 1 target for foreign espionage. As the FBI director has reported to Congress, foreign intelligence activities against the United States have grown in diversity and complexity since the end of the Cold War.

In addition to the intelligence services of friendly as well as unfriendly countries, sources of the threat to classified and other protected information include the following:

• Foreign or multinational corporations

• Foreign government-sponsored educational and scientific institutions

• Freelance agents (some of whom are unemployed former intelligence officers)

• Computer hackers

• Terrorist organizations

• Revolutionary groups

• Extremist ethnic or religious organizations

• Drug syndicates

• Organized crime

The intelligence services of friendly and allied countries are now more active in intelligence operations against the United States than during the Cold War. Espionage by friends in addition to adversaries has long been more widespread than generally realized. For example, here's an eye-popper: Since the mid-1980s, Americans have been arrested and convicted of spying for South Korea, Taiwan, Philippines, Israel, Greece, Saudi Arabia, Iraq, Jordan, Ghana, Liberia, South Africa, El Salvador, and Ecuador — in addition to Russia, the former Soviet Union, China, and the various formerly communist countries.

In many cases, foreign targets in this country have not changed. A continuing interest in penetrating national intelligence, defense, and economic sectors will continue as long as advances can be made. Almost every nation looks to advance its own science, technology, and defense efforts. Thus, the interest in obtaining such information — or actual products — are a continuing threat to a nation, which means that appropriate countermeasures must be mandated and upgraded. One of the best countermeasures are people, and the people must be trained through a variety of security education practices to understand and apply protective measures.

In a world that increasingly measures national power and national security in economic terms, foreign countries and corporations are placing increased emphasis on the collection of scientific, technical, and economics-related information of all types. The increasing value of trade secrets in the global and domestic marketplaces and the corresponding spread of technology have combined to significantly increase both the opportunities and the incentives for conducting economic espionage, as discussed in "Economic Collection and Industrial Espionage," which is provided further on in this appendix.

Important changes in the international economic environment and technological advances have increased our vulnerability to some types of foreign intelligence operations.

- The development of a global economy, with a rapid expansion in foreign trade, travel, and personal relationships of all kinds, now makes it easier than ever before for foreign intelligence officers or agents of foreign corporations to establish personal contact with and assess Americans with access to valuable classified, controlled, or proprietary information. As international contacts have become more common, it has become easier for foreign intelligence officers and agents to contact, assess, and develop targets without arousing suspicion.

- Computer networks and other developments in the information revolution increase exponentially the amount of damage that can be done by a single insider who betrays his or her trust.

Methods of operation that foreign countries or organizations use to collect information on the United States are discussed in "How Do I Know When I'm Being Targeted and Assessed?," "Getting Information Out of Honest People Like Me," "Risks During Foreign Travel," and "In the Line of Fire: American Travelers Abroad." Technical intelligence collection threats are addressed in "Computer and Other Technical Vulnerabilities." These articles will be published in future issues of the newsletter. If required immediately, individual copies are available from the security office. The National Security Threat List guides the FBI's counterintelligence strategy for protection against these threats.

ECONOMIC COLLECTION AND INDUSTRIAL ESPIONAGE

The United States encourages the free exchange of most scientific and technical information. Many government programs support the exchange of technology to facilitate economic development in a wide variety of foreign countries. However, a clear line must be drawn to protect information that is classified, concerns militarily critical technologies, is subject to export controls, or is proprietary information that is the intellectual property of a specific firm or individual.

Global economic competition has, to a large extent, replaced the Cold War political and military competition between East and West. As a result, friends and allies as well as less friendly countries now pursue their national interests through espionage against the United States. Their goal is to develop a competitive edge in the global marketplace or boost military readiness while drastically reducing their own research and development costs.

Intelligence collection is done by foreign corporations acting independently of their governments as well as by foreign intelligence services. Foreign economic espionage is a major national concern. Our economy and many jobs, as well as our military superiority, depend on our leadership in high-technology research and development. In testimony before Congress, the director of the FBI said the United States spends nearly $300 billion a year on basic research, making it "the test lab for the world" and a natural target of U.S. competitors, including some of the nation's former Cold War allies.

The foreign intelligence assault on the high-technology sector of our economy is sometimes called *economic espionage* or *industrial espionage*, but these terms can be misleading in two ways:

• Espionage is always illegal, but much intelligence collection today is done by legal or quasi-legal means. Traditional espionage, the use of spies and hidden microphones, is usually one part of a larger, coordinated intelligence collection program. The formal term now used by the National Counterintelligence Center is *foreign economic collection and industrial espionage*. This term includes both legal information collection and traditional espionage, but it's a bit of a mouthful for everyday use. We may have to live with some ambiguous terminology.

• The term *economic espionage* implies economic targets and economic consequences, but the distinction between economic and military targets has been blurred by rapid advances in technology. Most of the militarily critical technologies are now dual-use technologies. That is, the same technology has both military and civilian applications. As a result, the loss or compromise of unclassified but proprietary or embargoed technology damages military security as well as the economy.

Who Is Doing It?

Due to foreign policy ramifications and the sensitivity of sources, the U.S. government does not publicly name the countries that are most active in conducting espionage against the United States. However, several European and Asian nations have stated openly that their national intelligence services collect economic intelligence to benefit their industries at the expense of foreign competition. Considerable information on this subject is available in public sources.

For example, a statement by a former head of an allied Western European intelligence service illustrates the attitude of some friendly and allied countries toward economic and industrial espionage against the United States. When interviewed on the NBC television program *Expose*, this former high-government official was unapologetic about his country's espionage against the United States. He claimed credit for starting his country's program of economic and industrial espionage against the United States as a means of improving economic competitiveness. He said his country "would not normally spy on the States in political matters or in military matters where we are really allied. But in the economic competition, and in the technological competition, we are competitors. We are not allied."

Former FBI Director Freeh told a Senate committee that the U.S. counterintelligence community has specifically identified the suspicious collection and acquisition activities of foreign entities from at least 23 countries. Eight of these are now considered to be most actively targeting U.S. proprietary economic information and critical technologies. Previously, the FBI had announced it had 800 active espionage investigations involving 23 different countries. In some cases, the activity may be sponsored by a foreign corporation rather than the foreign government. The National Counterintelligence Center produces an annual, unclassified report to Congress on foreign economic collection and industrial espionage.

The Defense Security Service — for the Department of Defense — receives reports from U.S. defense industry contractors concerning suspicious intelligence collection activity by foreign entities. During the year 2000 alone, defense contractors reported incidents in which representatives from 63 countries displayed some type of suspicious interest in one or more of the 18 technology categories listed in the Militarily Critical Technology List.

The American Society of Industrial Security conducts a periodic survey of economic and industrial espionage incidents and losses experienced by U.S. corporations. In the survey completed in January 1998, 66% of respondents viewed domestic U.S. competitors as key threats to their data. Foreign countries perceived as key threats were China (41%), Japan (36%), France (30%), the United Kingdom (27%), Canada (25%), Mexico (20%), Russia (15%), Germany (12%), South Korea (10%), and Israel (10%). The survey did not distinguish between intelligence collection by foreign governments and by foreign corporations.

What Are They After?

It would be nice to know exactly what classified, proprietary, or other sensitive information foreign countries are trying to collect so that we could then concentrate on protecting information that is most at risk. Unfortunately, waiting for that kind of specific information before taking appropriate security measures would usually mean locking the barn door after the horses have already left.

Security measures must be based on what information needs to be protected rather than the latest report on what a specific country is trying to collect. The Militarily Critical Technologies List is a basic tool for making decisions about what technology needs to be protected. It is a detailed compendium of information on technologies that the Department of Defense assesses as critical to maintaining superior U.S. military capabilities.

FBI Director Freeh reports foreign collectors are particularly interested in "dual-use technologies and technologies which provide high profitability." The National Counterintelligence Center reports that the extent of foreign interest in specific categories of technology varies dramatically from country to country, and the leading-edge technologies are not the only technologies being targeted. Countries with less developed industrial sectors often prefer older off-the-shelf hardware and software that costs less and is more suitable for integration into their military programs.

The areas on the Militarily Critical Technologies List targeted most frequently during 1999, according to defense industry reports to the Defense Security Service, were Information Systems Technology, Aeronautics Systems, Sensor and Laser Technology, Electronics, Armaments and Energetic Materials, Marine Systems, and Space Systems.

The American Society of Industrial Security survey of trade secret theft, which includes theft by U.S. competitors, found the most common targets were customer-related information such as business volume and preferences, new product information, financial data, and manufacturing process information.

Security Countermeasures

All organizations that handle classified or other sensitive information need to have focused programs for employees and management to protect that information from theft or compromise. Employee awareness of the problem, alertness to indicators of suspicious activity, and willingness to report those indicators to management are keys to the successful protection of information.

Information on export controls is now available on the Internet in an up-to-date database at www.gpo.gov/bxa. This Web site contains the entire Export Administration Regulations (EAR), including the Commerce Control List, the Commerce Country Chart, and the Denied Persons List.

CO-OPTING FORMER EMPLOYEES: WHO DO THEY WORK FOR?

Introduction

There is a modus operandi (MO) in which formerly cleared U.S. employees go to work for a foreign company or institute, where their work concerns a project or technology similar to what they were working on for a cleared U.S. company. They may be recruited for employment by a foreign national and may be expected to use their U.S. contacts to obtain additional information. These reports clearly indicate foreign entities are attempting to collect classified, sensitive, or proprietary information using this MO. Foreign entities may view former U.S. employees as excellent prospects for collection operations because they consider these former U.S. employees less likely to feel obligated to comply with U.S. government or corporate security requirements once their U.S. employment has ended.

The Technique

As a variation of the modus operandi, the use of a visit by a formerly cleared U.S. employee is a good method to collect export-restricted and perhaps classified technical information from unwitting former coworkers. The export of defense articles and services (which includes both classified and unclassified technical data) is controlled under the International Traffic in Arms Regulations (ITAR). U.S. citizens working for foreign companies or institutes may wittingly or unwittingly take advantage of their former U.S. coworkers by incorrectly convincing them that "unclassified" technical discussions are appropriate or authorized.

Case Studies

Most countries, especially those that are our political and military allies, have active research and development programs for many of the 18 different technology categories listed on the Department of Defense Militarily Critical Technology List (MCTL). As such, some countries may also have an interest in acquiring this equipment or technology as previously described. The following two illustrations are classic examples of this MO:

A formerly cleared U.S. citizen, who was an engineer specializing in a militarily critical technology related to sensors, resigned from a cleared U.S. company, moved to a foreign country, and began working for a foreign university on the same technology in an effort to obtain a foreign government research grant. While employed by this foreign institution, the engineer made arrangements to come back and visit the cleared company and former coworkers in the U.S. in an attempt to obtain specific information related to the militarily critical technology. The information was clearly covered under the ITAR as export controlled. Fortunately, the employees of the U.S. company recognized the solicitation by the former coworker and U.S. citizen as a foreign request for export-controlled information and refused to discuss or release any information.

In another incident, a cleared U.S. citizen who worked on a major U.S. defense program for approximately three years for a cleared U.S. company went to work for a company in a foreign country. The former employee returned to the United States and visited the cleared company and coworkers several times each year. Each time she visited, she would go to dinner with a group of coworkers prior to leaving the United States.

Although the nature of these relationships may have been completely innocent, the foreign country where the former employee lives and works does not have an Industrial Security Agreement with the United States and has a history of technology diversions and exploiting Data Exchange agreements (DEAs) to gain access to otherwise restricted technology and equipment. Because of these circumstances, related security countermeasures in place at the company were readdressed as appropriate.

Lessons Learned

Security professionals should ensure their company employees are educated to recognize the possible co-opting of a former employee. Indicators of such an MO include living in a foreign country, working for a foreign company, working on the same technology, and frequently returning to their company of previous employment. If an individual encounters a situation similar to those described previously, the person should report the incident to his or her security representative and local FBI. The lesson learned here is that a cleared or formerly cleared U.S. citizen is not automatically entitled to classified or unclassified export-controlled information.

FOREIGN VISITS: WHAT IS INAPPROPRIATE?

Introduction

Over past years and into the future, we can expect to have inappropriate conduct by foreign personnel during the course of visits to the facilities. Inappropriate conduct during visits is a frequently reported modus operandi (MO) associated with foreign collection activity. Although visits may be more costly and slightly more risky to the foreign entity, visitors usually gain access to the targeted facility. For this reason, this MO, though not the most frequently used, is assessed to be the most damaging form of collection activity because it can result in the loss of some technology as a result of the visit. Once in a facility, good collectors can manipulate the visit to address some or all of their collection requirements. Visiting foreign scientists or engineers can take acquired technology back to their own country and apply it directly to their needs without having to wait for it to arrive through a bureaucratic intelligence collection process.

The Techniques

Although the vast majority of foreign visits take place without incident, many do result in some inappropriate or suspicious activity taking place. Reported cases involving inappropriate conduct during a foreign visit include "wandering" visitors who become offended when confronted, hidden agendas that involve questions beyond the scope of what was approved for discussion or the fraudulent use of data exchange agreements, arriving at a facility unannounced, taking notes and photographs, holding "commercial" discussions when the U.S. government refuses to officially sponsor the visit, and last-minute or unannounced additions to a visiting delegation. Many of these techniques are specifically designed to produce potentially embarrassing incidents for the host in order to obtain collection objectives as a result of the host attempting to be conciliatory.

Case Studies

Many reports of inappropriate conduct during a foreign visit involve taking advantage of the escort and making the escort a vulnerability instead of a security countermeasure. This happens most frequently when there is an insufficient number of escorts to control the size of the visiting delegation.

In other instances, the escort has not been properly briefed on what to protect and how to respond to questions. During a visit to an aeronautics facility, a foreign delegation of 10 people was provided with one escort. The visiting delegation recognized the vulnerability and used an opportunity during a restroom break to split the delegation, thereby causing half the delegation to be unescorted in an area with export-controlled technology.

A frequently used technique by several foreign military attachés within the United States is to arrive at a contractor facility unannounced in a three-piece suit with a business card. The civilian business attire makes the military attaché appear less threatening to the facility personnel. However, the technique itself is to arrive unannounced and rely on the courtesy of the company's management to permit the attaché access to the facility. On several occasions, and at separate facilities within the Washington, D.C., area, military attachés solicited unclassified papers and brochures and engaged in conversations to determine other venues for exploitation. What the company personnel may not have realized is that most foreign military attachés are either intelligence officers or acting in the capacity of intelligence officers.

Another popular technique is to add or switch a person at the last minute as part of a visiting foreign delegation. This technique also relies on the courtesy of the company's management to permit the person being added or switched into the facility. Sometimes the person being added or switched is a commercial or military attaché from an embassy or consulate. The reason for adding or switching a visitor is the visitor believes the available time is reduced in which the company can perform a check on the background of the visitor, thereby increasing the likelihood of slipping an intelligence officer into the facility.

Security Countermeasures

Some recommended security countermeasures to mitigate vulnerabilities associated with these collection techniques are relatively simple, inexpensive, and effective — if implemented:

- Do not allow suspicious unannounced foreign visitors access to the facility. Simply tell them no one is available and that they should schedule an appointment for another date.

- Do not allow last-minute additions or substitutions to a foreign delegation to have access to the facility. Ask them to remain in the lobby while the others are permitted access. This could potentially keep an intelligence officer out of the facility and encourage proper visitation procedures.

- Verify personal identification against the original visit request when foreign visitors arrive to ensure they are who they say they are.

- Ensure there is a sufficient number of escorts to control a visiting delegation if it should be split into multiple groups.

- Ensure escorts are briefed as to what is critical within the facility and that they know what requires protection from the foreign visitors.

- Ensure facility employees are briefed as to the scope of the foreign visit and to not discuss anything beyond what is approved.

- If a visitor becomes offended when confronted during a security incident, recognize the confrontation as a collection technique and ask the visitor to leave the facility if he or she cannot abide by the rules.

- Do not permit any cameras or note taking if something in the facility is sight sensitive.

SUSPICIOUS INDICATORS AND SECURITY COUNTERMEASURES FOR FOREIGN COLLECTION ACTIVITIES DIRECTED AGAINST THE U.S. DEFENSE INDUSTRY

The purpose of this brochure is to provide information and assist security professionals, counterintelligence personnel, and cleared contractors in recognizing suspicious contacts and implementing threat-appropriate, cost-effective, and rational-security countermeasures.

A summary of suspicious contacts in a recent year, reported by cleared defense contractors, indicates foreign entities employed a variety of modus operandi (MO) in attempting to acquire information. Reported MOs associated with various defense industry security concerns include the following:

• Unsolicited requests for scientific and technological (S&T) information

• Inappropriate conduct during visits

• Suspicious work offers

• Targeting at international exhibits, seminars, and conventions

• Exploitation of joint ventures and joint research

• Acquisitions of technology and companies

• Co-opting of former employees

• Targeting cultural commonalities

Identified activities or circumstances that are part of these MOs can serve as indicators. While these indicators do not always equate to an actual foreign collection threat, they can serve as a signal. A number of indicators in a given situation might warrant further examination.

Unsolicited Requests for Information

Unsolicited requests for U.S. defense industry S&T program information are the most frequently reported MO associated with foreign collection activity. Requests frequently involve faxing, mailing, e-mailing, or phoning to individual U.S. persons rather than corporate marketing departments. The requests may involve surveys or questionnaires and are frequently being sent over the Internet. Marketing surveys can elicit sensitive technological and business information. With this particular method, it is important to consider who is the end user of the information and who is completing the survey. Increasing use of the Internet provides a method of direct communication with government and U.S. industry for foreign collection purposes. Internet access to a company's bulletin board, home page, and employees provides a foreign collector with many avenues to broaden collection efforts.

Indicators

- The Internet address is in a foreign country.

- The recipient has never met the sender.

- Requester may be associated with an embargoed country.

- Technology requested is classified, controlled by International Traffic in Arms Regulations (ITAR), on the Militarily Critical Technologies List (MCTL), or has both commercial and military applications.

- The requester identifies his or her status as a student or consultant.

- The requester identifies his or her employer as a foreign government or states that the work is being done for a foreign government or program.

- The requester asks about a technology associated with a defense-related program, project, or contract.

- The requester asks questions about defense-related programs using acronyms specific to the program.

- The requester insinuates that the third party he or she works for is classified.

- The requester admits he or she could not get the information elsewhere because it was classified or controlled.

- The requester advises the recipient to disregard the request if it causes a security problem or if it is for information the recipient cannot provide due to security classification, export controls, and so forth.

- The requester advises the recipient not to worry about security concerns.

- The requester assures the recipient that export licenses are not required or are not a problem.

- Marketing surveys may be faxed or mailed to an individual via the company marketing office.

- Marketing surveys may be sent by foreign consortiums or a consulting company.

- Foreign companies with foreign intelligence involvement are likely to be a consortium of officials, military officers, or private interests.

- Marketing surveys often may exceed generally accepted terms of marketing information.

- There are strong indications that the "surveyor" is employed by a competing foreign company.

- Surveys may solicit proprietary information concerning corporate affiliations, market projections, pricing policies, program or technology director's names, company personnel working on the program, purchasing practices, and types and dollar amounts of U.S. government contracts.

- Customer and supplier bases for a company may also be sent marketing surveys that exceed accepted terms of marketing information.

Recommended Security Countermeasures

- Have a written company policy on how to respond to requests.

- Brief employees not to respond to suspicious requests.

- Brief employees to report suspicious incidents to the facility security officer (FSO).

- Review how much information you have in the open domain (i.e., what's on your Web site?).

- Have a technology control plan.

- Train employees to recognize and report suspicious marketing surveys.

Inappropriate Conduct during Visits

Foreign visits to cleared U.S. defense contractors can present potential security risks if sound risk management is not practiced.

Indicators

- Visitors are escorted by a foreign liaison officer or embassy official who attempts to conceal their official identities during a supposed commercial visit.

- Hidden agendas become evident, as opposed to the stated purpose of the visit (e.g., visitors arrive to discuss program X but do everything to discuss and meet with personnel who work with program Y).

- Last minute additions and unannounced persons are added to the visiting party.

- "Wandering" visitors act offended when confronted.

- Alternative mechanisms are used. For example, if a classified visit request is disapproved, the foreign entity may attempt a commercial visit.

- Visitors ask questions during briefing outside the scope of the approved visit, hoping to get a courteous or spontaneous response.

Recommended Security Countermeasures

- Brief all employees about threat issues surrounding foreign visits.

- Ensure that appropriate personnel, both escorts and those meeting with visitors, are briefed on the scope of the visit.

- Ensure that the number of escorts per visitor group is adequate to properly control the movement and conduct of visitors.

- Have a technology control plan.

Suspicious Work Offers

Foreign scientists and engineers will offer their services to research facilities, academic institutions, and even cleared defense contractors. This offer may be an MO to place a foreign national inside the facility to collect information on a desired technology.

Indicators

- Foreign applicant has a scientific background in a specialty/technology for which his or her country has been identified as having a collection requirement.

- Foreign applicant offers services for free. The foreign government, or the corporation associated with the government, is paying expenses.

- Foreign interns (students working on master or doctorate degree) offer to work under a knowledgeable individual for free, usually for a period of two to three years.

- The technology in which the foreign individual wants to conduct research is frequently related to, or may be classified as, ITAR, MCTL, or export controlled.

Recommended Security Countermeasures

- Have a technology control plan.
- Provide employees with periodic security awareness briefings with regard to long-term foreign visitors.
- Check backgrounds and references.
- Request a threat assessment from the program office.

International Exhibits, Conventions, and Seminars

These functions directly link programs and technologies with knowledgeable personnel.

Indicators

- Topics at the seminars and conventions deal with classified or controlled technologies or applications.
- The country or organization sponsoring the seminar or conference has tried unsuccessfully to visit the facility.
- Someone attending the convention receives an invitation to brief or lecture in foreign country with expenses paid.
- Requests for presentation summary are made 6 to 12 months prior to the seminar.
- Photography and filming appears suspicious.
- Attendees wear false name tags.

Recommended Security Countermeasures

- Consider what information is being exposed, where, when, and to whom.
- Provide employees with detailed travel briefings concerning the threat, precautions to take, and how to react to elicitation.
- Take mockup displays instead of real equipment.
- Request a threat assessment from the program office.
- Restrict information provided to what is only necessary for travel and hotel accommodations.

- Carefully consider whether equipment or software can be adequately protected.

Joint Ventures/Joint Research

Coproduction and various exchange agreements potentially offer significant collection opportunities for foreign interests to target restricted technology.

Indicators

- Resident foreign representative faxes documents to an embassy or another country in a foreign language.

- Foreign representative wants to access the local area network (LAN).

- Foreign representative wants unrestricted access to the facility.

- U.S. contractors are enticed to provide large amounts of technical data as part of the bidding process, only to have the contract canceled.

- Potential technology sharing agreements during the joint venture are one-sided.

- The foreign organization sends more foreign representatives than is necessary for the project.

- The foreign representatives single out company personnel to elicit information outside the scope of the project.

Recommended Security Countermeasures

- Review all documents being faxed or mailed, and have someone to translate when necessary.

- Provide foreign representatives with stand-alone computers.

- Share the minimum amount of information appropriate to the scope of the joint venture/research.

- Educate employees extensively on the scope of the project and how to deal with and report elicitation. Initial education must be followed by periodic sustainment training.

- Refuse to accept unnecessary foreign representatives into the facility.

Foreign Acquisition of Technology and Companies

Foreign entities attempt to gain access to sensitive technologies by purchasing U.S. companies and technology.

Indicators

- Companies of political and military allies are most likely associated with this activity.

- New employees hired from the foreign parent company or its foreign partners wish to access classified data immediately.

- Foreign parent company may attempt to circumvent or mitigate the Foreign Ownership, Control of Influence (FOCI) process.

Recommended Security Countermeasures

- Request a threat assessment from your security or program office.

- Scrutinize employees hired at the behest of foreign entity.

- Conduct frequent checks of foreign visits to determine if foreign interests are attempting to circumvent the security agreements.

- Provide periodic threat briefings to outside directors and user agencies.

Co-opting Former Employees

Former employees who had access to sensitive, proprietary, or classified S&T program information remain a potential counterintelligence concern. Targeting cultural commonalities to establish rapport is often associated with the collection attempt. Former employees may be viewed as excellent prospects for collection operations and considered less likely to feel obligated to comply with U.S. government or corporate security requirements.

Indicators

- Former employee took a job with a foreign company working on the same technology.

- Former employee maintains contact with former company and employees.

- The employee alternates working with U.S. companies and foreign companies every few years.

Recommended Security Countermeasures

- Brief employees to be alert to actions of former employees returning to the facility.

- Have a policy concerning visitation or contacts with current employees by former employees.

- Debrief former employees upon termination of employment, and reinforce their responsibilities concerning their legal responsibilities to protect classified, proprietary, and export-controlled information.

Targeting Cultural Commonalities

Foreign entities exploit the cultural background of company personnel in order to elicit information.

Indicators

- Employees receive unsolicited greetings or other correspondence from embassy of country of family origin.

- Employees receive invitations to visit country of family origin for purpose of providing lecture or receiving an award.

- Foreign visitors single out company personnel of same cultural background to work or socialize with.

Recommended Security Countermeasures

- Brief all employees on this MO and have a policy concerning the reporting of same.

- Monitor the activities of foreign visitors for indications of their targeting of company personnel.

If you believe that any of these situations apply to your company, you should immediately notify your security office. Likewise, notify security of any indication that your company or any of your employees may be the target of an attempted exploitation by the intelligence service or commercial interests of another country. Reports of actual, probable, or possible espionage should be submitted to the FBI.

REPORTING IMPROPER, UNRELIABLE, AND SUSPICIOUS BEHAVIOR

Reporting Responsibilities

If you are entrusted with safeguarding classified material, you are expected to report potentially significant, factual information that comes to your attention and that raises potential security concerns about a coworker. You are also strongly encouraged to help coworkers who are having personal problems that may become a security issue if the problems are not addressed.

Presidential Executive Order 12968 on "Access to Classified Information" states: "Employees are encouraged and expected to report any information that raises doubts as to whether another employee's continued eligibility for access to classified information is clearly consistent with the national security." It states further that the head of each agency that grants access to classified information shall establish a program to educate employees with access to classified information about their individual responsibilities under this order. This security guide meets that requirement.

What and when to report is a question of ethics and good judgment in determining what is in the best interests of your country, your organization, and your colleagues. The rules on this are very general, as there can never be enough rules to cover all the situations you might encounter.

In considering your responsibility to report potentially significant, factual information about coworkers, think carefully about the following: As Americans, we place a high value on our privacy. When we have to make intrusions upon another person's privacy in the name of security, this must be clearly justified and implemented in a fair and consistent manner. It is important for you to report indicators of illegal, improper, unreliable, or suspicious behavior by a coworker for the following reasons:

- The amount of damage that can be done by a single insider working for the other side has increased enormously with the growth of interconnected computer networks.

- It is now clear that employee and supervisor decisions to report adverse information about coworkers — or decisions not to report such information — have played a significant role in our counterintelligence successes and failures. See the next section, "People Who Made a Difference."

- Our goal is to help employees with problems *before* they get into serious trouble.

- If you are a contractor, compromise of the advanced technology on which your company's business is based will affect your company's bottom line. This could cause you (and your coworkers) to lose your job or your next raise.

Your vigilance is the best single defense in protecting information, operations, facilities, and people. Apathy, disbelief, or fear of what might happen if we become involved sometimes cause us to look away rather than confront troublesome behavior. But looking the other way from counterintelligence or security issues can pose a risk to a colleague's well-being as well as to your organization and the national security.

You are not expected to be an armchair security officer or psychologist, nor should you conduct your own investigation to verify or validate information. Your role is to be aware of potential issues and to exercise good judgment in determining what and when to report. The key is to intervene, when appropriate, in the interest of national security and your organization and to protect a colleague from his or her own potentially self-destructive behavior.

Information should be reported to a person in your chain of command, to your security office, or to a counterintelligence office. Report it to the person or office in which you have the most confidence that they will take appropriate action and protect your identity as the source of the information. You may also report it anonymously by calling one of the hotlines that many organizations have set up for this purpose.

The following section, "People Who Made a Difference," describes actual cases when an employee's decision to report or not report helped a colleague, caught a spy, or allowed a spy to continue unchecked.

Understanding your professional obligations will help you overcome the natural and understandable hesitation to report potentially adverse information about a coworker who may also be a friend. All reports will be checked out with the utmost confidentiality and discretion. If you so desire, you need not be identified as the source of the information. Security personnel have extensive experience handling such reports in a professional manner that protects your interests.

PEOPLE WHO MADE A DIFFERENCE

The following are actual cases in which a coworker's decision to report or not to report made a difference. Coworkers were helped, spies were caught, and other spies got away because of decisions made by people just like you.

Helping a Coworker

Financial Stress

A coworker reported to the security office that a senior intelligence official was experiencing serious financial problems. The problems were so serious that the individual had reportedly commented, "I don't know what I would do if someone offered me $100,000 for classified information."

Based on this report, a representative from the security office interviewed this official. It was learned that his financial problems had been snowballing over the previous six months. Although the official was making a serious attempt to solve his problems, these efforts were not helping.

As a result of the individual's cooperative attitude, the official was allowed to remain in a fully cleared status while formulating a plan to resolve his financial problems. He was assisted in securing a well-paying, part-time second job. While working that job for six months, he was able to resolve his financial problems and build up a small nest egg to deal with future eventualities.

Depression

A government employee in one of the intelligence agencies reported that her coworker, "Jim," appeared sad, lethargic, and inattentive. Jim had previously been somewhat shy but usually pleasant and alert. The coworker engaged him in conversation and found that he was quite despondent about his proposed reassignment. As the two spoke, the coworker was impressed by the degree of Jim's sadness, and she inquired as to just how badly the employee was feeling. Jim acknowledged that he had considered "just going to sleep forever." Concerned, she reported the conversation to her security officer, who arranged for Jim to be seen by an agency doctor.

The medical office confirmed that Jim was actually contemplating suicide. It arranged for Jim to receive treatment for depression, and management was able to address Jim's concerns about his reassignment. With his depression treated medically, Jim was able to begin his new assignment with a more realistic and optimistic point of view.

Alcohol Abuse

"Jane" was referred to the employee assistance program after several employees commented during a routine reinvestigation that their colleague drank heavily. Evaluation revealed that Jane had been drinking heavily for years and required an immediate referral to an alcohol treatment program. Regrettably, previous supervisors had recognized the problem but were unwilling to take action because the drinking did not impact Jane's work performance.

Jane successfully completed the treatment program and returned to work.

Catching a Spy

These are stories of people just like you who made a difference by helping to catch a spy. When they saw or heard something that raised a suspicion, they chose to act. They made a call that helped to protect our national security.

Reported Compromise of State Department Communication

Steven Lalas, an American of Greek descent, was a State Department communications officer stationed with the U.S. Embassy in Athens, Greece. He was arrested in 1993 and sentenced to 14 years in prison for passing sensitive military information to Greek officials. He began spying for the Greek government in 1977 while with the U.S. Army.

A report by a State Department official triggered the investigation leading to Lalas's arrest. He reported the apparent compromise of a State Department communication. In a conversation with an official of the Greek Embassy in Washington, the Greek official had revealed knowledge of information that could only have come from a Secret communication between the State Department and the U.S. Embassy in Athens. Investigation pointed to Lalas, and this was confirmed by a videotape of him stealing documents intended for destruction.

Unexplained Income

Dr. Ronald Hoffman managed a secret Air Force contract for Science Applications International Corporation (SAIC). From 1986 to 1990, he sold restricted space technology to four Japanese companies — Mitsubishi, Nissan, Toshiba, and IHI, Inc. — and was paid over $500,000. Hoffman was caught, prosecuted, and convicted because an alert secretary saw something that didn't seem right and reported it. She accidentally saw a fax from Mitsubishi to Hoffman advising of the deposit of $90,000 to his account and requesting his confirmation that the funds were received. The secretary's husband was also suspicious of Hoffman's lifestyle — two Corvettes, an Audi, a gorgeous sailboat, and fine home that didn't seem compatible with his SAIC income.

Here's the secretary's message to others: "No matter what your level in the company, whether you are an engineer or just a clerk or even a person in the mailroom, don't be afraid to stick your neck out and say something. Be accountable."

Excessive Use of Photocopier

A coworker reported in 1986 that Michael H. Allen was spending excessive time at the photocopier in their office. This report led to investigation by the Naval Investigative Service. A hidden camera was installed near the photocopier in Allen's office. The resulting videotape showed Allen copying documents and hiding them in his pocket.

Allen was a retired Navy senior chief radioman working at the Cubi Point Naval Air Station in the Philippines. He confessed to passing classified information to Philippine Intelligence in an effort to promote his local business interests. He was found guilty of 10 counts of espionage.

Removing Classified Information from the Office

Jonathan Jay Pollard was a naval intelligence analyst arrested for espionage on behalf of Israel. He used his access to classified libraries and computer systems to collect a huge amount of information, especially on Soviet weapons systems and the military capabilities of Arab countries. Over a period of 18 months until he was arrested in November 1986, he passed more than 1000 highly classified documents, many of them quite thick. He was sentenced to life in prison.

The investigation leading to Pollard's arrest was triggered by a coworker who reported seeing Pollard take a package of Top Secret material out of the building about 4:15 p.m. on a Friday afternoon. Although the package was appropriately wrapped and Pollard had a courier pass to carry such material to a neighboring building, which was not unusual, it did seem suspicious at that time on a Friday, especially because Pollard got into a car with his wife. Investigation rapidly confirmed that Pollard was regularly removing large quantities of highly classified documents.

Making a Serious Mistake

Many others have made serious errors by saying nothing, even when they had a clear obligation to do so. Our country suffered as a result.

Violations in Handling Classified Material

Navy spy Jerry Whitworth's work colleagues observed him monitoring and copying a sensitive communications line without authorization, saw classified papers in his personal locker, and knew Whitworth took classified materials home with him, but they believed he was doing it only to keep his work current. None of these Navy personnel reported these activities before Whitworth's arrest as part of the infamous John Walker spy ring. Their failure allowed the Walker ring to continue, with massive damage to U.S. national security.

Failure to Report

James R. Wilmoth was a U.S. Navy airman assigned to the carrier USS *Midway* in Japan. He was recruited by a Soviet KGB officer he met in a Japanese bar. As a food service worker, he had no access to classified information. In order to be able to earn money as a Soviet spy, he recruited a friend, Russell Paul Brown, who took classified documents from the burn bag in the electronic warfare center of the *Midway*. Although Wilmoth bragged about selling secrets to the Soviets, he wasn't taken seriously so no one reported him. When his Japanese girlfriend sent postcards to Wilmoth's shipmates from a vacation in Moscow, no one reported that either.

Excessive Use of Photocopier, Unexplained Affluence

Army Warrant Officer James W. Hall III was sentenced to 40 years in prison for spying for both the former East Germany and Soviet Union from 1982 to 1988. He compromised U.S. and NATO plans for the defense of Western Europe. After his arrest, Hall said there were many indicators that could have alerted those around him that he was involved in questionable activity.

Hall sometimes spent up to two hours of his workday reproducing classified documents to provide to the Soviets and East Germans. Concerned that he was not putting in his regular duty time, he consistently worked late to complete his regular assignments. Using his illegal income, Hall paid cash for a brand new Volvo and a new truck. He also made a large down payment on a home and took flying lessons. He is said to have given his military colleagues at least six conflicting stories to explain his lavish lifestyle, but Hall's coworkers never reported any of his unusual activities. After returning from Germany to the United States, he traveled to Vienna, Austria, to meet with his Soviet handler.

APPENDIX E

Security Articles:
Foreign Travel Risks

RISKS DURING FOREIGN TRAVEL

You Are the Target

The risk of becoming an intelligence target increases greatly during foreign travel. As an American government official, scientist, or business traveler with access to useful information, you can become the target of a foreign intelligence or security service at anytime in any country. The threat is certainly not limited to so-called unfriendly countries.

Never think, "They wouldn't dare risk something like that against me. They have too much at stake." Many countries do risk it, routinely, because the potential benefits are great and the risks are very low when an intelligence service is operating on its home turf. Even U.S. government cabinet level officials and corporate CEOs have been assigned to bugged hotel rooms and had all their documents secretly photographed or their laptop computers accessed.

Conversely, never think you are too low-ranking to be of interest. Secretaries, file clerks, and cleaning crew are targeted because they can often provide access to valuable information.

Foreign government scrutiny of you while visiting another country may occur by design or chance for any of the following reasons:

- You have government, business, scientific, or technical information of potential value to a foreign government or a local industry.

- You have relatives or organizational affiliations or speak the local language fluently in the country you are visiting.

- You fit a terrorism, narcotic trafficking, criminal, or other profile.

- You buy or sell on the black market.

- The local government discovers on your person or in your luggage literature that is banned or strictly controlled.

- You are associating with individuals the host government considers as political dissidents.

Here are some of the common methods that may be used. Most activities directed against you will be conducted in an unobtrusive manner that you are very unlikely to notice. Others are sometimes conducted in a rather crude manner that is observable.

Methods

Assessment. Friendly discussion with local contacts who assess whether you have information of value and seek to identify any personal attitudes, beliefs, problems, or needs that could be exploitable.

Elicitation. A ploy whereby seemingly normal conversation is contrived to extract intelligence information of value. Advantages of this technique are that it does the following:

- Puts someone at ease to share information

- Is difficult to recognize as an intelligence technique

- Is easily deniable

Eavesdropping. Listening to other peoples' conversations to gather information.

- Frequently done in social environments where attendees feel comfortable and secure and, therefore, are more likely to talk about themselves or their work.

- Frequent venues include restaurants, bars, and public transportation.

- Eavesdropping can occur in a radius of six to eight seats on public transportation or 10 to 12 feet in other settings.

Technical eavesdropping. Use of audio and visual devices, usually concealed.

- Relatively cost efficient and low risk.

- Concealed devices can be installed in public and private facilities such as hotel rooms, restaurants, offices, and automobiles.

Black bag operations. Surreptitious entry into someone's hotel room to steal, photograph, or photocopy documents; steal or copy magnetic media; or download from laptop computers.

- Often conducted or condoned by host government intelligence or security services or by operatives for local corporations
- Frequently done with cooperation of hotel staff

Surveillance. Occurs when someone follows you to determine your contacts and activities.

- Labor intensive if done correctly. Not usually done unless the subject is suspected of improper activity or a target of great interest.

Theft of information. Stealing documents, briefcases, laptop computers, or sensitive equipment.

- Laptop computers are especially vulnerable as they may contain a treasure trove of information.
- Theft of laptops from hotel rooms and while transiting airports is especially common.
- The laptop may have been stolen for the value of the laptop rather than value of the information it contained. You may never know whether or not the information was compromised.

Intercepting electronic communications. Telephones, fax, telex, and computers can all be monitored electronically.

- You are particularly vulnerable while communicating to, from, or within foreign countries, as most foreign telecommunications systems cooperate with their country's security service. Office, hotel, and portable telephones (including cellular) are key targets.

How to Protect Yourself

Common sense and basic counterintelligence (CI) awareness can effectively protect you against foreign attempts to collect sensitive, proprietary, and other privileged information. A few tips are listed here:

- Arrange a pretravel briefing from your security office.

- Maintain physical control of all sensitive documents or equipment at all times. Do not leave items that would be of value to a foreign intelligence service unattended in hotel rooms or stored in hotel safes.

- Limit sensitive discussions. Hotel rooms or other public places are rarely suitable to discuss sensitive information.

- Do not use computer or facsimile equipment at foreign hotels or business centers for sensitive matters.

- Do not divulge information to anyone not authorized to hear it.

- Ignore or deflect intrusive inquiries or conversation about business or personal matters.

- Keep unwanted material until it can be disposed of securely. Burn or shred paper and cut floppy disks in pieces and discard.

- Keep your laptop computer as carry-on baggage — never check it with other luggage and, if possible, remove or control storage media.

- If secure communications equipment is accessible, use it to discuss business matters.

- Report any incident to the relevant U.S. government agency or your local security office.

COUNTRY-SPECIFIC THREAT UPDATES

The State Department's Bureau of Consular Affairs maintains travel warnings and consular information sheets with rules and regulations pertaining to foreign travelers for every country in the world. This information is available by telephone, fax, and computer:

- Telephone: (202) 647-5225

- Fax: (202) 647-3000

- Internet: http://travel.state.gov, then click on Travel Warnings and Consular Information Sheets.

The State Department travel warnings and consular information sheets are a basic source of up-to-date, valuable information that all travelers should check prior to their departure.

Other Internet sites also have current information of value to travelers. Some of these are listed here. Note that the Internet addresses for these sites do change from time to time.

- Health information: Centers for Disease Control and Prevention (CDC) has a site devoted to health recommendations for various geographic areas, disease outbreaks, and vaccine requirements. The address is www.cdc.gov/travel/index.htm.

- Weather information: Worldwide weather information is available at several sites including http://weather.yahoo.com.

- Foreign exchange rates: Exchange rates are available at http://quote.yahoo.com. Click on World Markets, then Currency Exchange Rates.

- Online publications: State Department and other publications on various aspects of traveling and living abroad are found under Travel Publications at http://travel.state.gov.

- Business travelers: A consolidated index of information for business travelers and Americans residing overseas is at www.state.gov/e/eb/cba.

APPENDIX F

Security Articles: The Internet

INTERNET: THE FASTEST GROWING MODUS OPERANDI FOR UNSOLICITED COLLECTION

Based on reports of suspicious foreign contacts submitted, the Internet is the fastest growing modus operandi of unsolicited correspondence using computer elicitation between foreign entities and cleared U.S. companies and their employees. Foreign entities use the Internet to contact a wide variety of knowledgeable persons, with the intention to collect various pieces of information from each based on their area of expertise. This information is then put together in an amazingly clear mosaic, revealing a level of detail that no one individual would have been able to provide.

Use of the Internet offers a variety of advantages to a foreign collector. It is simple, low cost, nonthreatening, and relatively risk free for the foreign entity attempting to collect classified, proprietary, or sensitive information. These foreign entities can remain safe within their own borders while sending hundreds of pleas and requests for assistance to targeted U.S. companies and their employees. The unsolicited request for information, including use of the Internet, is the most frequently used modus operandi by "closed countries" and may often be worded to appeal to cultural commonalities.

One recent Internet request, sent from a foreign entity to cleared U.S. contractors, was a blatant unsolicited request for references to military projects that use software tools for networked, real-time operating systems (airborne, space, missile, tactical, intelligence, etc.). In the request, the foreign entity acknowledged much of the information would probably be classified. He also acknowledged his foreign "military customer" was too classified to be directly involved in sending the request over the Internet, so he was performing the request as a service to the foreign government.

In another report of suspicious activity involving the Internet, a cleared U.S. company received a request to market a software program, with intelligence applications, to intelligence and security organizations in an Eastern European country. The software program enables the quick integration of multiple data sources and millions of documents with incredible speed, and it can be used as an investigative tool to search various Web sites. At a minimum, foreign companies can use the software program to acquire competitive business intelligence off the Internet.

In many foreign countries, access to the Internet is potentially through a government host. Any foreign contact with these countries via the Internet is subject to intelligence and security service vetting and monitoring to prevent the loss of technical secrets and collection and exploitation of Western technology. Access to Internet search software will undoubtedly assist foreign intelligence and security services in searching and monitoring the Internet for both intelligence and counterintelligence purposes. In one East European country, the number of Internet hosts has grown exponentially, making it more difficult to isolate intelligence officers attempting to use the Internet to break into U.S. computer systems. Foreign intelligence services are known to use computers to conduct rudimentary online searches for information, including visits to government and defense contractors' online bulletin boards or Web sites on the Internet. Access to Internet advanced search software programs could possibly assist them in meeting their collection requirements.

While the use of advanced software tools by foreign intelligence and security services is inevitable, security lessons can be learned from these reported incidents, and we can implement security countermeasures to mitigate demonstrated vulnerabilities. We know foreign entities use the Internet because it provides an easy, low-cost, risk-free means to solicit information. We also know foreign intelligence and security services monitor the Internet and have the advanced software tools to make their searches and investigations much easier.

All requests for information received via the Internet should be viewed with suspicion. Only respond to people who are personally known and only after verifying the identity and address of the requester. Verification is important, as the possibility exists for foreign entities to present themselves as impostors. If a request is received from an unknown source or is not in character with the nature of requests normally made by a known source, a copy of the request should be provided to the security office and the request should not be responded to in any way.

The following is a list of suspicious indicators of foreign collection efforts via computer elicitation:

- The address is in a foreign country.

- The recipient has never met the sender.

- The sender identifies his or her status as a student or consultant.

- The sender identifies his or her employer as a foreign government, or states that the work is being done for a foreign government or program.

- The sender asks about a technology associated with a defense-related program, project, or contract.

- The sender asks questions about defense-related programs using acronyms specific to the program.

- The sender insinuates that the third party he or she is working for is classified or otherwise sensitive.

- The sender admits he or she could not get the information elsewhere because it was classified or controlled.

- The sender advises the recipient to disregard the request if it causes a security problem, or the request is for information the recipient cannot provide due to security classification, export controls, and so on.

- The sender advises the recipient not to worry about security concerns.

- The sender assures the recipient that export licenses are not required or not a problem.

APPROPRIATE USE OF COMPUTER SYSTEMS

Misuse of an automated information system is sometimes illegal, often unethical, and always reflects poor judgment or lack of care in following security rules and regulations. Misuse may, unintentionally, create security vulnerabilities or cause damage to important information. A pattern of inability or unwillingness to follow rules for the operation of computer systems raises concerns about an individual's reliability and trustworthiness.

As we store more and more information in computer databases, and as these databases become more closely linked in networks, more people have broader access to more information than ever before. Computer technology has magnified many times the ability of a careless or disaffected employee to cause severe damage.

Owing to the magnitude of problems that can be caused by misuse of computer systems, the misuse of information systems is now one of the 13 criteria used in adjudicating approval and revocation of security clearances for access to classified information.

Proper computer use is governed by your organization's IT security policies. Wherein the information stored on the computer system relates to national defense, sensitive infrastructure information identifies current or future projects and programs of a sensitive nature, financial and personnel data. Such information may also be covered under federal government regulations and even federal law. Many government agencies and defense contractors specify the security procedures and prohibited or inappropriate activities discussed next.

Security Rules

The following are basic rules for the secure use of the computer:

- Do not enter into any computer system without authorization. Unauthorized entry into a protected or compartmented computer file is a serious security violation and is probably illegal. It can be a basis for revocation of your security clearance. Whether motivated by the challenge of penetrating the system or by simple curiosity to see what is there, unauthorized entry is a deliberate disregard for rules and regulations. It can cause you to be suspected of espionage. At a minimum, it violates the need-to-know principle and in some cases is an invasion of privacy.

- Do not store or process classified information on any system not explicitly approved for classified processing.

- Do not attempt to circumvent or defeat security or auditing systems without prior authorization from the system administrator, other than as part of an authorized system testing or security research.

- Do not use another individual's user ID, password, or identity.

- Do not install any software on your computer without the approval of your system administrator.

- Do not permit an unauthorized individual (including a spouse, relative, or friend) access to any sensitive computer network.

- Do not reveal your password to *anyone* — not even your computer system administrator.

- Do not respond to any telephone call from anyone whom you do not personally know who asks questions about your computer, how you use your computer, or about your user ID or password.

- If you are the inadvertent recipient of classified material sent via e-mail or become aware of classified material on an open bulletin board or Web site, you must report this to the security office.

- Do not modify or alter the operating system or configuration of any system without first obtaining permission from the owner or administrator of that system.

- Do not use your office computer system to gain unauthorized access to any other computer system.

Inappropriate Use

Many offices permit some minimal personal use of office equipment when such personal use involves minimal expense to the organization, is performed on your personal nonwork time, does not interfere with the office's mission, and does not violate standards of ethical conduct.

The following activities are considered to be misuse of office equipment:

- The creation, download, viewing, storage, copying, or transmission of sexually explicit or sexually oriented materials (such computer use can cause you to be fired from your job)

- Annoying or harassing another individual, for example, through uninvited e-mail of a personal nature or using lewd or offensive language (such computer use can cause you to be fired from your job)

- Use for commercial purposes or in support of for-profit activities or in support of other outside employment, business activity (e.g., consulting for pay, sales, or administration of business transactions, sale of goods or services), or gambling

- Engaging in any outside fund-raising activity, endorsing any product or service, participating in any lobbying activity, or engaging in any prohibited partisan political activity

- The creation, copying, transmission, or retransmission of chain letters or other unauthorized mass mailings

- Any activities that are illegal, inappropriate, or offensive to fellow employees or the public (such activities include hate speech or material that ridicules others on the basis of race, creed, religion, color, sex, disability, national origin, or sexual orientation)

- Use for posting office information to any external news group, chat room, bulletin board, or other public forum without authority

- Any personal use that could cause congestion, delay, or disruption of service to any office equipment (this includes sending pictures, video, or sound files or other large file attachments that can degrade computer network performance)

- The unauthorized acquisition, use, reproduction, transmission, or distribution of any controlled information (this includes copyrighted computer software, other copyrighted or trademarked material or material with intellectual property rights [beyond fair use], privacy information, and proprietary data or export-controlled data or software)

E-mail

There are two big problems with e-mail. One is increased risk of accidental security compromise. The other is sending inappropriate materials by e-mail, which has caused many people to be fired from their jobs.

Security Risks with E-mail

As a result of the Internet and e-mail, there has been a sharp increase in security incidents involving the accidental disclosure of classified and other sensitive information. One common problem occurs when individuals download a seemingly unclassified file from a classified system and then fail to carefully review this file before sending it as an attachment to an e-mail message. Too often, the seemingly unclassified file actually has some classified material or classification markings that are not readily apparent when the file is viewed online. Sending such material by e-mail is a security violation even if the recipient has an appropriate security clearance, as e-mail can easily be monitored by unauthorized persons.

More important, even if the downloaded file really is unclassified, the electronic version of that file may have recoverable traces of classified information. This happens because data are stored in "blocks." If a file does not take up an entire block, the remainder of that block may have recoverable traces of data from other files. Your system administrator must follow an approved technical procedure for removing these traces before the file is treated as unclassified.

Some organizations have found it necessary to lock their computer drives to prevent any downloading of files from the classified system. If an individual wishes to download and retransmit an unclassified file from a classified system, the file must be downloaded and processed by the system administrator to remove electronic traces of other files before it is retransmitted.

Inappropriate Materials

Sending e-mail is like sending a postcard through the mail. Just as the mail carrier and others have an opportunity to read a postcard, network eavesdroppers can read your e-mail as it passes through the Internet from computer to computer. E-mail is not like a telephone call, where your privacy rights are protected by law.

The courts have repeatedly sided with employers who monitor their employees' e-mail or Internet use. In an American Management Association poll, 47% of major companies reported that they store and review their employees' e-mail. Organizations do this to protect themselves against lawsuits, because the organization can be held liable for abusive, harassing, or otherwise inappropriate messages sent over its computer network. In the same poll, 25% of companies reported that they have fired employees for misuse of the Internet or office e-mail.

In the past few years, *The New York Times* fired 23 employees for exchanging off-color e-mail. Xerox fired 40 people for inappropriate Internet use. Dow Chemical fired 24 employees and disciplined another 230 for sending or storing pornographic or violent material by e-mail.

Several years ago, Chevron Corp. had to pay $2.2 million to plaintiffs who successfully brought a suit of sexual harassment, in part because an employee sent an e-mail to coworkers listing the reasons why beer is better than women.

Security of Hard Drives

Secrets in the computer require the same protection as secrets on paper. Information can be recovered from a computer hard drive even after the file has been deleted or erased by the computer user. It is estimated that about a third of the average hard drive contains information that has been "deleted" but is still recoverable.

When you delete a file, most computer operating systems delete only the "pointer" that allows the computer to find the file on your hard drive. The file itself is not deleted until it is overwritten by another file. This is comparable to deleting a chapter heading from the table of contents of a book, but not removing the pages on which the chapter is written. Some networks may be configured to "wipe" or purge the hard drive when information is deleted, but most are not.

Computers on which classified information is prepared must be kept in facilities that meet specified physical security requirements for processing classified information. Special procedures may also be appropriate when working with some types of sensitive unclassified information. At a minimum, special procedures for clearing hard drives are appropriate prior to disposing of old computers on which sensitive information has been prepared.

Check with your security office concerning rules for traveling with a laptop on which sensitive information has been prepared. Laptop computers are a particular concern owing to their vulnerability to theft.

Computer Passwords

Passwords are used to authenticate an individual's right to have access to certain information. Your password is for your use only. Lending it to someone else is a security violation and may result in disciplinary action against both parties. Never disclose your password to anyone. Memorize it — do not put it in writing. If you leave your terminal unattended for any reason, log off or use a screen lock. Otherwise, someone else could use your computer to access information they are not authorized to have. You will be held responsible if someone else uses your password in connection with a system transaction.

Do change your password regularly. Use a password with at least six and preferably eight characters and consisting of a mix of upper and lower case letters, numbers, and special characters such as punctuation marks. This mix of various types of characters makes it more difficult for a hacker to use an automated tool called a "password cracker" to discover your password. Cracking passwords is a common means by which hackers gain unauthorized access to protected systems.

Social Engineering

"Social engineering" is hacker-speak for conning legitimate computer users into providing useful information that helps the hacker gain unauthorized access to their computer system.

The hacker using social engineering usually poses as a legitimate person in the organization (maintenance technician, security officer, inexperienced computer user, VIP, etc.) and employs a plausible cover story to trick computer users into giving useful information. This is usually done by telephone, but it may also be done by forged e-mail messages or even in-person visits.

Most people have an incorrect impression of computer break-ins. They think they are purely technical, the result of technical flaws in computer systems, which the intruders are able to exploit. The truth is, however, that social engineering often plays a big part in helping an attacker slip through security barriers. A lack of security awareness or the gullibility of computer users often provides an easy stepping stone into the protected system if the attacker has no authorized access to the system at all.

Laptop Computers: Vulnerability to Theft

Laptop computers are a prime target for theft for the value of the information on them as well as for the value of the computer. According to Safeware, a computer insurance firm in Columbus, Ohio, 309,000 laptop computers were stolen in the United States during 1997. There is also a high risk of theft during foreign travel.

The best protection for information on your laptop is to encrypt all sensitive files and e-mail. A variety of keys, cards, and other physical means of preventing unauthorized access to information on a laptop are now coming on the market. Evaluate the various alternatives to see if one of them meets your needs.

Here are some other guidelines for protecting laptops:

- Never let a laptop out of your sight in an airport or other public area. If you set it down while checking in at the airport counter or hotel registration desk, lean it against your leg so that you can feel its presence, or hold it between your feet.

- When going through the airport security check, don't place your laptop on the conveyor belt until you are sure no one in front of you is being delayed. If you are delayed while passing through the checkpoint, keep your eye on your laptop.

- Never, ever, check your laptop (or other valuables) with your luggage.

- Never keep passwords or access phone numbers on the machine or in the case.

- If possible, put your laptop in a bag that does not resemble a laptop carrying case.

- If your hotel room has a safe, keep your laptop in the safe while you are out of the room.

- Before traveling, back up all files.

Do not view sensitive material on your laptop while in a public place, especially not in an airplane. It is common practice for your airplane seatmate to look at what is on your screen.

INTERNET SECURITY: "WATCH OUT FOR THE UNDERTOW: THE RISKS OF CHATTING"

One of the highest risks you face on the Net is when you "chat" in real time with other users. Catching yourself midstream in an online conversation with a statement such as "I can't say anymore, it's a sensitive area," is an example of what not to do. Live chat doesn't allow time to fully think before responding. When you're online you also miss visual clues normally picked up in face-to-face conversations. Take the following precautions when chatting online:

- Think before you respond during live chat sessions. Report requests for information as well as foreign contacts on the Net to your local security office.

- The best way to protect your privacy is to refrain from giving out personal information.

- Remember to avoid discussions of your work, technical expertise, clearance/access level, employer, and job location.

- Remember that sometimes you may find information on the Net that you believe to be classified or is in some way related to classified information.

- Do not confirm or deny any information. Immediately report these incidents to your security office.

SPIES ON THE INFORMATION HIGHWAY

An old poster from World War II reads: "Loose Lips Sink Ships." The vision of Americans at war drowning at sea was a powerful reminder that security begins with each of us. Today we tend to think such concerns are outdated and ripe for the museum. We hear about economic espionage and our eyes glaze over. Do we really believe that the world we live in is still concerned with national security?

Consider the following. Deployments of Americans all over the world require that they will not be taken by surprise, that the equipment they use is capable of dominating any battlefield. Abstract ideas like this mean little to the average listener. Just try to personalize the idea. What if your son or daughter depended on you to keep them alive? You would do everything in your power. But first you would have to be fully informed about the threat facing them in the world.

Espionage today is hardly like we once knew it. For the most part, researchers make up today's spies. Yesterday's spy is today's collector. Yesterday's spy was equipped with poison pens and secret cameras. Today's collector is equipped with a laptop computer and modem, not to mention a current library card. These modern spies review data banks, technical journals, and open publications for profit. They look for indications of new ideas, trends, or new conditions that may affect their own country in some way. They do not need to steal what they can read free of charge.

Armed with this basic knowledge, today's spies set about to gather specifics. They look for the specific people who have specific information. Aware that most Americans protect classified information, the modern spies look for things "on the drawing board" that can be acquired before the classification stamp is affixed.

Being patient people, the modern collectors then listen. They listen to our open phones, open faxes, open computers, and after-hour discussions. We Americans love to talk. We are active, while the collectors can be passive. They know that our national trait of impatience with methodical security measures will ultimately betray us. They simply have to wait for us to talk about classified information in open restaurants, on planes, and especially on the telephone.

You'll notice that I have not mentioned which country the new collectors represent. They could even represent another company. Economic advisers openly advertise in our newspapers on ways to get a jump on the competition.

These ideas range from soliciting information for payment from enterprising or disgruntled employees to eliciting information at conferences and symposia open to the general public.

What is the best defense against this new method of economic voyeurism? Know what you must protect! Prior to any joint meetings, have your team discuss what will and will not be discussed, and then stick to it. Check before you publish! Assume that if you say it out in the open, it is compromised.

There is enough proof in the field today to show that there is no safe means of communication. Today's economic collectors won't break a law if they don't have to. They'll just listen.

APPENDIX G

Internet Security Links

The following is a selected listing of various Internet security links of relevance to the security manager, security educator, and other individuals who have an abiding interest in various facets of security.

From many of these sites you can identify items of interest for further development within your security education programs. In some cases, they can be used for discussion; the development of handouts or articles for newsletters; and a variety of security education pamphlets. When the information you find is not from a government site, or it is not stated that the information is approved for public release, please contact the site organization via regular mail, telephone, or e-mail for permission to use.

Neither the publisher nor the authors control or guarantee the accuracy, relevance, timeliness, or completeness of these sites. Further, the inclusion of the Web sites is not intended to assign importance to those sites and the information contained therein, nor is it intended to endorse, recommend, or favor any views expressed, or commercial products or services offered on these outside sites, or the organizations sponsoring the sites, by trade name, trademark, manufacture, or otherwise.

We hope that you find these sites useful. We are interested in any positive or negative comments from the specific to the general. Please forward all comments as well as recommendations for new sites or other Web resources to roperc@rcn.com.

PORTALS AND INFORMATION ARCHIVES

* www.defenselink.mil/ (Official DoD Web Site, Defense Portal)

* www.hqda.army.mil/library (Pentagon Library)

- www.firstgov.gov/ (General Services Administration's [GSA's] Government Portal)

- www.dss.mil/seclib/index.htm (Defense Security Service [DSS] Security Library)

- www.loyola.edu/dept/politics/intel.html (Loyola College of Maryland Strategic, Military, and Economic Intelligence Portal)

- www.odci.gov/ic/ (U.S. Intelligence Community Portal)

- www.senate.gov (U.S. Senate)

- www.house.gov (U.S. House of Representatives)

- www.ncix.gov/index2.html (National Counterintelligence Executive)

- www.cia.gov/cia/publications/factbook/index.html (CIA World Factbook)

- www.c3i.osd.mil/org/sio/index.html (C3I org, Links and Documents)

- www.dtic.mil/whs/directives (Washington Headquarters Services Directives and Records Branch [Directives Section])

- www.dia.mil (Defense Intelligence Agency Public Home Page)

- www.nro.gov (National Reconnaissance Office Public Home Page)

- www.nsa.gov (National Security Agency Public Home Page)

- www.ncts.navy.mil/nol (NavyOnLine, Technical Gateway to U.S. Department of the Navy [DoN] Online Resources)

- www.af.mil/sites (U.S. Air Force Sites)

- www.army.mil/public/installations.htm (Army Installations and Facilities)

- www.fbi.gov/publications.htm (FBI Document Library; mostly pdf type documents)

- www.cerias.purdue.edu/coast/hotlist (many Information and Computer Security links categorized)

- www.gwu.edu/~nsarchiv/ (George Washington University, Washington, D.C. National Security Archive)

- www.access.gpo.gov (U.S. Government Printing Office)

- www.nara.gov (National Archives and Records Administration)

- www.nara.gov/fedreg/ (NARA Office of the Federal Register)

- www.ioss.gov (Interagency OPSEC Support Staff [IOSS] Home Page)

- www.ioss.gov/html/prod_serv.htm (IOSS Products and Services)

- www.opsec.org (Operations Security [OPSEC] Professionals Society; furthers the practice of operations security as a profession)

- www.asc.wpafb.af.mil/sfs/sfa/opsec.htm (Wright-Patterson AFB OPSEC Home Page)

- www.energy.gov/security/index.html (National DOE Security Page)

- www.energy.gov/HQPress/releases00/janpr/soprog.pdf (DOE Security Progress Report, January 2000)

- www.nv.doe.gov/opsec (DOE Nevada OPSEC)

- www.info-sec.com/pccip/web (President's Commission on Critical Infrastructure Protection)

- www.nipc.gov (National Infrastructure Protection Center)

- www.ndpo.gov (National Domestic Preparedness Office)

- www.fema.gov (Federal Emergency Management Agency)

- www.cia.gov/ (Central Intelligence Agency)

- www.whitehouse.gov/nsc/index.html (National Security Council)

- www.nstissc.gov (National Security Telecommunications and Information Systems Security Committee [NSTISSC])

- www.nstissc.gov/html/library.html (NSTISSC, Index of Security Issuances)

- www.nstissc.gov/html/Working_Groups/eta.html (NSTISSC Education, Training, and Awareness)

- www.osti.gov/html/osti/opennet/od.html (DoE Office of Nuclear and National Security Information)

- www.state.gov (Department of State [DoS] Home Page)

- www.nato.int/ (NATO Official Homepage)

- www.legal.gsa.gov/intro2.htm (Federal Statutes and Regulations)

- www.dcfl.gov (DoD Computer Forensics Lab)

- www.dcitp.gov/index2.html (DoD Computer Investigations Training Program)

- www.orau.gov/se (DOE Security Education Special Interest Group)

- www.nssg.gov (U.S. Commission on National Security in the 21st Century)

- www.bxa.doc.gov (Bureau of Export Administration [BEA], Department of Commerce)

- www.bxa.doc.gov/OSIES/Default.htm (BEA, Office of Strategic Industries and Economic Security)

- www.treas.gov/ofac (Treasury, Office of Foreign Assets Control)

- www.customs.treas.gov (Customs)

- www.customs.treas.gov/travel/travel.htm (Customs, Traveler Information)

- www.pmdtc.org (DoS, Office of Defense Trade Controls)

- www.gsa.gov (General Services Administration)

- http://hydra.gsa.gov/pbs/fps/framest/t02fs.htm (Federal Protective Service)

- www.cia.gov/ic/cms.html (Community Management Staff)

- www.cia.gov/cia/publications/factbook/index.html (CIA World Factbook)

- www.securitymagazine.com/government (Government Security News)

- www.cdiss.org (Center for Defense and International Security Studies)

- www.cdi.org (Center for Defense Information)

- http://cisac.stanford.edu (Stanford University Center for International Security and Cooperation)

- www.tscm.com/index.html (Granite Island Group; technical surveillance countermeasures in the commercial sphere)

- www.fas.org/index.html (Federation of American Scientists; wide-ranging government and security information)

- www.dcs.ftmeade.army.mil/FlashWeb/default.asp (Defense Courier Service Article Tracking)

- www.ntis.gov (U.S. Department of Commerce; official source for government-sponsored U.S. and worldwide scientific, technical, engineering, and business-related information)

- www.perscom.army.mil/gendocs/ccfpage.htm (assists security managers and SSOs who have responsibilities providing security clearance/SCI access eligibility support to members of the U.S. Army)

- www.nationalsecurity.org (Heritage Foundation National Security Site)

- www.cicentre.com (Center for CI and Security Studies; providers of unclassified security and counterintelligence training and information)

- www.infosyssec.org (Security Portal for Information Security Professionals)

- www.ifpo.org/secsurf.html (International Foundation for Protection Officers)

- www.angelfire.com/ca7/Security/dodsec.html (J. R.'s Global Security Resources)

CURRENT NEWS

- http://ebird.dtic.mil (Early Bird; highlights Department of Defense news from open sources)

- http://ebwest.dtic.mil (Early Bird alternate site)

- www.govexec.com (Government Executive Magazine)

- www.govexec.com/defense (Government Executive Magazine, Defense Related)

SEARCH ENGINES

- www.SearchMil.com (1 million military pages indexed and ranked in order of popularity)

- www.google.com (a highly rated general search engine)

- www.google.com/unclesam (Federal Government Search)

- www.northernlight.com (a highly rated general search engine)

- www.acronymfinder.com (Acronym Decoder)

FORMS SITES

- http://web1.whs.osd.mil/icdhome/FORMTAB.HTM (DoD forms program where security forms can be found)
- www.fedforms.gov (search for any federal forms)

COUNTERINTELLIGENCE

- www.dss.mil/seclib/index.htm (DSS Security Library)
- www.dtic.mil/mctl (Militarily Critical Technologies Information)
- www.ncix.gov/index2.html (National Counterintelligence Executive)
- www.nacic.gov/pubs/pubs.html (Publications)
- www.nacic.gov/cind/2000/00news.html (News and Developments)
- www.ncis.navy.mil/activities/Counterintel/Counterintel.html (Naval Criminal Investigative Service [NCIS], Counterintelligence)
- http://public.afosi.amc.af.mil/ (Air Force Office of Special Investigations [AF OSI])
- www.dtra.mil/st/ts_index.html (Defense Threat Reduction Agency [DTRA], Technology Security)
- www.darpa.mil/sio (Defense Advanced Research Projects Agency [DARPA], Security and Intelligence Directorate)
- www.fbi.gov/hq/nsd/ansir/ansir.htm (FBI ANSIR — Awareness of National Security Issues and Response Program)
- www.fbi.gov/majcases.htm (FBI Major Investigations, e.g., Hanssen et al.)
- www.house.gov/hunter/CoxReport.htm (Cox Report on Chinese Nuclear Espionage)
- www.cicentre.com (Center for CI and Security Studies; providers of unclassified security and counterintelligence training and information)
- www.kimsoft.com/kim-spy.htm (intelligence and counterintelligence links)
- www.intelbrief.com (an assortment of intelligence and security-related links and information)

- www.spymuseum.org (International Spy Museum)
- www.tscm.com/index.html (Granite Island Group; technical surveillance countermeasures in the commercial sphere)

INDUSTRIAL SECURITY

- www.dss.mil/seclib/index.htm (DSS Security Library)
- www.dss.mil/isec/nispom.htm (National Industrial Security Program Operating Manual)
- http://defenselink.mil/dodgc/doha/isp.html (DOHA Industrial Security Program)
- http://defenselink.mil/dodgc/doha/industrial (Industrial Security Clearance Decisions by the Defense Office of Hearings and Appeals [DOHA])
- www.xsp.org (Extranet for Security Professionals; Features Virtual Security Offices; security information and exchanges etc. in a secure environment requiring password and authentication)
- www.fbi.gov/hq/nsd/ansir/ansir.htm (FBI ANSIR — Awareness of National Security Issues and Response Program)
- www.sed.monmouth.army.mil/114/isac (Monmouth County, NJ, ISAC)
- www.dtra.mil/st/ts_index.html (Defense Threat Reduction Agency [DTRA], Technology Security)
- www.darpa.mil/sio (Defense Advanced Research Projects Agency [DARPA], Security and Intelligence Directorate)
- www.nsi.org (National Security Institute; wide-ranging security awareness and training information)
- www.cfisac.org (Central Florida ISAC)
- www.sdisac.com (San Diego, CA, ISAC)
- www.asisonline.org (American Society for Industrial Security [ASIS])
- www.securitymanagement.com (ASIS)
- www.classmgmt.com (National Classification Management Society, Inc.; advances the practice of classification management as a profession)

- www.opsec.org (Operations Security [OPSEC] Professionals Society; furthers the practice of operations security as a profession)
- www.siaonline.org (Security Industry Association)
- www.dlis.dla.mil/CAGESearch (Defense Logistics Information Service CAGE Code Search)
- www.dss.mil/isec/briefings/gca/index.htm (GCA Training and Use of DD Form 254 briefing)
- www.ifpo.org/secsurf.html (International Foundation for Protection Officers)
- www.angelfire.com/ca7/Security/dodsec.html (J. R.'s Global Security Resources)

INDUSTRIAL SECURITY AWARENESS COUNCILS (ISACS)

- www.sed.monmouth.army.mil/114/isac (Monmouth County, NJ, ISAC)
- www.cfisac.org (Central Florida ISAC)
- www.sdisac.com (San Diego, CA, ISAC)
- www.greaterla-isac.com (Greater Los Angeles, CA, ISAC)
- www.isac-ok.org (Lawton, Oklahoma City, and Tulsa, OK, ISAC)

INFORMATION SECURITY AWARENESS

- www.classmgmt.com (National Classification Management Society, Inc.; advances the practice of classification management as a profession)
- www.dtic.mil/dtic/stinfo (DoD Scientific and Technical Information (STINFO) Manager Training Program)
- www.osti.gov/html/osti/opennet/od.html (DOE Office of Nuclear and National Security Information)
- www.orau.gov/se (DOE Security Education Special Interest Group)
- www.fbi.gov/hq/nsd/ansir/ansir.htm (FBI ANSIR — Awareness of National Security Issues and Response Program)
- www.nsi.org (National Security Institute; wide-ranging security awareness and training information, Information Systems Security Awareness)

- www.disa.mil/infosec/tsp.html (Defense Information Systems Agency [DISA] Information Assurance Education, Training, Awareness, and Products Branch)

- https://iase.disa.mil/index2.html (DISA Information Assurance Support Environment)

- www.cert.org (The CERT Coordination Center [CERT/CC] is a center for Internet security expertise located at the Software Engineering Institute, a federally funded research and development center operated by Carnegie Mellon University)

- http://csrc.ncsl.nist.gov (Computer Security Resource Center, National Institute of Standards and Technology)

- www.securityfocus.com (Security Focus, AIS-oriented information)

- www.darpa.mil/sio (Defense Advanced Research Projects Agency [DARPA], Security and Intelligence Directorate)

- www.fbi.gov/hq/nsd/ansir/ansir.htm (FBI ANSIR-Awareness of National Security Issues and Response Program)

- http://cisr.nps.navy.mil/Publications.html (Center for Information Assurance and INFOSEC Studies and Research, Naval Postgraduate School)

- www.pgp.com (PGP Security; assists companies to secure their e-business operations through firewall, encryption, intrusion, detection, risk assessment, and VPN technologies)

- www.cerias.purdue.edu (Center for Education and Research in Information Assurance and Security [CERIAS], Purdue University)

- www.cerias.purdue.edu/coast/coast.html (CERIAS, Computer Operations, Audit, and Security Technology [COAST])

- www.nsa.gov/isso/index.html (National Security Agency; information systems security organization)

- www.afcea.org (Armed Forces Communications and Electronics Association)

- www.nsi.org (National Security Institute; wide-ranging security awareness and training information)

- www.securityawareness.com (Security Awareness, Inc.; AIS-related awareness information)

- www.securityfocus.com (Security Focus; AIS-oriented information)

- www.tscm.com/index.html (Granite Island Group; technical surveillance countermeasures in the commercial sphere)

- www.fedcirc.gov/main.html (Federal Computer Incident Response Center is the central coordination and analysis facility dealing with computer security-related issues affecting the civilian agencies and departments of the federal government)

- https://infosec.navy.mil (Navy Information Security)

- http://chacs.nrl.navy.mil (U.S. Navy Center for High Assurance Computer Systems)

- www.ieee-security.org/cipher.html (Electronic Newsletter of the Technical Committee on Security and Privacy, IEEE)

- www.ciac.org/ciac (Computer Incident Advisory Capability, U.S. Department of Energy)

- http://doe-is.llnl.gov (DOE Information Security)

- www.infosyssec.org (Security Portal for Information Security Professionals)

PERSONNEL SECURITY

- www.dss.mil/seclib/index.htm (DSS Security Library)

- http://defenselink.mil/dodgc/doha/industrial (Industrial Security Clearance Decisions by the Defense Office of Hearings and Appeals [DOHA])

- www.navysecurity.navy.mil (Department of the Navy Central Adjudication Facility [DONCAF]; gives history, POCs, and brief summary of how the clearance process works; contains extracts from the espionage laws and federal statutes applicable to information and personnel security requirements)

- http://162.24.112.4/left_menu.html (Joint Personnel Adjudication System [JPAS]; JPAS is the DoD personnel security migration system for virtual consolidation of DoD CAFs; use by nonSCI security program managers; SSOs; and in the future by DoD contractor FSOs)

- www.kaba-ilco.com/index.asp (Kaba Holding AG)

PHYSICAL SECURITY AWARENESS

- http://locks.nfesc.navy.mil (DoD Lock Program)

- www.securitymagazine.com/government (Government Security News)

- www.sglocks.com (Sargent and Greenleaf Lock Manufacturer)

- www.unicangroup.com/intro2000eng.asp (Unican Security Systems, Ltd.; manufacturer and seller of key blanks, key duplicating machines, mechanical pushbutton locks, electronic access control systems, etc.)

- www.mas-hamilton.com/index1.html (Mas-Hamilton Group; safe lock manufacturer)

- www.nsi.org (National Security Institute; wide-ranging security awareness and training information)

- https://dodpse.spawar.navy.mil/infospc/index.html (Physical Security Knowledge Center)

- www.kaba-ilco.com/index.asp (Kaba Holding AG)

- www.lockmasters.com (Lockmasters, Inc.)

TERRORISM

- www.disastercenter.com/terror.htm (Counterterrorism Information)

- www.terrorism.com/index.shtml (The Terrorism Research Center)

- www.fbi.gov/publications/terror/terroris.htm (FBI Terrorism in the U.S. Reports)

- www.fbi.gov/hq/nsd/ansir/ansir.htm (FBI ANSIR — Awareness of National Security Issues and Response Program)

- www.nsi.org (National Security Institute; wide-ranging security awareness and training information)

- www.state.gov (Department of State [DoS] Home Page)

- www.state.gov/www/global/terrorism (DoS Terrorism Page)

- www.ds-osac.org (Overseas Security Advisory Council, DoS)

- http://travel.state.gov/travel_warnings.html (DoS, Travel Warnings and Consular Information Sheets)

- http://travel.state.gov/index.html (DoS, Bureau of Consular Affairs)

- www.travel.state.gov/links.html (links to U.S. embassies and consulates worldwide)

- www.cia.gov/cia/publications/factbook/index.html (CIA World Factbook)

- www.ds.state.gov/dspubs.htm (U.S. Department of State Diplomatic Security Service publications highlighting terrorism)

- www.dssrewards.net (U.S. Department of State Diplomatic Security Service Counter-Terrorism Rewards Program with information on terrorists and acts of terrorism)

- http://msanews.mynet.net/Scholars/Laden (information about Osama Bin Laden)

- www.gwu.edu/~nsarchiv/NSAEBB/NSAEBB55/index1.html (terrorism and U.S. policy)

- www.cia.gov/terrorism/index.html (CIA and terrorism)

- www.fas.org/irp/threat/terror.htm (terrorism background, threat assessments, and further links)

- www.linkvoyager.com/cgi-bin/serve.fcgi/terrorism (miscellaneous terrorism links and documents)

APPENDIX H

Security Articles: General Interest

PREVENTING VIOLENCE

Acts of extreme violence in the workplace are often preceded by some sign of extreme emotional pain, stress, mental disturbance, or some previous incident of violent behavior. Your awareness of these warning signs and action to report them if observed will help protect the safety of you and your coworkers. The following is a checklist for some actions that warrant reporting:

- Threats to harm others or endanger their safety

- Threats to destroy property

- Physical assaults

- Behaviors indicating potential for future violence (throwing things, shaking fists, destroying property)

- Obsession with a particular person(s), stalking, unwanted phone calls

- Other unusual behavior that might signal emotional distress

- Suicide threats and/or crisis intervention situations

- Verbal harassment (vulgar/profane language, highly disparaging or derogatory remarks or slurs, offensive sexual flirtations and propositions, verbal intimidation, exaggerated criticism or name calling)

- Visual harassment (derogatory or offensive posters, cartoons, publications, or drawings)

- Prohibited items (firearms, switchblade knives or knives with blades longer than four inches, any object intended for the purpose of injuring or intimidating)

Threats might be phrased in several different ways.

- Direct threats: I'll get him for this. I'll get even with him. He did me wrong. I'll kill him. He's gonna pay.

- Conditional threats: If they fire me, the system will crash. If they fire me, they'll never find the files. If they fire me, this place will look like the post office.

- Veiled threats: If the computer files were erased, there would be no project. Misplaced files are hard to find. Just a few mistakes and the whole system will crash.

Threatening or violent behavior is often triggered by some event that contributes to already existing stress or, as the saying goes, adds the straw that breaks the camel's back. This might include an argument with a supervisor over a poor performance review; problem with a coworker; failure to receive an expected promotion, termination of employment; or some non-work-related crisis.

There is no exact method to predict if or when an irate or disgruntled worker will become violent. One or more warning signs may be displayed before a person becomes violent, but this does not necessarily indicate that a person will become violent. The person's stress might be released through any one of a variety of behaviors — constructive as well as counterproductive.

In addition to the overt actions highlighted in the checklist, the following individual characteristics may be a basis for concern:

- Has difficulty controlling temper; displays unwarranted anger

- Is preoccupied with weapons or acts of violence

- Is intrigued by previous workplace violence incidents

- Has difficulty accepting authority/criticism

- Holds grudges, especially against supervisors

- Is argumentative/uncooperative

- Has a history of interpersonal conflict

- Expresses extreme opinions and attitudes

Remember that you are one of the keys for preventing workplace violence in your organization. You are in the best position to observe a potential problem in your working environment on a daily basis. If you have a concern, report it.

COUNTERINTELLIGENCE INDICATORS

Counterintelligence indicators are signs that an individual may already be involved in espionage or other improper use of classified information. The record of past espionage cases shows that coworkers and supervisors often overlooked or failed to report counterintelligence indicators that, had they been reported, would have permitted earlier detection of the spy.

Some of the following indicators are clear evidence of improper behavior. Others may well have an innocent explanation but are sufficiently noteworthy that your security office should be informed. If you become aware that any of the following indicators apply to one of your coworkers, you are expected to report this information directly to your security office or a counterintelligence office or by calling any one of the hotline numbers that various organizations have set up for this purpose.

The security office will evaluate the information in the context of all other information known about the individual. Depending on the circumstances, action may range from simply making a note in the individual's security file to conducting a discrete investigation.

If your reporting helps stop a case of espionage, you may be eligible for a reward of up to $500,000. The reward is authorized by an amendment to Title 18 U.S.C. Section 3071, which authorizes the attorney general to make payment for information on espionage activity in any country that leads to the arrest and conviction of any person(s):

- For commission of an act of espionage against the United States

- For conspiring or attempting to commit an act of espionage against the United States

- Or that leads to the prevention or frustration of an act of espionage against the United States

Indicators of Potential Motivation

These are several reportable indicators:

- Disgruntlement with one's employer or the U.S. government strong enough to make the individual desire revenge

- Any statement that, considering who made the statement and under what circumstances, suggests potential conflicting loyalties that may affect handling of classified or other protected information

- Active attempt to encourage military or civilian personnel to violate laws, disobey lawful orders or regulations, or disrupt military activities

- Knowing membership in, or attempt to conceal membership in, any group that (1) advocates the use of force or violence to cause political change within the United States, (2) has been identified as a front group for foreign interests, or (3) advocates loyalty to a foreign interest

- Repeated statements or actions indicating an abnormal fascination with and strong desire to engage in "spy" work; fantasies of oneself as a James Bond

Potential Indicators of Information Collection

- Asking others to obtain or facilitate access to classified or unclassified but protected information to which one does not have authorized access

- Obtaining or attempting to obtain a witness signature on a classified document destruction record when the witness did not observe the destruction

- Offering extra income from an outside activity to a person with a sensitive job in an apparent attempt to entice that person into an unspecified illegal activity

- Undue curiosity or requests for information about matters not within the scope of the individual's job or need-to-know

- Unauthorized removal or attempts to remove classified, export-controlled, proprietary, or other protected material from the work area

- Retention of classified, export-controlled, proprietary, or other sensitive information obtained at a previous employment without the authorization or the knowledge of that employer

- Extensive use of copy, facsimile, or computer equipment to reproduce or transmit; taking classified materials home or on trips, purportedly for work reasons, without proper authorization

- Working odd hours when others are not in the office without a logical reason or visiting work areas after normal hours for no logical reason

- Bringing cameras or recording devices, without approval, into areas storing classified or other protected material

Potential Indicators of Information Transmittal

- Storing classified material at home or any other unauthorized place

- Short trips to foreign countries, or within the United States to cities with foreign diplomatic facilities, for unusual or unexplained reasons or for reasons that are inconsistent with one's apparent interests and financial means

- Excessive or unexplained use of e-mail or fax

- Failure to comply with regulations for reporting foreign contacts or foreign travel; any attempt to conceal foreign travel or to conceal close and continuing contact with a foreigner, particularly a foreign official

- Foreign travel not reflected in the individual's passport to countries where entries would normally be stamped

- Maintaining ongoing personal contact, without prior approval, with diplomatic or other representatives from countries with which one has ethnic, religious, cultural, or other emotional ties or obligations, or with employees of competing companies in those countries

Potential Indicators of Illegal Income

- Unexplained affluence or lifestyle inconsistent with known income, includes sudden purchase of high-value items or unusually frequent personal travel that appears to be beyond known income; sudden repayment of large debts or loans, indicating sudden reversal of financial difficulties

- Joking or bragging about working for a foreign intelligence service or having a mysterious source of income

Other Potential Indicators

- Behavior indicating concern that one is being investigated or watched, such as actions to detect physical surveillance, searching for listening devices or cameras, and leaving "traps" to detect search of the individual's work area or home

- Any part-time employment or other outside activity that may create a conflict of interest with one's obligation to protect classified or other sensitive information and that has not been approved by the security office

• Attempt to conceal any activity covered by one of these counterintelligence indicators

HOW DO I KNOW WHEN I'M BEING TARGETED AND ASSESSED?

Introduction

It is important for Americans who have contact with foreign nationals to understand the process that all intelligence services use to spot, assess, and recruit agents. The following section, "The Road to Recruitment," describes the systematic, step-by-step process that intelligence operatives use to winnow down a large number of contacts until they eventually find the one or two exceptions who may be susceptible to recruitment. Anyone who during the course of his or her job has regular contact with foreign nationals should read "The Road to Recruitment."

Later, the section titled "Who Is Most Likely to Be Targeted?" discusses several factors that increase the possibility that you, or any other person, will be targeted and assessed. These include the following:

• Your access to information, people, or places of active intelligence interest

• Travel abroad where foreign intelligence operatives can gain access to you on their home turf

• Work in a position or geographic location in the United States where it is easy for foreign nationals to gain access to you

• Ethnic, racial, or religious background that may attract the attention of a foreign intelligence operative

It is important to note that all of the above factors that increase the chances of a person being selected for initial targeting and assessment are circumstances over which the individual has little or no control. Therefore, the fact that a person is targeted and assessed should never, by itself, be interpreted as casting doubt on the integrity or loyalty of that person.

Most foreign contacts are perfectly legitimate and well meaning. Your ability to recognize the few who are not will help you avoid problems. It will also help your security office help others avoid problems. Your assistance in identifying foreign intelligence collectors who may be cultivating you for ulterior purposes will make it possible to warn others and neutralize the foreign intelligence activity.

During the Cold War, most Americans who betrayed their country by spying for foreign intelligence services were not targeted, assessed, and recruited on the initiative of the foreign service. They were volunteer spies — Americans who took the initiative in contacting and passing secret information to a foreign country. The strong preponderance of volunteers over recruits may have been due, in part, to the Cold War barriers that limited opportunities for Communist intelligence officers to take the initiative in contacting, assessing, and cultivating American targets.

In today's global economy, the environment for espionage operations is totally different. Foreign intelligence collectors are pursuing a broader range of targets, and it is relatively easy for them to establish contact with and assess Americans who have access to valuable classified, controlled, or proprietary information.

THE ROAD TO RECRUITMENT

Are you a target? How would you know? Foreign intelligence operatives are not obvious. They don't wear trench coats or have shifty eyes. In today's world, they're usually friendly people who pursue their trade under the guise of activities that appear normal and natural. They want to cultivate you as a "friend."

The only thing you can be certain of is that you are a *potential* target if you have access to classified, controlled, or sensitive proprietary information. That's why it's important to be careful what you say when talking with *any* foreign national.

This goes beyond just being careful in what you say about your work. You must also be careful in what you say about yourself and your coworkers. Don't talk about the cost of putting two sons through college at the same time or the cost of medical help for your daughter's leukemia. Don't talk about your stupid boss, how you hate the IRS, problems with your spouse, or your colleague's drinking problem. A foreign intelligence operative may interpret any of these as clues that you (or your colleague) may be worth cultivating.

You already know that you must report anything that suggests you may be the target of a foreign intelligence service or other hostile group. That sounds simple. What you may not realize is this: If you haven't learned how intelligence services operate, you likely won't recognize when you are being targeted and assessed until the process is far advanced. The purpose of this description of the "road to recruitment" is to help you recognize an intelligence operative even before he or she does anything overtly suspicious.

Foreign intelligence personnel look for any legitimate activity that lets them meet and gain some assessment of the people who have access to the information they want. They then become a part of this activity. The rituals of espionage like secret meetings and dead drops are often avoided, at least during the early stages of most cases.

If I'm trying to get information from you, my goal is to make it easy for you, not to give you sleepless nights. We meet over lunch, become friends. I learn what makes you tick, sympathize with your problems, and feed your ego. If it seems like you may be amenable, we talk about information that is easy for you to rationalize talking about. I look for ways to gain one small step of cooperation at a time. To gain your sympathy, I may talk about my country's need for economic development or the threat from my country's enemies. If it's done right, you may not know its a spy operation until you are so far down the road that you are either afraid to turn back or don't want to turn back.

One of the most succinct descriptions of the spotting, assessment, development, and recruitment process used by all intelligence services was provided by a former Soviet KGB officer. He called it the "road to recruitment." While the terminology he used is typically Russian, the process is similar to that used by all intelligence services. A thousand initial contacts lead to 100 operational contacts, which lead to 10 developmental contacts, which lead to three trusted sources, which lead to one recruitment. Like a sales or marketing plan, the road to recruitment is a guide on how to proceed and what to expect. It is a gradual process of sorting through and winnowing down a large number of possibilities in order to succeed in eventually making just a few small sales (trusted sources) and perhaps one big one (full recruitment as an agent).

The foreign agent's goals at each stage on the road to recruitment are as follows:

- *Initial contact.* If not already known, confirm whether or not you have information of value. If you do have information of value, establish some logical basis for continuing contact and obtain your agreement to meet again. This is generally expected to be successful in about 1 out of 10 cases. Scientific conferences, international business development programs, seminars, exhibits, and meetings of all types where networking is encouraged are spy heaven. They offer ideal opportunities for making a large number of initial contacts in a short period of time.

- *Operational contact.* Look for some indication of exploitable vulnerability or susceptibility. In other words, determine whether it's worth spending time and money developing the contact with you. The faster the foreign agent accomplishes this goal, the more time he or she has available to devote to promising developmental contacts. Again, the expectation of many intelligence collectors is to be successful in about 1 out of 10 cases. One indicator of success is your willingness to talk about topics or people of intelligence interest. Elicitation of useful — but not necessarily secret — information is an interim goal, or way station, on the road to recruitment.

- *Developmental contact.* At this point, the goal is to establish a relationship of friendship and trust, get to know what makes you tick as a person, determine your weaknesses and your unfulfilled goals and ambitions, give you some sense of personal interest or pleasure in maintaining the contact, cause you to feel a sense of obligation. The objective is to start you down the road of providing information, beginning with easy and innocent requests for professional advice, discussion of developments in your professional field, discussion of your work colleagues and the best way to deal with them, and your explanation of the rationale behind your company's policy or American government policy. This may progress to requests for articles from professional journals that are ostensibly difficult to get in your "friend's" home country or technical information about your company's products that is not protected but also not readily available. Anything to establish a regular pattern of your coming to meetings prepared to provide information, no matter how innocuous that information may be. A request for your organization's internal phone book is not innocuous. It's a red flag. For an intelligence organization, a phone book is a basic tool for identifying the names of people who have access to the key information the organization is seeking.

- *Trusted source.* Of each 10 developmental contacts, maybe three can be developed into trusted sources. These are regular sources of useful information. They are trusted in the sense that the foreign intelligence organization believes its source is telling the truth and is not reporting the contact to his or her security office. If a trusted source is providing classified information, it will usually be in oral discussions rather than in documentary form. Trusted sources may not know (or will not admit to themselves) that their "friend" is an intelligence officer. Of every three trusted sources, perhaps only one will become fully recruited as a knowing agent who regularly provides classified documents or who accepts money in exchange for information or other services.

If you are the target, you should be reporting to your security officer by the time you are classified as an operational contact (being assessed). If you haven't reported it by the time you've graduated to a developmental contact, you may be close to getting into trouble. Your goal is to recognize this process and report it to your security officer. The foreign intelligence operative's goal is to make it so easy for you to get involved or to put yourself in a compromising position that you won't want to report or will be afraid to report it to your security officer.

Your main defense is awareness and reporting on your foreign contacts. If you report, we can alert you when you are dealing with a known foreign intelligence operative, or we may identify a foreign intelligence operative as a result of your reporting. That's part of our job — identifying the few intelligence officers or agents among the many legitimate government officials, businesspeople, or scientists you meet. Your reports on your contacts are an important contribution to the database that makes these identifications possible.

If the FBI or a military service counterintelligence office learns about your contact, it will probably ask your security office if you are reporting on it. If you are not reporting it, security will be obliged to open an investigative case on you. In other words, if you do report, you are part of the solution. If you don't report, you can become part of the problem.

You should not avoid contact with foreigners or distrust all persons from abroad. Your encounters with foreign colleagues and cultures should be among your most treasured experiences. But you must be aware that among the millions of foreigners who come to our country or whose countries you visit, there are some who would exploit your trust.

If you do find yourself in contact with a foreign intelligence operative, there's no need to be afraid, only careful. You won't be hurt, but you may be manipulated and used — if you let that happen. You are much more likely to be charmed by a "friend" than blackmailed by an enemy.

If the contact goes so far that you are asked to provide information, perhaps as a "consultant," you should listen carefully, be observant, and remember as many details as possible. Keep all options open by neither agreeing nor refusing to cooperate. Remain calm, be noncommittal, ask for time, and report immediately to your security office.

The following tables examine in greater detail the first three stages on the road to recruitment. They look at it from the perspective of what you might observe as a target and what this means your contact might be trying to do.

Initial Contact	
What You Observe	**What It May Mean**
Questions about the nature of your work at first meeting	Trying to determine as rapidly as possible whether you are someone worth spending time on
Invitation to lunch or any other request for follow-up meeting	Testing your willingness to maintain contact
An erroneous statement made about an activity or person that you are familiar with	Tricking you into providing the correct information or testing your willingness to do so
Pretending or falsely implying to be a representative of a particular firm, organization, or country	Attempting to use cover story to gain your confidence and make you more comfortable with the contact
Unsolicited request for information via mail, phone, or the Internet directed to you by name, rather than to other appropriate addressee such as corporate marketing department	Trying to collect openly available information or testing your willingness to be helpful by responding to such a request, especially if request comes from a foreigner with the same national, ethnic, or religious background as you (If you respond, you may then be targeted and assessed by other means)
Operational Contact	
What You Observe	**What It May Mean**
Discussions that lead in the direction of sensitive or classified topics	Testing your willingness to talk about sensitive topics
Inquiries about your own job satisfaction or professional rewards	Looking for exploitable weaknesses, such as bitterness or alienation
Talk about his or her country's need for economic development or threat from foreign enemies	Eliciting sympathy for his or her country's problems and motivate you to be helpful

Requests for technical explanations from a person who, because of his or her alleged credentials, should already know the answer	Getting you accustomed to responding to questions; testing whether you respond to flattery about your knowledge or have a need to feel important; or maybe the alleged credentials are not real
Disclosure to you of what you would consider to be sensitive information	Provoking you to verify facts or findings. Making you feel that it's okay to talk about such information; trying to put contact on a "confidential" basis
Royal treatment during a foreign visit	Developing a sense of obligation to somehow reciprocate; setting the stage for relaxed discussion and further assessment
Your advice is sought on subjects of common interest	Setting the precedent for you providing information, no matter how innocuous it may be; testing whether flattery and making you feel important makes you more open and talkative

Developmental Contact	
What You Observe	**What It May Mean**
Offer of a consulting fee on a private basis, even for providing innocuous information	Developing your financial motivation; getting you into the habit of providing information for money
Request for introduction to another person or to provide innocuous information (such as unclassified reports from your library or an organizational telephone book) with no mention of compensation	Testing your inclination to be helpful or establishing a pattern of your providing information
Attempts to get you inebriated while engaging in a technical discussion	Trying to elicit privileged information or testing whether you can be led into a compromising situation while drunk
Invitation for an expenses-paid visit to a foreign country to attend conference, share technical expertise, or for sabbatical	The invitation may be entirely innocent, but if the intelligence service arranged it you may be in an advanced developmental stage; the goal may be to reward you for your assistance, create a sense of obligation, or get you on their home turf where they can try to compromise you by heavy drinking, black market currency exchange, or sexual provocation
Attempts to gain inside or privileged information by offering favors or money	This is past the assessment and development stage, moving toward recruitment

366

If you are targeted and assessed by a foreign intelligence officer, this certainly does not mean that you have done anything wrong. It does not in any way reflect on your reliability. You are a natural target because of your access to protected information and because your job or other circumstances brings you into contact with foreign nationals. You have done nothing wrong unless you start maintaining a regular contact without reporting it to your security officer.

WHO IS MOST LIKELY TO BE TARGETED?

The likelihood of your being targeted for initial assessment usually depends on circumstances over which you have little or no control. Circumstances that increase the chances include the following:

*   The most obvious consideration, but not necessarily the most important, is the value of the information, people, or places to which you have access. The greater the value of your access, the more likely you are to be selected for contact, assessment, and (if you appear susceptible) recruitment. Your value to a foreign intelligence service does not depend on rank. Support personnel such as secretaries, computer operators, and maintenance personnel may be able to provide access to very valuable information. It is easy to overemphasize the extent to which the value of your access determines your chances of being targeted. Foreign intelligence officers are under pressure to recruit agents just as salespeople are under pressure to make sales. Their career advancement depends on it, but they also need to avoid getting caught. As a result, they may go after the easiest or most available target rather than take the risk of going after the most valuable target.

*   You are more likely to be targeted and assessed if you are stationed in a foreign country or often travel there. All foreign intelligence or security services have far more resources available in their home country than in the United States. There is much less risk for them when they are operating on their home turf, and they are far more active and aggressive there.

*   Even within the United States, you are more likely to be targeted if you are in an area and in a position where it is relatively easy for foreign nationals to contact and assess you. For example, foreign diplomats, jour-

nalists, and lobbyists are constantly working Capitol Hill in search of contacts and information. Personnel at industrial sites and national laboratories that have foreign scientists onsite and many foreign visitors are more likely to be targeted than personnel at sites with few foreign nationals onsite and few foreign visitors.

- If your cultural, ethnic, or religious background differs from some so-called norm in any obvious way, you are also more likely to be targeted and assessed. Many foreign intelligence operatives have limited understanding of American culture and commonly think in stereotypes. If they put you in any stereotypical category of persons they believe are more likely to be supportive of their interests or to be disadvantaged, bitter, or alienated, you are more likely to be targeted for initial contact and moved quickly into the operational contact phase. Foreign intelligence operatives find it easier to contact, build rapport with, assess, and manipulate individuals with whom they can claim to share a common interest — including a shared national, ethnic, or religious background.

Personnel in these more vulnerable categories need to be aware of their vulnerability and be especially prompt in reporting any significant foreign contact. The more attractive you are as a target, the greater the chances that a foreign national who befriends you is an intelligence operative.

There is no reason to suspect that personnel in any of these categories are more susceptible to recruitment than any other American. Vulnerability to being targeted is very different from susceptibility to being recruited.

Lest there be any misunderstanding on this point, there is no evidence that naturalized citizens are less loyal than native-born citizens. Many naturalized citizens have a stronger loyalty to the United States than native-born citizens, who often take their country for granted. There is also no evidence that members of any disadvantaged or minority group are more susceptible to recruitment than other Americans.

Opportunities for foreign intelligence officers and agents to arrange face-to-face meetings to assess targets in the United States have increased dramatically. The openness of the post–Cold War environment, growing global commerce, and increasing espionage by our friends in addition to our adversaries have increased the vulnerability of all of us to assessment by multiple foreign intelligence collectors.

PROJECT AND OPERATIONS SECURITY AND YOUR TRASH

There's an old saying that "one man's trash is another man's treasure." Regardless of what you call it, sensitive and unclassified trash has its own unique value in the world of intelligence and business competition.

As a new year begins, and as we continue on various company-sensitive projects and programs, many of you may take the time to review and consider various files to be discarded. Please keep in mind the policy for destruction of unclassified-sensitive information. The policy directs that such material be destroyed in a manner that will ensure that its information, data, or value cannot be reconstructed or discerned by rigorous study.

Unclassified-sensitive information, products, and materials include proprietary or contractor source selection information, export-controlled, privacy act, distribution limitation items, financial, project and program status items, and those that may fall under the Freedom of Information Act. When in doubt, contact the security office for review and guidance.

So what's the big deal about trash? Who really cares? Of what possible value can the trash be? "Trash cover" is a traditional intelligence methodology used by virtually every intelligence agency in the world. It involves the collection and analysis of trash. Even the FBI collects trash during its surveillance of criminal suspects. (Remember the value of Rick Ames's trash?) Competitors and foreign businesses use it as a technique to learn about what we are doing and, more important, what we will be doing in the future. When trash covers are conducted as part of a security survey, they reveal only a snapshot of what's going to the dump. If organizational unclassified-sensitive/technical data, organizational charts, mission statements, staff directories, and so forth are recovered during a trash survey, how much else is going out the door?

Take a realistic look at your environment. All the necessary security precautions have been taken, people have been cleared, equipment has been accredited, standard operating procedures are in place, but information of value still gets out with the trash. Project and operations security only works when put into practice. This is the only way to ensure information remains protected within proper channels.

Appendix I

Audiovisuals: Getting the Word Out to the Right Audience — The Right Way

In today's business world, there is an infinite assortment of communication media and know-how available for getting out the company message. Any firm with the right amount of money can have access to a wide variety of state-of-the-art communication technologies. And for smaller activities with more limited budgets, there are lower-cost options as well. A great many audiences need to be reached. The business community often finds itself communicating to anyone who will listen — and to many who don't.

Good communication is also essential to efficiency and teamwork within the organization and its workforce. To be successful in business these days, management knows it must do a good job of communicating internally. Employees want to know what is going on and where the organization is heading. There is a multitude of communication devices — from newsletters and magazines to letters from the front office — vying for the employee's attention. All are designed with internal communication in mind. But certainly the most popular in this technological age are audiovisual products.

AV OPTIONS: VIDEOTAPE, FILM, AND SLIDE-TAPE

Audiovisual media combine both sound and visual elements. They include a broad range of products, the more common being motion pictures, television, and slide-tapes. While more expensive to produce than some printed alternatives, audiovisuals appeal to large audiences and are relatively easy to use.

It has been said that television keeps us in touch. Certainly television has impacted our society dramatically as an information and entertainment medium. Now, with the explosion of videocassettes and CDs on the market, video systems are fast becoming the newest dimension in internal communication for business and industry. In fact, video is widely regarded as the most effective means of corporate communication since the origin of speech. Its uses range from job training to security education. Several video end products available to government and contractors promote security education and awareness as part of a security education program.

The more common video systems come in three-quarter inch videocassettes (U-MATIC) and the popular half-inch videotapes used with commercial home recording and playback systems. VHS and BETA are two principal half-inch formats on the market. Each of these, three-quarter-inch formats require different equipment for viewing.

Motion picture products have long enjoyed widespread use as instructional-educational tools. They are produced in 16-mm, 35-mm, and 70-mm sound-on-film. Generally, they are more expensive to produce than other AV products, but they can be projected on a large screen and are better suited for large audiences than videotape. The technology has now been perfected for producing good-quality films from videotape masters.

The least expensive audiovisual mode is the slide-tape combination of 35-mm slides with audiocassettes. The audiotapes can be pulsed for automatic advance, or the slides can be advanced (or reversed) manually.

This medium is ideally suited for individual, self-paced learning packages, providing the viewer with direct control of the presentation. Also, while it may not lend itself to presentations before large audiences, it does offer an inexpensive method of presenting programmed, easy-to-operate packages to groups of perhaps 10 or fewer.

VISUALS: PART OF THE COMMUNICATION PACKAGE

Use of audiovisuals should be part of a thoughtfully planned training process. Planning means selecting good programs for viewing. But first and foremost it means using audiovisuals for suitable purposes, using them to do the things that they do well while meeting other training needs with other training approaches.

Audiovisual products normally do not do a good job of communicating large quantities of information in great detail. But they do the job when it comes to informing, persuading, motivating, and entertaining. Audiovisuals can be the "spoonful of sugar" that helps to make the security message a little more palatable.

A short film can help to make the audience more receptive to that rather detailed briefing for document custodians or even the security educator's "Dutch-uncle" speech about the latest inspection deficiencies. Audiovisuals won't do the job alone, but they can be a dramatic means of highlighting a topic, while the details or "valleys" can be supplemented more cost-effectively through printed materials, lecture and discussion, or other media. Visual media are a supplement — not a substitute — for an active multimedia security awareness and education effort, to include person-to-person communication and instruction by security professionals. They provide the balance and continuity to such an effort but should not be considered a cure-all or quick fix, even though the temptation to use them as such may sometimes be there. For the security manager who wants to be innovative, security awareness training can employ the full range of communication skills and media from the company newsletter to posters to a guest appearance by the boss or an outside expert.

Personal messages from the head of the organization will carry some weight and bosses are often agreeable about supporting a cause, particularly if someone asks them and can put together some appropriate remarks for the occasion. What better way to emphasize security awareness within the company and at the same time introduce your training session?

Likewise, a few well-phrased remarks from the top can be used to precede that videotaped security presentation. In any case, an introduction to the program is essential. Preview and screen any audiovisuals you intend to show. Make sure that they apply to your organization and can be expected to appeal to your audience. Then tell your people that you have chosen this material for their viewing, and tell them why — not at agonizing length, just a brief introduction. Following the running of the film or tape, solicit comments and questions and invite discussion, perhaps with some leading questions of your own. In short, promote audience involvement and ensure that they got the message and understand its relevance to their work.

FINDING AND USING GOOD PRODUCTIONS

In getting down to the logistics of the matter, let's face up to a couple of realities: Security is not a subject with high popular appeal, and the production and distribution of security films and videotapes are not lucrative enterprises, as enterprises go. Not as many videotapes are available for security trainers as there are for rock music fans — and there never will be. We do not, and we never will, spend as much money selling security as we do selling some of the more obscure brands of soft drinks.

These are facts of life, constraints that we've got to live with. They affect the production "polish," which we can expect from training materials of this type, and that means that such programs on security cannot be obtained with a quick trip to your local video club. Good-quality products are available, but we are not pretending that there isn't some effort involved.

WHO HAS THESE AUDIOVISUAL MATERIALS? HOW DO YOU GET THEM?

These questions are not the easiest to answer, but visual products on tape are available. The Department of Defense, for example, including Department of Defense contractors, will find that the greatest quantity of relevant materials are available from the Defense Audiovisual Agency (DAVA) and the AV centers located on most military bases. These activities provide materials on loan to contractors and government activities.

Yes, the Department of Defense activities have many of these materials, but remember, you want up-to-date visual products; many activities keep products on their shelves for several years, and often the subject matter has gone by the wayside due to changes in policy and procedures or the subject matter itself. The government also sells audiovisual programs to the public, at somewhat below going market rates, through the National Audiovisual Center (NAVC).

Contractors under the industrial security program can turn to their Defense Security Service (DSS) cognizant security offices for the loan of various products. Each DSS regional office has an education and training (E&T) specialist who maintains a library of security education programs.

Consider going onto the Web and looking under "security videos" or "security awareness." You will find a myriad of private-sector companies that have produced many fine products. Unfortunately, you may not find what you want, because many are so specialized.

Other places to turn to include the American Society for Industrial Security (International), located in Alexandria, Virginia. If you are a member of ASIS, you can check out videos. ASIS maintains an ever-increasing collection from a great many sources. Also, consider other companies and organizations in your area of the country. When local or area security managers get together to discuss security concerns and the topic of training, the types and topics of videos typically arise. From such get-togethers, you can usually find a good selection of videotapes right in your own backyard. Pooling resources between companies also provides a variety of tapes for training sessions, especially when without such an informal program, you would be in a world of hurt, having only a very few on hand, and those have probably been shown over and over to the same people, who are — frankly — getting tired of seeing them every year or two.

Perhaps a group of smaller facilities could rent equipment jointly. There are a number of ways in which this kind of networking can be accomplished. And your participation in professional groups concerned with security can be an ideal source of assistance from other security professionals in your area. If you're not currently involved in one of these groups, consider it as a viable and profitable method to meet, greet, know, and work with your peers for the benefit of all.

Index